MW01014147

# St. Paul's
# Cosmic War Myth

# The Westminster College
# Library of Biblical Symbolism

Peter W. Macky
*General Editor*

Vol. 2

PETER LANG
New York • Washington, D.C./Baltimore • Boston
Bern • Frankfurt am Main • Berlin • Vienna • Paris

Peter W. Macky

# St. Paul's
# Cosmic War Myth

## A Military Version
## of the Gospel

PETER LANG
New York • Washington, D.C./Baltimore • Boston
Bern • Frankfurt am Main • Berlin • Vienna • Paris

**Library of Congress Cataloging-in-Publication Data**

Macky, Peter W.
St. Paul's cosmic war myth: a military version of the Gospel / Peter W. Macky.
p. cm. — (The Westminster College library of biblical symbolism; 2)
Includes bibliographical references and indexes.
1. Bible. N.T. Epistles of Paul—Criticism, interpretation, etc.
2. Theomachy in the Bible. I. Title. II. Series: Westminster College
library of biblical symbolism; vol. 2.
BS2655.T543M33   227′.064—dc21   97-13443
ISBN 0-8204-3829-4
ISSN 1079-5723


**Die Deutsche Bibliothek-CIP-Einheitsaufnahme**

Macky, Peter W.:
St. Paul's cosmic war myth: a military version of the Gospel / Peter W. Macky.
–New York; Washington, D.C./Baltimore; Boston;
Bern; Frankfurt am Main; Berlin; Vienna; Paris: Lang.
(The Westminster college library of biblical symbolism; Vol. 2)
ISBN 0-8204-3829-4 Gb.

Cover design by James F. Brisson.

The paper in this book meets the guidelines for permanence and durability
of the Committee on Production Guidelines for Book Longevity
of the Council of Library Resources.

© 1998 Peter Lang Publishing, Inc., New York

Printed in the United States of America.

*DEDICATION*

To Peter

Scholar, Teacher, Husband, Father Extraordinaire

from Nancy, Cameron and Christopher

## AUTHOR'S NOTE

As days become hours, God's goodness becomes greater and greater than ever. I stand with His glorious light calling me, and I know I shall see and rejoice in Him forever.

Dictated by author 4/10/97, 9:45 a.m.
Peter W. Macky died 4/10/97, 6:30 p.m.

## ACKNOWLEDGEMENTS

Had Peter lived to write these acknowledgements, surely the list would have been longer. Many contributed to his conversations about this book over several decades.

His Oxford University examiners, in 1967 awarding him a D.Phil., suggested that he take his dissertation and try to publish it one day. Here, reworked, he has done so 30 years later, dictating the author's note on the morning he died.

Grateful to those who took up the task of finishing it by proofreading, checking the indices, typing, mailing, I mention only those I observed; others perhaps unmentioned may rest assured that Peter would have thanked them by name. Dr. Jesse Mann relieved Peter's mind by agreeing to oversee the project to its completion; he has shepherded it masterfully and with grace. Dr. John Deegan generously allowed staff time for the project.

Drs. Bardarah McCandless, Jeff Kripal, Warren Hickman all spent hours proofreading the text, as did our son Cameron. Victoria Mann, Lucinda Hickman, Elizabeth and James Hines donated several intensive hours to the index. Alissa Sprow gave many hours typing. All were gifts to a great man, a superb scholar's creation. His family and those who will benefit from this work for years to come call them blessed.

Nancy Macky, Ph.D.

# TABLE OF CONTENTS

# INTRODUCTION

In this posthumously published volume, Peter Macky makes a significant contribution to Christian scholarship by means of a seminal work on biblical theology and language. Each of these subjects in this original study merits serious attention.

With regard to biblical theology, the author focuses upon the still unresolved issue of coherence in Paul's interpretation of the gospel. He argues that the apostle to the Gentiles viewed the early Christian kerygma through four metaphorical "windows," which are identified as the cosmic war myth, the judicial story Paul tells, his organic (body) symbolism, and the metaphor of the royal family. Each of these "models" (established symbols) is deemed an appropriate metaphor for attesting to the good news of God's action in the world, but Macky limits his study to the first, Paul's "military version of the gospel," which is both the most intellectually difficult and theologically significant of the four. For the conflict between good and evil is identified here as "the inner driving force of the story of Christ."

Macky's hermeneutical strategy is to make coherent a variety of disparate and apparently disconnected Pauline texts attesting to this moral struggle--"tips of an iceberg" they are called--by recognizing their common ground beneath the textual surface in **"the cosmic war myth."** The bulk of the book is devoted to reconstructing this singular symbolic "iceberg" from the pieces of the puzzle found in the Old Testament and intertestamental apocalyptic literature. Themes such as God as a Man of War, Satan and his hosts, angelic armies, the victory of light over darkness, and the eschatological battle are addressed. As he fits these together into a recognizable whole, Macky concedes that the resultant unified cosmic war myth (with variations) is based more upon probabilities than proofs. Yet of such is the kingdom of historical reconstruction. What emerges in this study is a plausible picture of the way the ancients articulated their understanding of the conflict in human life and history between good and evil. That the apostle Paul would have been exposed to and influenced by this symbol does not strain credulity. That it provides a productive heuristic assumption in the interpretation of these Pauline texts if evident from Macky's exposition.

The question of what to make of these results remains, however. How are we to construe this "cosmic war myth" and the "military version of the gospel" it spawned? The former is dismissed as cognitively vacuous by the modern mind, and the latter is considered politically incorrect by postmoderns. The author builds upon his earlier work, *The Centrality of Metaphors to Biblical Thought: A Method for Interpreting the Bible* (1990), in addressing this question.Macky is convinced (with most others) that the theological language of scripture is metaphorical. But he wisely agrees with the cautious realism of a Janet Martin Soskice, rather than the mere expressivism of a Sallie McFague. Metaphors have cognitive value, in other words, because they refer to realities that transcend language and human consciousness, yet not in a literal manner. Angels function, for example, as guardians and avengers of justice. They are imaginative symbols of the reality and seriousness of divine law. In dependence upon C. S. Lewis, Dr. Macky calls such symbolic **representations** a "true myth."

Given the author's death soon after the completion of his manuscript, it is poignant to consider these words from his treatment of the power of death in Paul's military version of the gospel.

> In Paul's military gospel, Christ's death and resurrection was the way God created the new Kingdom of Light (in the midst of this Kingdom of Darkness), into which neither Sin nor Death can enter: just as Sin no longer can enslave believers, so also Death no longer has an eternal hold on them. However, as the children of light carry on their lives in the flesh as **continuing** participants in this present age, they remain subject to the power of temporal, physical Death, just as Christ himself was. Still, even when they die they remain in Christ, for the new realm of the dead in Christ is an extension of the Kingdom of Light into the world of the dead. (145)

As one privileged to know Peter Macky from the earliest days of our respective ministries, I affirm with him that this is the heart of the "true myth" proclaimed by the apostle Paul and believed by Christians across the centuries. Peter Macky was an extraordinary scholar, as this, his last book attests, but he was first and foremost a believer in Jesus Christ and a member of his Church. On the basis of Paul's military version of the gospel, we may confidently believe that in death, as in life, Peter is among those who "remain in Christ."

Thomas W. Gillespie, President
Princeton Theological Seminary

# I. PAUL'S MULTIPLE WINDOWS

# ON THE GOSPEL MYSTERY

## Introduction

> God disarmed the principalities and powers, making a public
> example of them, triumphing over them in him (Christ). (Col
> 2:15)
>> Put on the armor of light. (Rom 13:12)
>> Then comes the end, when Christ delivers the kingdom to
>> God the Father, after destroying every rule and every
>> authority and power. (1 Cor 15:25)
>> The God of peace will soon crush Satan under your feet.
>> (Rom 16:20)

In these and a variety of other passages in Paul's writings we recognize that one of his ways of presenting the gospel was by using military symbolism, imagery taken from the realm of warfare—armies, soldiers, weapons and physical destruction. The conflict between good and evil, which is the inner driving force of the story of Christ, is pictured here as a long-running cosmic war: battles ebb and flow between two armies which face each other down through the ages until one wins the final confrontation by destroying the other completely. In this symbolic picture, which is rooted in the Old Testament and in Jewish Apocalypticism, God in Christ battles the Kingdom of Darkness. After initially (and only partially) defeating it in the cross and resurrection, God in Christ continues the battle through the Spirit in the Church, and wins it at the Eschaton.

In this book we will explore and elaborate Paul's cosmic war myth, his military version of the gospel. Our primary purpose is to make this Pauline picture as imaginable as possible by delving into its depths in order to present it in full. Our view is that most of his brief references to the great battle are tips of an iceberg. The great hidden body of the iceberg is the detailed myth of the great battle between Good and Evil, which he had learned when young, and had adapted to fit his new faith in Christ. Our primary goal in this book is to describe the iceberg as fully as we can, which we will do in chapters II to VII.

When we have painted as complete a picture of Paul's military (and apocalyptic) myth as we can, then we will begin the task of deciding how Paul probably meant it. In chapter VIII we will focus on one central element of the myth, the two angelic hierarchies, the heavenly armies of light and darkness. The question we will ask is what realities these images probably symbolized for Paul. Finally we will suggest in chapter IX what the value of the military symbolism seems to be. It suggests that Christian life now is warfare, an ongoing battle in which courage, faithfulness, discipline, training, acceptance of suffering, and hope are essential.

The other major symbol systems Paul used (somewhat indiscriminately) in his letters include the judicial story that Paul tells: God is the law-giver and judge, humans are guilty law-breakers, Christ's death was the means by which believers are acquitted, and the end of the story comes in a Last Judgment. Further, Paul uses organic (especially body) symbolism in which all humans are members of the mortal body of Adam, all believers are included in the eternal Body of Christ, are therein enlivened by Christ's own Spirit, and will in the end be raised in Christ when he returns. The fourth major symbol system he uses is a royal family picture according to which God is the father from whom the children are alienated, but God reconciles believers through Christ, adopts them into the royal family, and will give them crowns and glory at the end. Each of these four is extensive enough for us to speak of them as models.[1]

We call these Paul's four windows on the gospel: each symbolic picture is a window in a garden wall enabling us to see differing (but complementary) views of the garden as we move from window to window. Our hypothesis is that Paul used all four of these symbol systems as basic windows on the gospel (along with many other symbols taken from other areas of human experience). Each of these four pictures is an appropriate and traditional way to express the good news of God's action in the world. Paul knew all four from his upbringing and found all four to be powerful as ways to enable his hearers to imagine something of the wonder of what God had done, is doing and will do in and through Christ.

First of all in this chapter, we will provide **A. A Sketch of the Four Windows**, to show that there are in fact these four major distinctive windows onto the mystery of the gospel. Then we will present **B. The Argument for a Multiple Windows** approach, which is the foundation for the book. Next we will consider as background **C. The Tradition of Interpretation of Paul's Writings**, showing how Pauline interpreters have for a century or more noticed the different types of imagery the apostle used. This variety of approaches will provide substantial support for our theory that Paul imagined and employed multiple windows on the gospel. Then we will outline **D. A Theory of Symbolism**.

## A. A SKETCH OF THE FOUR WINDOWS

### (1) The Military Window: Victory Over The Powers of Evil

George Caird, in his classic work *Principalities and Powers*, says, "the idea of sinister world powers and their subjugation by Christ is built into the very fabric of Paul's thought, and some mention of them is found in every

---

[1] See Peter W. Macky, *The Centrality of Metaphors to Biblical Thought: A Method for Interpreting the Bible*, 55–56 for our use of "model."

epistle except Philemon."[2] Caird's small book provides an introduction to Paul's military gospel, which had the following elements:

(a) God is the warrior at the head of the eternal Kingdom of Light, with Christ as his regent over the earthly realm of light. In the opposing army Satan is the Prince of Darkness, with the powers (the angelic rulers of the nations) immediately under him as his commanding generals. On earth, human rulers (e.g. the Caesars) are the earthly agents of darkness, and all people opposing the gospel are the armies of the children of darkness. Hidden within the earthly armies is Satan's agent Sin, which Paul pictures as an evil spirit that invades the lives of individuals. Finally, Paul pictures Death as the most pervasive of Satan's agents, the one that has penetrated all organic creatures, but will in the end be defeated.

(b) Paul apparently thought of the battle as going on during Christ's lifetime (1 Cor 2:8). Then in Christ's death God conquered the principalities and powers (Col 2:15). As a result of the resurrection Christ has begun to rule over the powers (Phil 2:9-11; Eph 1:22), as Prince Regent in a Kingdom of Light into which believers can enter (Col 1:12-13).

(c) When believers in the present enter Christ's Kingdom of Light, they are protected from any eternal harm by the "armor of light" (Rom 13:12), so no evil forces can harm them spiritually. However, the evil powers fight on in the world and can still make believers suffer physically. Further, in this imagery Sin is pictured as a saboteur spirit from Satan that still seeks to rule over believers if they allow it to enter their lives again (Rom 6:12).

(d) Those past and present military images then lead to a future military vision, most vividly given in 2 Thessalonians 2, but also elaborated in 1 Thessalonians 4 and 1 Corinthians 15. Once evil in incarnate form (a Man of Lawlessness) rises to supreme power, then Christ will return and destroy all evil forever (2 Thess 2:8). In that battle Christ will destroy [*katargese*] "every rule [*archen*] and every authority [*exousian*] and power [*dunamin*]...The last enemy to be destroyed is death" (1 Cor 15: 23-24). At that moment Satan's rule will be forever ended (Rom 16:20).

---

[2] George B. Caird, *Principalities and Powers: A Study in Pauline Theology*, viii.

This military symbolism is very effective as a window onto the mystery of Paul's gospel. The picture it provides is concrete, memorable, easily imagined and contemplated as a way to make sense of the painful suffering of daily life for Christians in Paul's day. Its main limitation is that war is a process that most people wish to avoid, so many will find the picture of the Christian life as war a distasteful one.

## (2) The Organic Window: The Body of Christ (Present and Future)

A second major type of symbolism Paul uses as a window onto the mystery of the gospel is organic, especially the metaphor of believers as members of Christ's body in which the Spirit is the life-giving power uniting all. Believers being "in Christ," or having "Christ in them," or "dying (or rising, or ascended) with Christ," are all probably allusions to the metaphor of the body of Christ.

The major elements of Paul's organic symbolism seem to be the following:

(a) Paul apparently pictured all people as having been born "in Adam," i.e. into the body of Adam, members of that universal human body which is inhabited and dominated by Sin (Rom 5:12), which sends death to all: "In Adam all die" (1 Cor 15:22).[3] In this organic symbolism Sin and Death seem to be diseases that hiddenly enter into their victims and debilitate them.

(b) Then, by the resurrection of Christ a new corporate reality comes into existence—the body of the Second Adam, who is the life-giving Spirit (1 Cor 15:45): "You are the body of Christ and individually members of it" (1 Cor 12:13, 27; see also Rom 12:4–5; Eph 4:12; Col 1:18). This earthly body receives a foretaste of the eschatological gifts, because all that happened to Christ has happened to the body: those in the body have been crucified with Christ (Rom 6:5–6), buried with him (Col 2:12), raised with him (Col 2:12), and now sit with him in the heavenly places (Eph 2:6).

A second organic symbol Paul uses to speak of the community is the

---

[3] E. E. Ellis emphasized this corporate life, using the phrase "the body of Adam" in his article "*Soma* in First Corinthians" (*Interpretation* 44 [1990] 138–140).

olive tree which symbolizes God's people from Abraham on (Rom 11:17–24). A third organic symbol of God's corporate people is "the seed [*sperma*] of Abraham." Paul points first to Christ as the single seed of Abraham (Gal 3:16) and then says that all those who belong to Christ are thereby also Abraham's seed (Gal 3:29; see Rom 9:7–8).

(c) Paul's evangelistic ministry, when imagined in organic terms, is planting a garden (1 Cor 3:5–9). In this gardening, others contribute to the growth by watering (and probably weeding and pruning) but God is the life-giver, the one who makes the garden grow.

(d) In the future, all those who are "in Christ" (i.e. are "members of the body of Christ") will be "made alive" (1 Cor 15:22). Apparently, in Paul's organic version of the gospel, the resurrection is a gift given only to those who are in Christ, who are members of the body of Christ, who already have the Spirit within them uniting them to the Risen Christ and to all other believers (1 Cor 15:22–23; Rom 8:11). When Christ returns, the earthly body of Christ will apparently be transformed into a spiritual, eternal, body of Christ (2 Cor 5:1).[4]

(e) In this organic symbol system God can be aptly pictured as the life-giver (1 Cor 3:6–7). First he is the planter, the farmer who grows this organism, e.g. the olive tree Paul describes in Romans 11. Then in 1 Corinthians 15 Paul elaborates this organic metaphor by speaking of God giving life to the seed that has been buried.

Paul's organic symbolism thus is the clearest window through which one can understand the life of the believing community and the hope of resurrection to eternal life in union with God and all the faithful. The main limitation of this organic symbolism is that its corporate emphasis obscures the responsibility and freedom of individuals, both of which the judicial window emphasizes admirably.

---

[4] Ellis spoke of the glorious, heavenly body of Christ, but not of this humble, earthly one that we postulate; see E. E. Ellis, *Paul and His Recent Interpreters* (Grand Rapids: Eerdmans, 1961) 41–42.

## (3) The Judicial Window

Alongside God as the Warrior (the military model), and God as the Giver of Life (organic), Paul and the Hebrew-Jewish tradition knew of God as the Judge, e.g. in Daniel 7 (especially verse 10). The central characteristics of this model are these:

(a) God is imagined as a law-giver (Rom 1:32) and judge (Rom 2:5-6). By this judicial power and authority God seeks to uphold the good and deter evil. God's purpose is harmony, which depends first on order, so God provides a judicial system of order, law, testing, accusation, condemnation (or acquittal) and punishment (or reward).

(b) Human beings are subjects far beneath the exalted ruler. Thus they are pictured as related only indirectly and impersonally to this judge who does not take personal relationships into consideration, for God "shows no partiality" (Rom 2:11).

(c) In this system, the central value is equal justice, i.e. the practice of giving each person exactly what they deserve for what they have done (Rom 2:6; 2 Cor 5:10).

(d) All human beings have transgressed, i.e. wilfully broken God's law (Rom 3:12), either the written law of Moses or the Gentiles' law written on their hearts (Rom 2:15). This wilful transgression makes them all guilty (Rom 3:19).

(e) Therefore human beings all deserve punishment. Sometimes on earth they get what they deserve (1 Cor 11:30; 1 Thess 2:16), but often they do not get caught and overtly punished. Acting with forbearance, God sometimes passes over sins (Rom 3:25). As a result, some people continue to sin, thinking they will permanently escape responsibility.

(f) Still God's punishment (called his wrath) is visited internally on all sinners, driving them deeper into their sinfulness (Rom 1:18-32).

(g) The heart of the symbolism is a perfect Judge, one who in the End will make rewards and punishments precisely reflect what is deserved, for all secrets, both of action and motivation, will be uncovered (Rom 2:16). Then justice will be seen to be done in the lives of all.

(h) At the same time, and somewhat mysteriously, Paul pictures God the Judge as acquitting (justifying, declaring Not Guilty) any repentant sinners who have faith in Christ (Rom 3:24). They were under God's curse, but somehow (perhaps because by faith they come into Christ) Christ's becoming a curse relieves them of it (Gal 3:13). Here Paul renews the ancient Hebrew picture of the Judge acting in an un-judgelike fashion: the wrathful Judge relents "for his own [or his name's] sake" (Ezek 20:44, Dan 9:17).

(i) Even following the acquittal in Christ, the divine Judge maintains very high standards which (apparently) people must attain at the End in order to receive the rewards. Paul says God will accept those who are "holy, blameless and irreproachable before him" (Col 1:22–23; see also 1 Thess 5:23; Phil 1:9–10). Those who measure up will be rewarded for their achievement (1 Cor 3:14).

(j) Of course, on the guilty the Judge will send punishment, destruction, on "the Day of Wrath" (Rom 2:5; see also 1 Thess 1:10; Rom 12:19; Eph 5:6). How believers in Christ (all of whom are presumably still sinners to some extent) will escape that wrath is not entirely clear in Paul's picture of the Last Judgment. Perhaps they will not escape it entirely, but in their case the fire will purge rather than destroy, preparing them for eternal life (see 1 Cor 3:15).

Undoubtedly this judicial model was very significant for Paul the ex-Pharisee, the Jew brought up on Moses and the Torah. Not only does it speak to Jews, but it is universally vivid and powerful, touching the imaginations of people in all cultures, for all know of law, transgression, guilt and punishment. Thus a theological system modelled on this human judicial system is immediately understandable to almost all people older than five.

Of course, this is not a literal description of God's relationship to the world, but rather one symbolic way to portray that mystery. The main limitation of this symbolic window is its image of God as a judge, i.e. one who is impersonal, concerned about law not persons, normally imposing justice not mercy. This image needs to be corrected by bringing in the alternative symbolic windows, especially the loving parent, to which we now turn.

### (4) The Royal Family Window

In the first three models just sketched God is pictured as far above human beings, dealing essentially impersonally with them. Now, in the familial symbol system, we find Paul emphasizing God's direct, personal involvement with human beings, for they will be God's children who become members of the heavenly royal family and so inherit crowns, glory and kingdoms.

(a) God is the royal parent, the one who rules over all creation yet may be personally involved, in love and mercy, with human creatures. As the "father of mercies" (2 Cor 1:3), who has a "household" (Eph 2:19), God invites all who are willing to believe to join and receive the love spread by the family Spirit (Rom 5:5).

(b) Christ is the prince of this royal household, the one who gave up wealth and glory to become one with the slaves on the bottom of the hierarchy. "He was rich, yet for your sake he became poor, so that through his poverty you might become rich" (2 Cor 8:9). As a result of that sacrifice, Christ has been elevated to God's right hand, becoming ruler of all creatures (Phil 2:9), in "the kingdom of God's beloved Son" (Col 1:13).

(c) The human problem according to this symbol system is that the children have rejected their Father by running away from home into exile. There they are estranged from him, alienated, looking upon him as their enemy (Rom 5:10).

(d) By Christ's presence and Spirit in them, believers may be reconciled (Rom 5:10) and so become God's children (2 Cor 6:17-18), for "all who are led by the Spirit of God are children of God" (Rom 8:14-16). Of course this present adoption is only a foretaste, for Christians also "wait for adoption [*huiothesian*]" (Rom 8:22-23), the final and eternal inclusion in the family of God.

(e) As children of God already, believers in Christ are heirs of God. Though they are God's children already in some senses, the great gifts that this royal family status entails are still in waiting for the End: "We are children of God...heirs of God and fellow heirs with Christ" (Rom 8:16-17). Since God is the owner of the world, the inheritance awaiting the children is the one promised "to Abraham and his descendants, that they should inherit the world" (Rom 4:13).

(f) Thus one of the central gifts God gives is that believers, those who receive the Spirit of Christ, will "inherit a kingdom" (1 Cor 6:9; 15:50; Gal 5:21; Eph 5:5). Paul's meaning seems to be that God's children will share in the royal prerogatives, for they are united with Christ as co-heirs and receive all the blessings he receives. Thus, as Christ reigns in glory, so believers will in the end become God's royal children and "reign in life...through Jesus Christ" (Rom 5:17). As a sign of this royal status Paul pictures them as receiving crowns (1 Cor 9:25; Phil 4:1; 1 Thess 2:19).

(g) Next, along with the kingdom they inherit, they will receive the glory which belongs naturally to God, which will engulf all those who become part of the divine family. Glory (*doxa*) is the beautiful but awesome radiance, the dazzling light surrounding the Monarch of All (as in Isaiah 6 and Ezekiel 1). Since God is engulfed in glory, Paul pictured the adopted royal children as eventually receiving "glory and honor" (Rom 2:7; see also Rom 5:2; 8:30).

(h) The glory that God has and shares with the royal children apparently includes eternal life, for they will receive "glory and honor and immortality" (Rom 2:7). Paul says that the mortal body is "sown in dishonor [but] raised in glory [*en doxe*]" (1 Cor 15:43; see also, Rom 8:23; 2 Cor 4:17).

These various elements of the royal family model show us that Paul knew this as a fourth relatively complete window on the mystery of the gospel. Unlike the other models, this one emphasizes personal intimacy between God and believers, for they become children who share God's glory, honor, immortality and reign. Grace, mercy, love, friendship, personal intimacy and sharing of life, are the central divine attributes in this picture. Thus they provide a striking contrast to the others, especially to the judicial model in which God is no respecter of persons, acting mainly on the basis of justice, what people deserve. This unique personal emphasis is the central contribution this family symbolism makes, but of course it has its limitations too: it does not bring out the ontological difference between God and humankind that the Grower does, nor the moral and authority difference that the Judge does, nor the great conflict between good and evil that the Warrior does.

## B. AN ARGUMENT FOR THE MULTIPLE WINDOWS APPROACH

In presenting these four Pauline windows opening onto the gospel we have sketched the central evidence for the basic presupposition of this book—that Paul knew and used four relatively distinct symbolic expressions of the gospel. Clearly these are all different symbol systems, ones that are not immediately compatible with each other: for example, one cannot at the same time, with the same person, act as a personal, loving parent and as an impartial, justice-abiding judge; further, the image of sin as human action producing guilt is not immediately compatible with the image of Sin as a saboteur spirit that needs to be defeated; thirdly the corporate emphasis of the organic symbolism stands in great tension with the individual emphasis of the legal perspective, in which individuals are responsible for their own transgressions and guilt. Therefore, the most appropriate way to take them is as complementary windows onto the mystery. The following are a few further arguments for adopting this hypothesis.

**(1) The Hebrew Tradition**

The Hebrew tradition uses all four of these symbol systems as complementary windows onto the mystery of God, so it is plausible to believe that Paul did the same. In the tradition, God and the supernatural world are constantly pictured by means of multiple metaphors, each of which provides a glimpse of the reality, but none of which is to be taken literally. Indeed, each of the windows we propose Paul looked through is traditional:

Military: God is often pictured as a warrior (Isa 63:1-6), as the one who in the end directs the destruction of the enemies of Israel (e.g., Ezek 39:3; Zech 14:3-4) and of the monstrous forces of evil (Isa 27:1).

Judicial: God is clearly pictured as the Eternal Judge in the eschatological scene in Dan 7:9-10 and as the Law-giver in Exodus 20.

Organic: God is the planter and gardener of the vineyard Israel (Isa 5:1-7). Further, the people of Israel are one body, a corporate personality, known as Jacob or Israel, and pictured in the image of "one like a son of man" in Dan 7:14.

Familial: Israel is God's child (Exod 4:22), whom God loves despite his sinning (Hos 11:1-9). In the end Israel will sit on the throne beside God, ruling over the world (Dan 7:13-14, 18).

In the Old Testament these are clearly complementary symbol systems for speaking of the mysterious divine interaction with the world. In addition, of course, the ancient writers used many other symbols to picture God—as shepherd, fortress, panther, mother, eagle, fire, wind, maker, High One, and many more. Thus it is plausible to conclude that Paul thought this same way, picturing the mystery of the gospel through complementary windows.

## (2) Multiple Symbols for the Cross

In Paul's own writings the multiple metaphors for a single mysterious reality are obvious, especially when speaking of the way God reaches out to the world through the Cross. In the outline of the Four Windows given above, we have presented that point clearly, for the cross to Paul can be viewed through all these windows and many more:

Military: in the Cross, God has defeated the powers of evil (Col 2:15).

Judicial: through the Cross, God has justified, acquitted, those who believe in Christ (Rom 3:24), because Christ has suffered the curse of the law that was due to sinners (Gal 3:13).

Organic: believers have died in and with Christ, been buried with him, and raised with him to new life (Col 2:11–12), for by faith they become integral elements of the body of Christ (1 Cor 12:12–13, 27; Rom 12:5).

Familial: in Christ's death God showed his love and reconciled to himself those who were estranged, forgiving their trespasses (Rom 5:8–10), and adopting them into the family (Gal 4:5).

In addition to those four major windows on the Cross, Paul speaks of that mystery in these other kinds of symbolism:

Religious: Christ is our passover lamb which has been slain, probably to protect us from the Angel of Death (1 Cor 5:7).

Economic: Christ has bought us back, redeemed us, by paying the price that was required to get us out of slavery (Eph 1:7).

Artistic: in Christ God has created a new kingdom, so all who are in Christ are new creations (2 Cor 5:17).

While these other windows on the Cross are certainly valuable, and must be considered when seeking Paul's probing of that mystery, they are not as complete as the four outlined above. Therefore we will leave them in the background most of the time. Their presence, however, makes clear that Paul saw the cross as a mystery so profound that he needed many different metaphors to provide adequate insight into it.[5]

---

[5] See F. W. Dillistone, *The Christian Understanding of Atonement* (1968) for an example of the way that the atonement can be illuminated using the array of different models found in the NT.

### (3) No Literal Description

The only significant alternative to the multiple windows theory is that one of them is not a window but is Paul's literal view of the reality. Of course the most popular candidate for that literal system is his legal/judicial symbolism, for many interpreters have taken much of it to be literal speech, especially when the relatively abstract "righteous" family of words is used to define it: God is righteous; God demands righteousness from creatures; God's standard for measuring their compliance is a righteous one; God acts righteously; in Christ God has revealed the divine righteousness; indeed, through Christ, God has given the divine righteousness to believers; therefore God has declared them righteous (justified, acquitted); righteousness remains the standard by which God will judge the world at the end; God is the righteous Judge.

The argument for the conclusion that all these statements are metaphorical is not a simple one, for we gave many pages to it in the book on metaphor we will mention below. Some of the statements can be more easily seen as metaphorical than others: for example that God "gives the divine righteousness to believers" pictures righteousness as a commodity, or perhaps a spirit, something that can be transferred from one person to another, whereas it is more mysterious than that. God as the Judge is also clearly metaphorical, for it is based on a human role and God does not have the substantial limitations of humans playing that role. Therefore God as "Judge" is one who transcends what we know of literal judges, and that transcendence cannot be fully described literally.

The most likely candidate for literal speech among all the theological uses of the "righteous" family of words is "God is righteous" (see Rom 3:26). The argument for it as literal speech is this: we only know what it is to be "righteous" from a perfect example of it; God is the only perfect example of it; therefore we use "righteous" literally of God, based on revealed knowledge, and use it in a secondary sense with human beings. Our reply to that argument is that we do not know what perfect righteousness is, for we define the word in terms of human beings whom we know directly.[6] Thus when we use the term

---

[6] It is even possible that "being righteous" used of human beings is a metaphorical concept, i.e. one that we can only define and understand by analogy with more concrete realities in our experience. For example we may

of God, we use it in an exalted sense, saying that God is "perfectly righteous" (i.e. righteous in a way that is mysterious, beyond our understanding). Thus "righteous" is a term we use metaphorically with God.[7]

Our conclusion is thus that there is no realistic alternative to our theory that Paul saw through multiple windows onto the mystery of the gospel. There is no detailed literal account of the gospel, so some particular symbolic window must be used to express it (though some elements in each of the accounts may well be literal, as we will see). We stress that we have no "detailed" literal account of the gospel because we can sum up the gospel literally by saying "God saves those who repent and believe in Christ." However, as soon as we try to express that in any detail, e.g. saying who "God" is, and what "God saves" means, and how God does it, then we must turn to particular symbols.


## C. TRADITIONAL INTERPRETATION OF PAUL'S WRITINGS

This hypothesis of four complementary symbolic windows onto the gospel is a modification and development of modern approaches to Paul's thought. First of all, in the nineteenth century, scholars distinguished in Paul's thought between his inherited Judaism (with its emphasis on law and righteousness), and his supposedly adopted Hellenism (with its emphasis on the problem of the flesh). These two alternative perspectives were then often called incompatible, with interpreters taking one or the other as the authoritative one. Then Schweitzer proposed three different symbol systems, claiming his "mystical" one (similar to the one we call organic) was Paul's most important. Later scholars suggested that Paul's thought developed from his early military (apocalyptic) and judicial (Pharisaic) types to his later cosmic and mystical types. Most recently Beker has suggested that the apocalyptic form is the framework into which all other types must be fit.

---

understand it on analogy with a line that is perfectly straight and so is a standard by which to measure the straightness of other lines. See Macky, *Metaphors* (159–161) for a discussion of metaphorical concepts.

[7] See Macky, *Metaphors* (235–241) where we discuss the perfections God is "perfect" and "good" and show why it is appropriate to take them as metaphorical rather than literal speech.

**(1) Schweitzer's Trilogy**

Albert Schweitzer refined the Jewish v. Hellenistic dualism into a three-fold heritage, pointing to "three different doctrines of redemption which for Paul go side by side: an eschatological, a juridical and a mystical."[8] By "eschatological" Schweitzer meant the apocalyptic picture of a battle against evil powers, what we call the military symbolism. By "juridical" he meant what we call the judicial symbolism. By "mysticism" Schweitzer referred to what we are calling Paul's organic symbolism, the way he pictures all human beings as members of the body of Adam, and all believers as incorporated in the body of Christ.

Clearly, Schweitzer believed that the mysticism was the most profound of the approaches, one that should have banished the others, for he thought they were incompatible: "The co-existence of such disparate views is in itself difficult enough to conceive, [but] it becomes a complete enigma when we find it in a mystic," (25) which is what Schweitzer believed Paul was. Here is a clear example of one problem in interpreting the multiple windows: a reader can take one symbol system as the most profound and try to explain the others in terms of it. Schweitzer at least recognized the difficulties in this process rather than letting them disappear in a cloud of mysticism. His problem, however, was that he thought Paul had three distinct theories, whereas it is more plausible to suggest that they were distinct but complementary symbolic windows.

**(2) Paul's Developing Thought?**

Another nineteenth century approach to the varieties in Paul's pictures was the theory that Paul's beliefs evolved. For example, when considering Paul's eschatology some scholars postulated four stages of development. R. H. Charles saw the military imagery of the Thessalonian letters and First Corinthians as Paul's early, more primitive, thought. The organic and cosmic imagery of the Prison Epistles he then took to be more advanced.[9]

More recent scholars, e.g. Shires, argue that the four-stage scheme is

---

[8] *The Mysticism of Paul the Apostle*, 25.

[9] R. H. Charles, *Eschatology: The Doctrine of a Future Life in Israel, Judaism, and Christianity. A Critical History*, 437–438.

imposed upon Paul's letters, not found there.[10] The main argument against the scheme is that the various kinds of symbolism pervade his letters from beginning to end. For example, military symbolism is present in the Thessalonian letters but also in Romans and Ephesians; organic symbolism begins early, in Paul's image of believers being "in Christ" (1 Thess 4:16), and continues throughout his writing.

Shires' own theory was that Paul spoke figuratively in his eschatological passages but intended to give his readers a set of abstract propositions. Shires said that despite his figurative language, Paul "attempts a logically consistent whole" (32) which is integrated by "underlying principles" and "central truths" (34). Those abstract truths are so general, however, that they seem hardly to fit the concrete, vivid, narrative vision Paul offers. For example, Shires proposed this as one of Paul's intended truths: "Time is not an illusion or a relativity but a concrete reality" (42). Our alternative theory is that Paul provided multiple windows which can be combined in the imagination of the reader, even though the mysterious reality cannot be expressed in literal abstractions.

### (3) The Triumph of the Divine Liberator

A more recent trend has been to emphasize the military (apocalyptic) imagery, since Schweitzer and Weiss popularized it near the end of the last century. Later, Aulen in *Christus Victor* argued that the military symbolism is the oldest type of cross symbolism. Then liberation theologians stressed the importance of Christ as liberator of the oppressed.

Most recently Beker has pictured Paul as primarily an apocalyptist. Beker rejected Schweitzer's theory of three inconsistent doctrines, with mysticism as the deepest. Instead, Beker asserted that the apocalyptic symbolism of triumph over evil forces is Paul's deepest, most pervasive, perspective. Then, he claimed, Paul uses a variety of symbols from other realms, judicial, personal, political, organic, whenever they were appropriate for his particular audience.

The specific types that Beker mentions in connection with salvation provide a close parallel to those we develop: (1) "Liberation symbolism" speaks of the defeat of the powers and the freeing of slaves, which is what we call

---

[10] H. M. Shires, *The Eschatology of Paul in the Light of Modern Scholarship* (1965), 38–39.

military symbolism; (2) "Justification symbolism" uses the symbols of guilt, law, acquittal, punishment, which we have labelled judicial symbolism; (3) "Reconciliation symbolism" deals with personal categories of enmity, love, and alienation, which we call Royal Family symbolism; (4) Finally Beker refers to "the organic images" in which changes are of "biological structures," just what we have labelled organic symbolism.[11]

## (4) Complementary Symbol Systems

Our approach is like Beker's in seeing all these perspectives as complementary symbolisms and not as inconsistent doctrines. However, we do not adopt the apocalyptic/military symbolism as the most basic, as Beker does, for it seems to be one among equals, not the sole foundation. Though this book will explore that military window in detail, still we emphasize that it needs to be corrected by the visions provided by the other windows. For example, we see the Reformation interpreters as correct in stressing Paul's judicial imagery—law, transgression, justice, wrath, justification and condemnation—as central. Their error, we propose, was in taking this imagery virtually literally and isolating it from symbolic correction that would have come by viewing the mystery through the windows offered by the other central symbolic perspectives. Likewise we find Schweitzer's mysticism approach as valuable, but one-sided. The same should be said of the Liberal Protestant emphasis on the familial symbol system, which was expressed in the slogan "the Fatherhood of God and the brotherhood of man."

Our proposal is that all these symbolic perspectives, these windows on the mystery, are of central value and need to be interpreted together, the way we take Jesus' parables and interpret them in the light of each other. However, the military symbolism is the one that we plan to develop, elaborate and explore first.

The book that has explored this trail most fully heretofore is Ragnar Leivestad's *Christ the Conqueror: Ideas of Conflict and Victory in the New*

---

[11] J. C. Beker, *Paul The Apostle: The Triumph of God in Life and Thought* (1980), 256–258. Beker is here summarizing and endorsing the analysis of Gerd Theissen in "Soteriologische Symbolik in den paulinischen Schriften," *Kerygma und Dogma* 20 (1974) 282–304.

*Testament* (1954). Leivestad discussed the wide array of passages throughout the NT which used military symbolism as a way to provide insight into the gospel, giving eighty pages or so to Paul. Unfortunately, he wrote before the widespread dissemination of the Dead Sea Scrolls, so he was not able to use the detailed military background in those documents to elaborate Paul's picture.

We will follow Leivestad's lead in many cases, but depart from him in these general ways: our emphasis is on developing Paul's picture fully, so we use the Scrolls and other writings to extrapolate from his explicit imagery in order to create that more detailed and complete picture. We will then go beyond Leivestad in providing an interpretation of part of Paul's military myth, suggesting what his angelic battle imagery may have symbolized for him. That process in turn is based on the past generation's detailed study of metaphor, imagery and symbolism, especially as they are used in literary ways to evoke insight into mysteries. Our theory of the way symbolism works in imaginative writings is background that we will now outline.

## D. A THEORY OF SYMBOLISM

By the term "symbolism" we refer to the use of symbols (defined in the sense given below) to communicate. In *The Centrality of Metaphors to Biblical Thought* we presented in detail the theory that undergirds this present exploring of Paul's use of symbols. Among the central elements of that theory are the following:

### (1) Definitions
These are our definitions of the central concepts:

(i) **Analogy**: a relationship between two realities in which there are significant similarities and noticeable differences.
(ii) **Symbol**: a reality (an object, quality, process, state of affairs or image) that stands for and gives insight into some other reality because of the analogy between the two.
(iii) **Metaphor**: that figurative way of speaking (and meaning) in which a subject is spoken of in terms of a symbol, which is related to it by analogy.
(iv) **Model**: an established symbol, one that has become

conventionally used to illuminate a particular subject. (56)[12]

Among the more important points suggested by these definitions are these: Analogies can be expressed in the rhetorical form called "analogy," e.g. "just as the body is one and has many members . . . so it is with Christ" (1 Cor 12:12). Secondly, the same analogy can be expressed in a metaphor, e.g. "you are the body of Christ and individually members of it" (1 Cor 12:27). Such metaphors use a symbol (body) and connect it explicitly with a subject (Christ and you Corinthians). Thirdly, speakers may use symbols without putting them in metaphors, i.e. without explicitly mentioning the subject they are intended to illuminate. For example, 1 Cor 12:14-26 focusses solely on animal bodies, beginning with this statement: "For the body does not consist of one member but of many." Normally, as here (27-30), the context makes adequately clear what the subject was that the speaker was symbolizing.

## (2) Varieties of Metaphors

Not only did Paul and the biblical writers use these different literary forms, but also used a considerable variety of types of metaphor. When considering "The Varieties of Metaphor" (chap. III) the most important distinction is the spectrum that runs from novel to retired (dead) metaphors. Novel metaphors, e.g. God's "word runs swiftly" (Ps 147:15), are those in which the speaker makes a connection between symbol and subject that is unusual (73-75). Next come familiar metaphors, e.g. God "refines" his people by sending suffering (Isa 48:10), ones that were used by more than one writer and ceased to be novel but did not become so widely used that they could be called standard (75-76). Standard metaphors, like "God is my fortress," are those that have become ingrained in the tradition. Some, such as God is the judge, are so common that many users of the language will not at first notice that they are metaphorical. But when the question is raised, most mature speakers will recognize that God is not literally a judge, but is symbolized as that for certain purposes (77-79). The most important categories for biblical interpretation are the next two: hidden metaphors and retired ones.

---

[12] The page and chapter references in this section are all to Macky, *Metaphors* unless otherwise noted.

The fourth category, "Hidden Metaphors: Saboteurs of our Thinking" differs from the third in that many users find it almost impossible to recognize the symbolic nature of the utterance (79–80). For example, when we ask "what meaning did you get out of that paragraph?" we probably are understanding meaning as a kind of treasure that can be plucked out of the carrying case of the words. However, meaning is more appropriately thought of as something the readers create by using their knowledge and imaginations. So "finding meaning" is a hidden metaphor for most users. Though most readers are probably not familiar with this category of hidden metaphors, an array of authors have documented this pervasive reality in our speech, for example Lakoff and Johnson in *Metaphors We Live By* (1980). The continuing debate focusses on which usages are residents of this foggy realm.

The root of that dispute concerns distinguishing hidden metaphors from the final line on the spectrum, retired (dead) metaphors, those that have ceased to be metaphorical uses and become literal ones for some users (80). We call them "retired" because all of them can be recalled to active service, re-used as metaphors whenever an author wishes.

Our theory is developed in detail in chap. IV "Retired Metaphors," where we argue that we can recognize such usages by the following characteristics, all of which must be present for the usage to be literal: (a) the usage has become commonplace, as for example is our speaking of a fork in the road; (b) the user must be able to apply the usage directly to the reality, by knowing the reality directly. That is no problem with observables like road forks, but becomes more difficult when using mental and psychological phrases like "I see your point." It becomes even more difficult when speaking of abstractions, e.g. the "foundation" of a theory. (c) The speaker must be intending to speak literally, for in all examples of retired metaphors a speaker can intend to use them metaphorically, e.g. to make a joke about a giant using the fork in the road for his supper.

## (3) Theories of Interpretation of Metaphor

Once we have discerned how best to draw the line between metaphors (whether novel, familiar, standard or hidden) and literal speech, then we can mark out a spectrum of theories held by scholars on the interpretation of metaphors (163). At one end of the spectrum is **Absolute Literalism**, the theory that all metaphorical speech can be re-expressed literally (137–140). Next to it is **Sophisticated Literalism**, the view that all the cognitive (informative, assertive, truth-conveying) content of metaphors can be re-expressed literally and accurately, though all the other speech functions and effects may be distorted or even lost in the translation (162–164; 169–176). At the other end of the spectrum is **Radicalism**, the theory that almost all speech is metaphorical so there is hardly any literal speech into which to translate it (141–142; 156–161). Somewhat less extreme is **Modified Radicalism**, the view that all speech about supersensible realities (those that cannot be observed by our senses) is and must be metaphorical (177–183).

In the middle of the spectrum is the view we argue for, which we call **Critical Metaphoricalism** (183–187). Among the main branches of this theory are the following: (a) Metaphor is distinctly powerful in fulfilling the deeper speech functions, those that go beyond information and argument (e.g. expressive, dynamic, exploratory and relational speech functions). When pursuing those purposes literal speech often cannot successfully take its place.[13] (b) When we speak informatively, we can speak literally to some extent about any reality we know directly, provided there are adequate observable concomitants to the reality which other members of our speech community can recognize and thus know what reality we are speaking about. (c) When we come to speak about supersensible realities only a very little of what we know directly (by experience) can be expressed literally. For example, we can say "I understand you" and mean it literally. However, when we try to explain what it is to understand ("It's like seeing; e.g. like seeing our destination clearly after wandering in a fog"), we turn to metaphor (with its inherent symbols and analogy). Thus most of our speech about supersensible realities is metaphorical.

When applying this theory to theological speech we ask in chapter VIII "Did the Biblical Writers Speak Literally of God?" Our answer is that in a very few assertions they did. First of all, negative assertions were probably meant literally, e.g. that God is invisible, incorruptible, immortal, without iniquity, uncreated, non-temporal (eternal) and unchangeable (217–221). Secondly, a few

---

[13] See ch. X, "Doing Things Metaphorically," which discusses how metaphors can accomplish the array of different speech act purposes (which are summarized earlier on 15–17).

positive assertions probably were meant literally, that God is "real" (true, 195–209), "active" (living, 209–216) and performs a few very general positive activities, e.g. God saves, helps, blesses, does good (221–229).

All the rest of biblical speech about God, so we argue, is symbolic (and much of it also metaphorical). That of course includes all physical symbols applied to God, because God is not physical, e.g. God is my rock and my fortress. It includes all the specific interpersonal activities that God is said to perform, e.g. calling, forgiving, justifying, adopting, guiding, chastening, punishing. In all these cases the symbol is the human activity, which is then applied to God metaphorically (231–232). Even more certainly metaphorical are assertions of God's "inner" activities, that God feels, thinks, intends, wills, repents and loves (233–235). Finally, it is likely that all the perfections are meant metaphorically by the biblical writers also, i.e. that God is perfect, good, wise, just and holy (235–241). Those are terms used first and literally of earthly realities, and are then applied to God metaphorically.

The implication of this view, that most of our speech about God is metaphorical, is this: we cannot translate the obvious biblical metaphors into literal speech because there is hardly any literal speech about God to translate it into. Thus, for example, the whole system of legal/judicial symbolism which Paul uses is not mainly literal speech, but (as we argued briefly above) one more symbolic window onto the mystery. It uses the human experience of a legal system (law-making, police, judges, guilt, condemnation and a penal system) as the model by which to picture some aspects of God's interaction with the creation. It is a highly significant system, but it is a symbol system, not a literal one. As such, it needs to be corrected by the perspectives offered when we see the mystery through the other major windows.

Further, we cannot take the symbolic windows and combine them fully and adequately into a literal system based on abstract philosophy rather than on concrete human experiences. We can of course create such abstract systems, e.g. based on Platonism, or on Aristotelianism, or on Hegelianism, or on Existentialism, or on Process Philosophy. But—and this is one of the central points of the book—those more abstract systems are still largely symbolic, based on hidden metaphors, those that their users mistake for literal speech. Thus the symbolic windows that Paul (and the tradition) used are not preliminary, popular, simple forms that must be transcended by philosophical theology.

Instead, the philosophical theology is preliminary: it may be useful as a way to help us see more deeply into the way to combine the various windows. But the final revelation comes when readers are able to see as clearly as possible through the multiple windows, by learning to take them together in a single vision. That final seeing is the application of this theory of interpretation, which is presented in ch. XI "Reaching the Depths: Participating in a Speaker's Metaphorical Thinking."

In this book we will look into the depths of Paul's military gospel, showing how we elaborate the symbolic picture and then begin to interpret and evaluate it.

**Outline**

In chapters II to VII we will show that Paul did have a relatively complete military version of the gospel.

The next chapter will present the Old Testament and Jewish background, in **II. The Lord is a Man of War**. Then in **III. The Enemy Commander-in-Chief**, we will explore Paul's references to Satan, whom he saw as the Ruler of the Kingdom of Darkness, the top of the evil hierarchy which constitutes this present age of darkness. Next in **IV. The Army of the Kingdom of Darkness** we will describe how Paul imagined the rest of the members of the Kingdom of Darkness—principalities and powers, the human rulers of this present age, the children of darkness, and Satan's two dread spirits Sin and Death.

Those three chapters provide the background and setting for Paul's story. The first act of his Cosmic War Myth is **V. God's Initial Victory** when **Through Christ God Establishes the Kingdom of Light**. There the children of light, who have all been spiritually transferred into the new age of Christ's Kingdom of Light, are spiritually protected as if they were inside an impenetrable fortress. Though the Kingdom of Darkness has been defeated, still the battle goes on outside. We will describe that battle in **VI. The Ongoing War between the Two Kingdoms**. Finally the conflict will rise to a consummation in **VII. The Last Battle**, in which Paul pictures Christ destroying every principality and power and authority that stands in opposition to God.

After this elaboration of Paul's cosmic war myth, we will explore **VIII.**

**The Reality Behind Paul's Angelic Armies Symbol**, asking what Paul probably saw as the subjects lying hidden behind his symbolic picture of the two angelic hierarchies in their age-long war against each other. We will argue that for Paul Satan and the principalities symbolize the mysterious, transcendent power of divine justice that cannot be literally described. Finally we will evaluate Paul's myth in **IX. The Treasures in Paul's Earthen Vessel**.

In these chapters that develop Paul's military symbolism, we will go far beyond the explicit assertions that Paul makes in his writings—seeking to look down through the water to the part of the iceberg that is hidden. By drawing in the Hebraic background which Paul absorbed in his upbringing, we can expand considerably the sketch of a war myth that Paul provides in scattered passages in his letters. Our theory is that he had a complete picture in mind, even though he never presented it fully in any passage. Ultimately, the best evidence supporting this approach will be its fruitfulness in making comprehensive sense of what Paul wrote. If at the end we have seen more deeply into Paul's imagining than we had before starting, then that will be adequate support for the value of this approach.

# II. THE LORD AS A MAN OF WAR

Military Symbolism in the Hebrew Theological Tradition

## Introduction

From the beginning of her national experience Israel pictured the Lord as acting on her behalf as "a man of war" (Exod 15:2), an almighty champion who enters into powerful and victorious physical combat with the enemies of the chosen people. Thus military symbolism for the Lord's action in the world is as old as the people of Israel itself.[1] Therefore, Jews like Paul who were familiar with the Hebrew tradition inherited a picture of God as (among other things) a victorious warrior. In this chapter we will sketch that picture, so it can serve as the background against which we can see Paul's own military symbolism.

As Paul later envisioned the Messianic Kingdom of Light beginning by a preliminary Conquest of Evil Powers, so also in the Hebrew tradition God's Kingdom in Israel began with **A. The Man of War's Initial Victory**, over Egyptian tyranny. That Exodus story, especially the ancient poetic version in the Song of Moses, provides some of the most basic military symbolism for the Hebrew picture of God.

---

[1] See Lind, *Yahweh as Warrior*, 23 and Longman and Reid, *God is a Warrior*, ch. 1.

As a result of that victory, God became the protector of Israel, indeed God was pictured often as the fortress in which Israel could dwell securely if she lived faithfully. However, for centuries she endured **B. The Continuing Siege of the Fortress**, as the Lord personally fought for her and also commanded human armies in battle. This picture of the fortress under seige was the foreshadowing of the Pauline picture of Christ's followers securely dwelling in Christ's fortress-like Kingdom of Light while the forces of darkness continued to attack them (sometimes quite subtly) whenever they ventured outside.

The reason the battle continued was that **C. The Enemies of Heaven** constantly sought to destroy God's people. Some enemies were human, e.g. the evil empires, especially Assyria, Babylon and the Seleucid Empire; others were pictured as fantastic monsters, Leviathan, Rahab and Daniel's Fourth Beast; still others were angelic, the rebel sons of God (Ps 82:1-7) who were the supernatural princes of Greece and Persia (Dan 10:20) and other nations. In the end, the Jewish people developed a cosmology that combined all these enemies into a Kingdom of Darkness under the command of a single "Angel of Darkness" known as Belial and Satan (e.g. 1QM xiii). These same enemies, especially the supernatural ones, are alive and still threatening destruction to God's people in the Pauline mythology.

Finally, the Hebrew tradition proclaims, God will destroy the forces of evil, the enemies of God, in **D. The Last Battle**, which will usher in the new age of peace and goodness. The evil empires (e.g. Gog and the northern armies, Ezek 38-39) will be finally wiped out; the demonic powers of wickedness will be destroyed (e.g. Leviathan, Isa 27:1, and the Fourth Beast of Daniel 7:11); and the Angel of Darkness will lose power forever (1QM xv-xvi). Here, in the Hebrew and Jewish pictures of the End, is the clearest source of all for Paul's military symbolism of God's victory over all evil.

## A. THE MAN OF WAR'S INITIAL VICTORY

In the beginning of Israel's national history God fought and conquered the sea monster Rahab, thereby rescuing the children of Israel from age-long slavery (Isa 51:9-11; Ps 74:13-16). At first the story was told as the Lord's battle against the Sea and the army of Pharaoh, which together were the anvil and the hammer that threatened destruction to the fleeing followers of Moses

(Exod 14–15). Later this creation-of-Israel story was mythologized by depicting the Sea as the monster Rahab, the destructive power of chaos in human affairs. In both cases the Lord was symbolized as the single warrior who faced the enemy alone and defeated it as the people of Israel watched from the sidelines.[2]

This story and other battle stories like it provide the most vivid military symbols of the Lord's involvement in Israel's quest. These stories tell of God as a mountain-sized warrior who brings physical force directly to bear on human enemy armies, defeating them by stirring up natural or supernatural forces against them. Here, the Almighty is imagined, portrayed symbolically, as a warrior, one who wields arms, bearing the sword or shooting out fire that destroys the enemies. Of course there is great variety in the way Israel's Champion exercises power: fire and wind, earthquake and thunderstorm, flood and hail are arrows in the divine quiver.

Most of all in the Song of Moses (Exod 15:1–12) this image of the divine warrior stands out. This song is not only the foundational Divine Warrior portrait, but also one of the most vivid. In it the singer proclaims that the Lord alone, without any human help, triumphed over the vast army of Pharoah, drowning them in the depths of the Red Sea. When the fleeing people of God were threatened by Pharaoh's hosts, the Lord came among them as their refuge, defending them from attack and thus delivering them from death. Descending into their midst, the divine warrior acted as the champion of the helpless refugees who had no other defense. Their enemy rushed forward in chariots, seeking to kill the fleeing slaves and retrieve the spoil they had taken from Egypt, but in their way stood the Lord Almighty. Like a giant, thousands of feet tall, he swung his strong right hand and smashed the attacking army (Exod 15:6), sweeping them into the sea where they drowned. Like a terrifying tornado, the warrior's angry breath burst forth and piled the seas up as walls: "at the blast of your nostrils the waters piled up…You blew with your wind, the sea covered them" (Exod 15:8, 10). Thus, when the Egyptians had entered the trap, God let the waters return, drowning the blood-seeking army as they approached the defenseless Israelites.

---

[2] See John Day, *God's Conflict with the Dragon and the Sea: Echoes of a Canaanite Myth in the Old Testament* (Cambridge: Cambridge University Press, 1985).

The people of God were merely spectators at this battle, so no actual human fighting took place. Instead, the singer pictures the Divine Warrior acting alone, using the powers of nature, which were all at his command, to destroy the attacking army.[3]

As a result of this Red Sea victory the Lord comes to be the Ruler of Israel, the one who will "reign for ever and ever" (Exod 15:18). As Lind concludes: "The experience of Yahweh as the sole warrior at the sea results in the experience of Yahweh as the sole king at Sinai."[4] Their Champion will lead the rescued slaves to Canaan and plant them safely on the divine mountain, to dwell in the sanctuary built by God's own hands (Exod 15:16–17).

That defeat of Pharoah was later pictured as a defeat of supernatural forces—the sea serpent called Rahab and Leviathan—which was imagined as giving power to the Egyptians.[5] Rahab and Leviathan were two of the names of the monstrous serpent who ruled the seas in ancient myths. The monsters came from the sea because the sea was the unknown chaos that threatened the settled life of the land.[6] Rahab was an underwater dragon which stirred up storms when it thrashed around. The Lord was the giant warrior who stepped out into the sea with sword flashing, fighting off Rahab's attack and then driving the sword into the monster's heart. In this battle myth the Almighty cut the dragon up and tossed it on the land for the wild animals and birds to eat. This Yahweh v. Rahab battle imagery was one symbolic way the Israelite writers spoke of the wondrous victory of the Lord at the Red Sea (Isa 51:9–11; Ps 74:13–14; see also Ezek 32:1–6).

This fantastic symbolism for the historical event of the Exodus rescue, the myth of a supernatural battle with a sea monster, provided the inspiration for

---

[3] See D. N. Freedman, "Strophe and Meter in Exodus 15," in H. N. Bream et al (eds), *A Light Unto My Path: Old Testament Studies In Honor of Jacob M. Hyers* (Philadelphia: Temple University Press, 1974), 193.

[4] Lind, *Warrior*, 51.

[5] See Neil Forsyth, *The Old Enemy: Satan and the Combat Myth* (Princeton: Princeton University Press: 1987) ch.4 "Combat at the Red Sea: The Exodus Legend" (90–104).

[6] This sea monster imagery probably goes back to Tiamat the sea serpent killed by Marduk in the Babylonian creation story, imagery echoed in Genesis 1. See Forsyth, 48–50.

later apocalyptic pictures of the Lord's heavenly triumph over the monstrous beasts of Daniel 7 (see also Isa 27:1). In particular they often provided the crucial parallel detail that they "come up from the sea" (Dan 7:3), the world of chaos which is symbolized by Rahab/Leviathan. Those sea monster images, and later ones in the Apocalyptic Jewish writings (e.g. 1 QM i), were the prototypes for the early Christians' similar pictures (e.g. 2 Thessalonians 2).

## B. THE CONTINUING SIEGE OF THE FORTRESS

In God's initial defeat of the powers of evil in the Exodus, the Rescuer of Israel became their protector, the one who surrounded them with cloud and fire, and came in power to drive away their enemies. When they reached the promised land, God eventually centered them in Jerusalem, the walled city of God. There rose the sanctuary where God's Name dwelled (Deut 12:5), i.e. where God was personally present. There God was imagined as **(1) Israel's Shield and Fortress**, the one in whom they found refuge from the dangers of the world. At times their divine protector went forth to fight outside the fortress, against their enemies, and then they painted word pictures of **(2) The Gigantic Heavenly Warrior** smashing all opponents. A third military image the Hebrew writers used portrayed **(3) The Lord as Commander of Earthly Armies,** a hidden figure whose plans were carried out by human soldiers.

### (1) Israel's Shield and Fortress

God the heavenly warrior has a special concern for Jerusalem, the place where the divine Name dwells. Therefore, Isaiah proclaims that when the city is attacked: "the Lord of Hosts will come down to fight upon Mount Zion...[and] will protect Jerusalem" (Isa 31:4-5). Descending from on high when the city is besieged, the Champion of Israel becomes a shield over the people, like a mother bird hovering over her young. By this shielding presence the Protector will save Jerusalem from attackers, delivering the people to safety, whenever they turn to their Ruler in faith and true worship. The enemies outside her gates will fall by the heavenly sword, for the Lord is a fire that blazes in Zion, shooting out flames to destroy her enemies (Isa 31:9).

Here God the heavenly warrior is pictured as a protective shield outside, and fire within, the fortress city on Mount Zion. Indeed God is often pictured as their tower, stronghold, refuge and shield. Most of all the Hebrew writers often speak of the Lord as their Rock and Fortress, suggesting a picture of a great rock fortress on the heights, within which God's people can find refuge. One psalmist calls God: "my rock [*sela*], who trains my hands for war...my help which never fails, my fortress [*metsudah*], my strong tower [*misgab*, high place] and my rescuer [*palat*], my shield [*magen*] in which I trust [*chasah*, find refuge]" (Ps 144:1–2). One psalmist sings eloquently of Jerusalem the fortress: "God's holy mountain, beautiful in elevation, is the joy of all the earth, Mount Zion in the far north. Within her castle [*armon*, high place, citadel] God has shown himself a sure refuge [*misgab*, tower, high place]" (Ps 48:2–3). The psalmist is here thinking of God as the protector of the fortress city (10–11, 12–14)

Clearly the images of fortresses, towers, and castles are closely related to the warrior image because fortresses were central elements in ancient warfare (e.g. Dan 11:7, 10). When writers also refer to God as Israel's shield the military allusion is even more certain, e.g. Ps 144:2, where God is called "My rock and my fortress, my stronghold and my deliverer, my shield and he in whom I take refuge..."[7]

The main image these poems evoke as their symbol is of a great rock fortress set on a high mountain. The mountain itself is steep and rocky at the top, with cliffs most of the way around. Built up from those cliffs, the walls at the top are impregnable. Towers stretch up into the sky providing even greater vision and strength to those who find refuge within them. No enemy, no matter how huge and powerful its army, could break into that kind of stronghold. Therefore, those who are willing to find refuge there, and trust to the power of the rock, will be safe.

In the ancient world such mountain-top fortresses were common. For example we find references to literal fortresses, strongholds etc., in at least sixteen different OT books.[8] Such high fortresses provided power as well as

---

[7] Among the many other passages which speak of God as a fortress, or rock, or stronghold, the following are especially notable: Isa 25:4; Jer 16:19; Ps 18:2; 31:3; 42:9; 71:3.

[8] Num 13:19; Jud 6:2; 1 Sam 23:14; 2 Sam 24:7; 2 Kgs 8:12; Isa 23:11; Jer 48:18; Lam 2:2; Ezek 33:27; Dan 11:24; Hos 10:14; Amos 5:9; Mic 5:11; Nah 3:12; Hab 1:10; Zech 9:3.

safety, for those who occupied the high place could see for miles around and so detect an attack before it took place; further, those on high could look down on their enemies and so had the force of gravity on their side when they fought, so their spears and rocks and arrows were considerably more effective than those of the attackers trying to move and fight uphill. Even a small hill of the size of Zion could provide protection when the walls of the city-fortress were strong enough, as the story of Hezekiah makes clear: a huge Assyrian army camped out in front of it, but never got inside (2 Kgs 19:31–36).

In sum, God is pictured in the Hebrew tradition as such a rock-solid fortress, a shield that protects all the faithful from the destructive attacks of enemies. As long as they remain within this refuge, standing in the shadow of the Lord, the divine power protects them for no one can break through the Lord's high walls around faithful people.

When this metaphor—God as the fortress Mt. Zion into which his faithful people can come for refuge—reached Paul, it probably had a little less vividness and emotive power than it had for the ancient Hebrews. Of course Jerusalem still had its walls, but the Romans were too strong to be kept out by them. Indeed, very few fortresses existed in Paul's day that were invulnerable to Roman attack, for Masada was perhaps the only exception in Palestine. Instead of fortresses, in Paul's day only strong kingdoms could withstand the Romans. Thus for Paul the fortress image for God was expanded into a kingdom image. He pictures believers finding refuge in the Kingdom of Light that Christ is and rules (Col 1:12–13; Rom 13:12; 2 Cor 6:14–15; Gal 1:4). They too, like the ancient Israelites, found that no enemy could harm them once they had by faith entered this fortress refuge.

## (2) The Gigantic Heavenly Warrior

In prophetic and wisdom books God is sometimes pictured as in Exodus 15—the warrior directly battling human enemies. Once, in Isaiah 63, the Lord is portrayed as a gigantic warrior who simply overwhelms enemy armies by crushing them under foot (Isa 63:1–6). In others this gigantic warrior is pictured brandishing a sword, one that waves over the earth and then descends to destroy all God's foes (Isa 34:1–8; Ezek 21:3–14; 32:10). Finally, in some poems the heavenly warrior is pictured brandishing the forces of nature as weapons of destruction (e.g. Psalm 18).

In Isaiah 63 the prophet pictures the Lord as a giant humanlike figure striding forward, his muscles bulging under garments stained blood red. The gigantic size of this heavenly warrior is implied by the fact that human beings, and perhaps even nations, are only grapes crushed under his feet (3). In his fury at the nations' oppression he treads down the vast armies of his enemies, bringing vindication, vengeance, victory (1–6). Here the Lord is imagined as a warrior who is as huge, overpowering, and unbeatable, as a human being is to an army of grapes.

The gigantic heavenly warrior strides forth in the prophetic literature most commonly as the bearer of a heavenly sword which descends on his enemies. When God's people have become oppressed, they look to their heavenly swordsman to rescue them, as in the oracle of Isaiah 34:1–8. "My sword has drunk its fill in the heavens, behold it descends for judgment upon Edom...The Lord has a sword; it is sated with blood, it is gorged with fat" (5–6). Here the poet sees the sword appear in the heavens, destroying supernatural enemies, probably the rebellious sons of God (Ps 82:1–6), before swooping down in judgment on the enemies of God's people. The Lord will descend as the champion of the chosen people, slaughtering their enemies by the heavenly sword as easily as the priests slaughter the helpless sacrificial animals in the temple (Isa 34:6–7).

Of course God's sword does not just decimate the enemies of Israel, but also Israel herself when she becomes God's enemy (Ezek 21:3, 9–10). This passage, like Isaiah 63, evokes the image of a gigantic warrior, perhaps thousands of feet tall, because he needs only one sword to devastate the nation as easily as a scythe cuts through grain stalks.

The same kind of picture—the Lord wielding a supernatural sword—symbolizes the End, when God conquers the sea monster which is the symbol of evil: "On that day the Lord will punish with his cruel sword, his mighty and powerful sword, Leviathan that twisting sea-serpent, that writhing serpent Leviathan, and slay that monster of the deep" (Isa 27:1). Here Leviathan seems to symbolize all evil, for the previous verse announces a general punishment upon earthlings (26:9).[9] Since Leviathan is a huge dragon of the

---

[9] See Day, *God's Conflict with the Dragon and the Sea*, 143, for a discussion of this passage.

sea, the swordsman conquering him must be bigger and stronger, more agile in battle and able to fight even in the chaos of the sea. Hardly any image could suggest more fully the immeasurable destructive power of the heavenly warrior than this image of God using the divine sword to destroy the sea dragon, which represents chaos and evil itself.

Though the heavenly sword is the most commonly mentioned weapon in God's arsenal, it is just one of the images used to suggest the divine warrior's destructive power. In Psalm 7 the poet adds a bow and fiery arrows to make the threat even more palpable. In other passages fire is God's weapon. OT writers pictured God as a "consuming fire" (Deut 4:24), or alternatively as one out of whose "mouth came devouring fire" (2 Sam 22:9; see Isa 30:27).

In other visions God brandishes other forces of nature as weapons. In Psalm 18 the poet imagines God almost as a dragon, saying that God gets angry at the oppression of his people, making the earth tremble:

> *Smoke* went up from his nostrils
> and devouring *fire* from his mouth...
> Then the channels of the sea were seen,
> and the foundations of the world were laid bare...
> At the *blast of the breath* of your nostrils. (Ps 18:8, 15)

This blast of breath that uncovers the sea floor reminds the reader of the victory at the Red Sea crossing (Exod 15:8). The sea is chaos, the symbol of evil, so driving it back and laying bare its foundations is God conquering it.

In these various passages we discover that the Hebrew writers often pictured God as a gigantic heavenly warrior. This champion wielded a sword that could decimate armies, both angelic and human, indeed could kill the sea dragon Leviathan, the symbol of chaos, of evil. Indeed this warrior could tread underfoot tens of thousands of human enemies, squashing them like grapes. Further this cosmic soldier's arsenal included a bow and arrows of fire and lightning, along with thunder and hail and fiery coals falling everywhere. Indeed simply the breath of the heavenly warrior was enough to lay bare the foundations of the earth, blasting like a hurricane anything that got in his way. This imagery then paves the way for Paul's pictures of Christ conquering the Man of Lawlessness by the breath of his mouth (2 Thess 2:8), or God crushing Satan underfoot (Rom 16:20), thereby bringing an end to all evil.

### (3) Commander of Earthly Armies

In the previous sections we have shown God pictured as Israel's Fortress protecting her and as the Gigantic Warrior directly conquering her enemies. Now we turn to the imagery of God as the Commander-in-Chief standing invisibly behind, directing, and sometimes empowering, earthly armies, or even individual warriors (e.g. David, 1 Sam 17:45–47). There we see David as the weapon in God's hand used to conquer the defiant enemy.

At times the Lord's weapon is a whole national army. Ezekiel connects this picture with the one we previously depicted of the Lord brandishing his sword, having the Lord say to the King of Egypt: "I will make many peoples appalled at you...when I brandish my sword before them...on the day of your downfall...The sword of the King of Babylon shall come upon you" (Ezek 32:10–11). Similarly, Jeremiah's God says of the Babylonian army's attack on Judah: "I myself will fight against you [Judah] with outstretched hand and mighty arm, in anger, in fury, and in great wrath" (Jer 21:5).

Perhaps the most important of these stories for the development of biblical theological-military symbolism is Isaiah's account of God sending the Assyrian army as punishment for Israel and Judah (5:26–30). Though the visible attacker is the Assyrian army, Isaiah declares that God is the commander standing behind it: "Ah, Assyria, the rod of my anger, the staff of my fury!" (10:5)

Secondly, however, Isaiah proclaims that this Assyrian weapon in God's hand is not completely under God's control. As a people determined to get their own way in the world, they go beyond God's justice and become oppressors (Isa 10:7–13). Here Isaiah shows how the "weapon in God's hand" symbol is limited, for the Assyrians have their own intentions, so God's punishment of Israel eventually becomes evil, oppression from which God will have to rescue his people. Later we will see that this same imagery is applied to Satan by Jews and Christians: Satan was God's agent of punishment, but he went off on his own, going far beyond justice, and so became an oppressor from whom God will rescue his people.

In this section we have presented three symbolic pictures of God, as the fortress surrounding Israel, as the gigantic warrior, and as the commander-in-chief hidden behind the armies sent out to do the divine will. Putting these together forms a more complex myth:

Israel takes refuge in the divine fortress (often pictured as on Mount Zion) but is continuously assaulted by enemy armies. When the enemies attack the faithful people, then the Lord strides forth as their champion using his sword, his feet, and the powers of nature including his hurricane breath, to crush the attack and preserve the people. However, at times Israel leaves the fortress, by ceasing to trust and worship the Lord alone. Outside the fortress she becomes vulnerable to destruction from foreign armies which are sent into battle by Israel's own God. Those armies stand under this ultimate commander of all armies, the one who wields them as a rod to punish, a sword to conquer, an axe that will cut down even the greatest tree. In the end, after the sword has run amuck, God will come and destroy it. Paul's myth is remarkably similar to this one.

## C. THE ENEMIES OF HEAVEN

The Lord as commander of earthly armies uses those armies to punish the chosen people. However, at times, as we noted, the foreign conquerors go far beyond God's just sentence and so become **(1) Evil Empires**, which themselves must be overthrown in order for God to rescue their victims. Sometimes these empires are pictured as **(2) Fantastic Monsters**, e.g. Rahab, Leviathan and Daniel's fourth beast. In addition to (and standing hidden behind) human armies, the Hebrews pictured God as commanding punishing angelic armies, but some of them also go beyond the divine will and so become **(3) Angelic Enemies**. These angelic evil forces eventually (in the Qumran writings) are pictured as gathered under the command of a single rebel archangel, known there as **(4) Belial/Satan: God's Agent who Becomes the Angel of Darkness**.

### (1) Evil Empires

Foreign conquerors as God's agents, who then become oppressors, is a story that is told often in the Book of Judges. The author's common plot contains four acts: the Israelites do evil; God's wrath visits them as a foreign conquering army; the people cry out to God for help (presumably because the conquest becomes oppression); God raises up a judge as their savior (Jud 3:7-9, 12-15; 4:1-4; 6:1-8) thereby apparently agreeing that the conquest has become undeserved oppression.

Isaiah uses the same plot, but makes the conqueror-becomes-oppressor theme explicit (Isa 10:5-15). A similar story involves Babylon, which Jeremiah and Ezekiel proclaim is the Lord's agent of punishment on Judah, the agent from whom the Lord will eventually rescue them (Jer 20:4; Ezek 17:20; 37:1-14). Later still, Second Isaiah speaks of the Babylonian exile as a punishment that went too far (Isa 40:2). Therefore the Lord comes to look upon the exiles as oppressed people he will rescue (Isa 49:10).

Similarly Daniel looks upon the Seleucid conquest of Judah as punishment brought by the Lord for the sinfulness of the nation (Dan 9:11-12). However, God's agent of punishment has run amuck, becoming the most ferocious of the fantastic monsters coming out of the sea (Dan 7:7), so God eventually conquers it.

Thus the Hebrew prophets saw the conquering empires under two images: the sword in God's hand bringing just punishment to his own people (and others); the monster arising from the chaos of the sea which symbolizes evil, from whom God will rescue his oppressed people. Paul, too, apparently assumed this dual understanding of the evil empires (ruled by the principalities and powers)—God's agents and God's enemies.

## (2) Fantastic Monsters

The imagery of the oppressor nations as fantastic monsters may have arisen because of the use of animal and nature symbolism for attacking armies (Am 3:12; Jer 5:6). The second foundation for the attacking armies as monsters is the ancient mythology mentioned already in describing God as the heavenly warrior who battles the sea monster, the symbol of chaos and evil. God conquers Rahab (also named Leviathan)[10] the sea serpent, at the Exodus (Isa 51:9-11; Ps 74:12-14). When Ezekiel foresees the future conquest of Egypt he pictures it as God conquering the great dragon of the Nile: "I am against you Pharaoh, King of Egypt, the great dragon sprawling in the midst of its channels" (Ezek 29:3). Later, when Ezekiel pictures the battle of God against Gog of Magog, God says: "I will turn you about, and put hooks in your jaws" (Ezek 38:4), which suggests a great fish, or perhaps "a dragon in the seas" which is

---

[10] Day says "Rahab may simply be an alternative name for Leviathan" (*God's Conflict with the Dragon*, 6).

the imagery the visionary uses to speak of Egypt earlier (Ezek 32:2–4). Likewise when the apocalyptic writer of Isaiah 24–27 pictures the final conquest of evil he speaks of it as the Lord using his sword to conquer Leviathan, the twisting serpent, the dragon in the sea (Isa 27:1). In other places this monster is called "Sea" (*Yam*) as when God "trod on the back of Sea" (Job 9:8). Therefore, "when the waters saw you, they were afraid, the very deep trembled" (Ps 77:16) for "You (God) trampled Sea with your horses, churning the mighty waters" (Hab 3:15).[11]

The OT culmination of this fantastic monster imagery comes in Daniel 7, where the Fourth Beast goes far beyond God's ordered punishment (25) and so must be finally conquered. This fourth beast proceeds to "devour the whole earth" (Dan 7:7, 23), suggesting that it is imagined as a cosmic dragon, the symbol of all evil. In the end God will overcome this evil, for the Fourth Beast is destroyed by divine fire, clearly as an act of righteous conquest (7:10–11, 26). This beast seems to be a symbol for supreme evil, the final evil, the embodiment of all evil, perhaps Evil Itself, for when it is destroyed then the new age of God's saints ruling forever begins (Dan 7:26–27).

### (3) Angelic Enemies: The Rebel Sons of God

While evil human empires were the visible form of cosmic evil, the writers of Israel (especially after the Persian overlordship from 545–330 BC) sometimes pictured angelic enemies of God hidden behind or within the human empires. In this myth, those angelic enemies were originally the "sons of God," God's agents or ambassadors, to each of whom God had given rule over a particular nation. Somehow, enmity arose between them and God, perhaps when these angelic ambassadors rebelled against God by claiming independent rule and then sent their nations to oppress Israel. As a result, the myth of God's army fighting for Israel sometimes includes warfare against oppressive angelic powers, with God's own heavenly host of faithful angels as normally the fighters on the side of heaven.

The angelic (i.e. supernatural) enemies probably first appeared in

---

[11] Mary K. Wakeman, in *God's Battle with the Monster*, suggests that when Yam is parallel to one of the other monster names, then it may simply be another name for Rahab/Leviathan, or it may be a different monster (97).

Hebrew stories as the gods of the nations, who were seen as real powers, but early on depicted as subordinate to Yahweh. Various passages hint that the standard pre-exilic Hebraic myth pictured Yahweh as Emperor and the gods of the nations as local kings under his command, "subordinate powers acting under the supreme authority of Yahweh."[12] Among the clear references to this picture are these: "Who is like you, O Yahweh, among the gods?" (Exod 15:11). The story suggested in Deut 4:19 is that "each nation...has its own angelic ruler and guardian, except Israel, which comes under the direct sovereignty of God" and is thus forbidden to worship the foreign gods/rulers.[13]

These angelic rulers/gods of the nations, though originally appointed by God (Deut 32:8–9), eventually, according to this Hebraic myth, abused their positions and so became objects of God's wrath (Ps 82:1–2, 6–7). The myth this suggests is that the princes (sons of the king) were given authority over the outlying provinces of the divine empire but abused that authority by becoming tyrants, accepting (or perhaps even demanding) worship of themselves as Caird suggests.[14] These rebel angelic princes then mobilized their earthly slaves in battles against each other and against God's people.

Those rebel angels are eventually pictured in apocalyptic imagery as battling God's loyal host of heaven, the battles clearly symbolizing (and perhaps explaining) the battles between human armies and nations. In Daniel, for example, such battles between loyal and rebel angels are clearly mentioned. In one of his visions Daniel sees an unnamed human-like angel who tells him that the angelic rulers of the nations are fighting:

> The Prince of the Kingdom of Persia withstood me twenty-one days, but Michael, one of the chief princes, came to help me, so I left him there with the Prince of the Kingdom of Persia...now I will return to fight against the Prince of Persia; and when I am through with him, lo, the Prince of Greece will come...there is none who contends by my side against these except Michael, your (Israel's) prince. (Dan 10:3, 20–21)

---

[12] Caird, *Principalities and Powers*, 2.
[13] Caird, 5.
[14] Caird, 9.

Apparently, in this apocalyptic myth, the earthly battles between nations are visible expressions of heavenly battles between those nations' angelic guardians. Collins suggests that in Daniel 10-12, "while the battles go on on earth, the decisive struggle is being carried on on another level between Michael and Gabriel, on the one hand, and the princes of Persia and Greece on the other (x:20-21)."[15] In the end, therefore, God will have to conquer both heavenly and earthly enemies, a view explicitly stated in the Isaiah Apocalypse: "On that day the Lord will punish the host of heaven, in heaven, and the kings of earth, on the earth" (Isa 24:21, see also 34:2-5). Presumably mentioning these two groups together implies that the heavenly host stands behind the earthly kings as the supernatural powers behind their thrones.

One important question we cannot easily answer is what the relationship is between the rebel angels and the fantastic beasts. In Daniel 7 God's arrival destroys the beast which symbolizes the oppressive Seleucid Empire. The Prince of Greece (10:20), however, seems to be a spirit, and probably invisible to ordinary human eyes, the supernatural spirit that is hidden within and behind the Seleucids. Thus the author may have used the beast symbol to suggest how destructive the Seleucid empire was, and used the prince/angel symbol to suggest that that power was supernatural. If so, the two symbols together provide the author's fullest suggestion of the power and destructiveness of the evil empire.

Later, in the intertestamental literature, the battle between God's loyal angels and the rebel angels becomes more prominent. In *1 Enoch* 54, for example, the archangels Michael, Gabriel, Raphael and Phanuel conquer "the hosts of Azazel" who were guilty of "becoming subject to Satan and leading astray those who dwell on earth." These hosts of Azazel are probably both angelic and human, all those who are members of Satan's kingdom.[16] Another example of the same symbolism is found in *The Assumption of Moses* 10, which says that "the chief angel," presumably Michael, shall conquer Satan and punish

---

[15] J. J. Collins, "The Mythology of Holy War in Daniel and the Qumran War Scroll," 600.

[16] See D. S. Russell, *The Method and Message of Jewish Apocalyptic: 200 BC-AD 100*, 249-252, for a discussion of Azazel, Semjaza and the rest of the fallen angels in *1 Enoch* and *Jubilees*.

all those who have oppressed Israel (1–2). Thus the enemy angels are almost always portrayed as on the ontological level of the loyal angels, never as direct opponents on the level of God.

In the Septuagint these angelic armies are referred to in relatively abstract terms that Paul later also uses. Caird notes that in the Greek version,

> we find the terms powers (*dunameis*), authorities (*exousiai*), principalities (*archai*) and rulers (*archontes*) applied for the first time to angelic beings. Where the Hebrew speaks of God's hosts, the Greek sometimes speaks instead of his powers. (11)

For example the title "Yahweh of Hosts" is often rendered in the Psalms as *Kurios ton dunameon* (Lord of the powers). Thus the Pauline terms for supernatural forces come from the Septuagint language for the angels. That provides important evidence for the widely supported conclusion that by his terms principalities and powers, etc., Paul was referring to the Hebraic mythology of evil angels lying behind the nations, especially behind the oppressive empires.

Finally, in the War Scroll, the enemy is pictured as a single Kingdom of Darkness, including Belial/Satan at the top, angels of destruction as subordinates, national armies as the earthly children of darkness fighting God's people, and evil spirits within human beings to lead them astray. Thus the last battle is one in which "the assembly of gods and the hosts of men shall battle" but the victory is due to God's intervention (1QM i).[17] In this picture God seems to be the hidden power at work within the loyal angels and humans, the reason why they are victorious.

Clearly the traditional Hebrew myth which came down to the early Christians included the imagery of rebel angels, led by the gods or "princes" of the Gentile nations. These national angelic guardians had been given their rule by God but they had gone their own evil ways and so ceased to be fully God's servants, though they were still forced at times to carry out God's just sentences of punishment. Never does the OT speak of God directly fighting the rebel

---

[17] All quotations from the Scrolls, unless otherwise noted, are from Geza Vermes, *The Dead Sea Scrolls in English*.

angels, which suggests that they were pictured as on a lower level and could not threaten God's own position. They did, however, hinder the loyal angels and humans in their attempts to carry out the will of God on earth, so the conflict between loyal and rebel angels provided the unseen background to the conflicts between nations. These rebel guardians of the nations are called in Greek principalities, authorities, powers, rulers of this present age. Eventually they all became pictured as members of a single Kingdom of Darkness, led by Belial/Satan, to whom we now turn.

## (4) Satan/Belial: God's Agent who Becomes the Angel of Darkness

When Paul spoke of Satan as "the god of this present age" (2 Cor 4:4) he ascribed to him a position of extraordinary, perhaps even cosmic, power that probably never entered the imaginations of OT writers. Those writers seldom mentioned Satan and saw him essentially as a judicial spirit carrying out God's will. Only in the intertestamental period did this angel rise to prominence, at first under such names as Azazel, Semjaza, Mastema, and finally as Belial/r or Satan. Only in the Dead Sea Scrolls is he called the Angel of Darkness, the ruler of all forces of evil, essentially the same position that Paul ascribes to him. Thus the Qumran picture is the most of important of all these for enabling us to see the background that Paul and the early Christians probably assumed.

In the Old Testament no single ruler of the forces of evil steps on stage, for the Hebrews had not yet developed a picture of a unified evil angelic or demonic kingdom. Satan appears, but only as an agent directly under the command of God. As "the satan," one of the sons of God whose role is to be "the adversary" of humankind, he tempts, brings pain and causes death and destruction—all with God's permission (Job 1–2; 1 Chron 21:1). In his last brief appearance in the Old Testament story (Zech 3:1–5), he is named Satan and plays the role of the accuser of sinners before God. In this case God rebukes Satan and cleanses the sinner, clearly suggesting some opposition between God's will and Satan's. But there is no combat. Satan is a bureaucrat who does largely what he is told, though sometimes he oversteps the line in his zeal for justice.[18]

---

[18] Forsyth goes farther, arguing that Satan in Zechariah has become independent of God (*The Old Enemy*, 121–122).

Further background for Satan the god of this world can be found in other servants of God in the Hebraic tradition. A second destructive servant is the avenging angel of death whom God sends to punish whole cities and nations. During the Passover God sent "the destroyer," presumably an angel, to kill the firstborn of the Egyptians (Exod 12:23). Later, as punishment for David's sin of taking a census, God sends an angel (perhaps the angel of the Lord) with a pestilence to kill thousands of the people. But God did not let the angel destroy Jerusalem (2 Sam 24:15–17). Later still, according to the 2 Kings version of the escape of Hezekiah, "the angel of the Lord went out and struck down 187,000 men in the Assryian camp" beseiging Jerusalem, thus driving Sennacherib away (19:35). To those angels Forsyth adds other literary ancestors of the character Satan: The "evil spirit" that God sends into Saul (1 Sam 16:14–16 etc.), and the "lying spirit" God sends against Ahab (1 Kings 22:23).[19]

During the intertestamental period, these various angels who did the dirty work of God apparently became combined in a single figure, who eventually was depicted as the leader of the forces of darkness. For example, *Jubilees* presents Mastema as the leader of the evil spirits which God ordered imprisoned for persecuting Noah and his family. Mastema appeals to God to let a few of the spirits remain free, or else, "I will not be able to execute the power of my will on the sons of men; for these are for corruption and leading astray before my judgment, for great is the wickedness of men." God agrees, leaving one tenth of the evil spirits free for Mastema to use as punishment (*Jub.* 10:8–9). Given Mastema's appeal to God this clearly suggests this spirit is still God's agent, not an independent power of evil.

Perhaps the oldest picture of an independent cosmic enemy of God comes in *The Testaments of the Twelve Patriarchs* where Beliar is the ruler of the evil spirits and is doomed to be trodden under by God's angelic host in the end. Beliar in the *Testaments* is called "the Prince of Deceit" (*T. Sim.* 2:7) and

---

[19] *The Old Enemy*, 111–112. J. B. Russell, in *The Prince of Darkness*, sees a gradual process of the destroying angel becoming more and more distinct from God. Thus the "lying spirit" is "prince of lies and lord of deceit." Russell writes: "Gradually the *mal'ak* obtained its independence from God; gradually its destructive aspect was emphasized; finally it became the personification of the dark side of the divine nature. The *mal'ak* was now the evil angel, Satan, the obstructor, the liar, the destroying spirit" (38).

"Satan" (*T. Gad* 4:7). He rules over "the kingdom of the enemy" (*T. Dan* 6:4), otherwise known as "Satan and his spirits" (*T. Dan* 6:1). These Beliar-ruled "spirits of deceit" act like demons which invade human beings and cause them to produce the sins of hatred, envy etc. Further these spirits also are directly connected with the gods the Gentile nations worshipped: "The Gentiles went astray, and forsook the Lord, and changed their order, and obeyed stocks and stones, spirits of deceit" (*T. Naph.* 3:3). Thus these demonic spirits are similar in some ways to the rebel sons of God in the Old Testament.[20]

In the Scrolls, the *Testaments'* satanology seems to have developed in an apocalyptic direction. The picture painted is of Belial/Satan as the Angel of Darkness, the commander of a Kingdom of Darkness in open conflict with God's Kingdom of Light: "All the children of righteousness are ruled by the Prince of Light and walk in the ways of light, but all the children of falsehood are ruled by the Angel of Darkness, and walk in the ways of darkness" (1QS iii). The enemy commander, the Angel of Darkness, is also called Belial and Satan. This angel combines into one character the Old Testament roles of the satan (testing and accusing), of God's punishing angel of death, and of the evil empires/beasts that ceased to carry out God's will and so became God's enemies.[21]

Though Belial/Satan, the Angel of Darkness, was created by God and exercises punishment as God desires, still he is almost entirely evil: "Satan, the Angel of Malevolence, thou hast created for the Pit; his rule is in Darkness and his purpose is to bring about wickedness and iniquity. All the spirits of his company, the Angels of Destruction, walk according to the precepts of Darkness" (1QM xiii). Thus the Scrolls' Satan is the ruler of a hierarchy, with

---

[20] For a fuller description of the *Testaments'* demonology, and its close parallels with Paul's picture of Sin as an agent of Satan, see Peter W. Macky, *The Problem of Sin in Romans: The Relationship in the Thought of St. Paul between Man's Freely Willed Sins and the Demonic Power Sin* (Oxford: Oxford University D. Phil dissertation, 1967) chapter 9, "Spirits of Deceit."

[21] Forsyth describes the development in this way: "at Qumran...the combat terminology of many Old Testament passages...has now become a radical apocalyptic myth of an ongoing battle between two rival forces in the cosmos, led by the spirit of light and the spirit of darkness" (*Enemy*, 199).

evil angels directly under him, and the human children of darkness under them.[22] Because sin is prevalent in the world, God allows Belial the punisher to hold sway until the End. Of course, by his domination of the children of darkness this ruler forces them to sin even more. He does it through "the spirit of perversity" at work within individual human children of light and darkness, as an evil spirit leading them astray (1QS iii).

The line between the two kingdoms and their armies is clear, according to the Scrolls: those who join the Qumran community, inhabiting its monastery near the Dead Sea, thereby leave the Kingdom of Darkness and join the Kingdom of Light, becoming "in some way citizens of the kingdom of heaven."[23] Within the community, the children of light are ruled and protected by "the spirit of truth" within them, also called the "holy spirit."[24] In that community of light, the Angel of Darkness cannot enter, so the people who remain there are relatively safe from its temptations, lies and destruction. One Qumran psalmist portrays this safety in traditional imagery: "I shall be as one who enters a fortified city, As one who seeks refuge behind a high wall" (1QH vi). However, as long as they are alive on earth, they can be tempted by "the spirit of perversity (or darkness, or error)," which along with "the spirit of truth" is a permanent part of the make-up of all human beings. Thus the Angel of Darkness in Qumran is the head of the Kingdom of Darkness, but can only tempt but not directly oppress those who are within the Kingdom of Light, a view later taken up by Paul.[25]

---

[22] Collins argues that in the Scrolls for the first time Belial/Satan is the equal in power of Michael, and evil is an everpresent reality ("The Mythology of Holy War," 608).

[23] H. Ringgren, *The Faith of Qumran*, 127.

[24] Ringgren, 89.

[25] The story of a pre-mundane fall of Satan appears to be a late addition to the Jewish demonology, for it is not directly reflected in the New Testament. The story is told in *2 Enoch* 29–31 and *The Books of Adam and Eve* 12–17, both of which are probably first century AD works (Russell, *Jewish Apocalyptic*, 58–62). When the fall of Satan did come into the Christian story, in Revelation 12, it came in a uniquely Christian version: Satan does not leave heaven in the pre-mundane period, but at the death of Christ, when God's grace extends to all believers, whom Satan wishes to punish for their sins. Thus the story of Satan falling from heaven during the creation period is not part of the tradition to

**Conclusion**

The complete traditional Hebrew picture of the Enemies of Heaven, the myth that the early Christians probably took over, included the following elements of setting and character:

**The unified Kingdom of Darkness** stands opposed to God's Kingdom of Light, and dominates the whole corrupted earth in the present age.

At the head of the kingdom is Satan, otherwise known as Mastema, Belial or **the Angel of Darkness**, one of God's former agents (perhaps an archangel) who went astray. He continues to do God's will by tempting all people, and accusing and punishing those who do evil. However, he has rebelled, for he does more harm than God orders or desires.

Directly under Satan is **the army of angels of destruction** who carry out his will. These are first of all apparently the sons of God, the princes of the nations (called in the Septuagint principalities, powers, authorities, rulers of this age), to whom God gave the guidance of their nations. Unfortunately (perhaps in late works due to Satan's temptation and instigation) they rebelled against God and became oppressors, both of their own nations and through them of foreigners. Further, rebellious guardian angels, some of the masses of the host of heaven, probably fill out the ranks of Satan's angelic army.

In addition to his angelic subordinates the Jewish Satan also deploys evil spirits. Satan's power invades individuals by **spirits of deceit** which produce greed, anger, envy, hatred and all the other sins. To some extent these are due to inborn impulses (the Scrolls' "spirit of perversity"), but their power and oppression are due to humans accepting their temptations.

The people who are dominated by these evil spirits are the human **children of darkness**, the followers of Satan. They include kings and emperors who then make their people into the evil empires that punish, and then oppress, God's people, the children of light. These evil empires are sometimes pictured as fantastic monsters of destruction, with the chief example being Daniel's fourth beast.

Though God created and sends all the forces of darkness on missions of **punishment**, still they go **far beyond the divine will** in carrying out their

which Paul and the early Christians alluded.

own selfish wills. Human beings oppressed by all these evil powers deserve the suffering to some extent, as punishment for their sins. Some people, however, those who seek to walk in God's way by faith and obedience, are **victims of oppression** far beyond what they deserve. Therefore, God will in the end rescue them and destroy their oppressors forever, just as he sent his anointed one, Cyrus the Persian, to destroy forever the empire of Babylon.

This **final destruction of enemies** comes as the climax of history, the Last Battle.

## D. THE LAST BATTLE

**Introduction**

The final act in the symbolic military drama of the Hebrew tradition is the vision of a last battle in which the Divine Warrior will conquer all evil, end this evil age, and thus usher in a new one. Perhaps the battle of God against Gog in Ezekiel 38-39 is the oldest last battle vision, but the picture of God conquering evil and thus providing a new start for Israel is as old as the Exodus. Therefore, the last battle imagery grows directly out of the root of the traditional Divine Warrior imagery, with the ingrafting of the promise that this battle will end evil forever because it will change the world decisively. Between the Exodus and the Exile the prophets envisioned the coming Day of the Lord, when God would appear and conquer his enemies. Amos was perhaps the first to proclaim it, seeing it as a day of darkness and distress, a day of judgment and punishment, not only on Israel's enemies but also on Israel herself (Am 5:18-20). Eventually that image turned into the vision of a last battle, when evil would be finally destroyed.[26] In this section we will briefly describe five visions of the battle, those in Ezekiel 38-39, Zechariah 14, Isaiah 24-27, Daniel 7-12 and the War Scroll. Our theory is that Paul knew these pictures and probably combined them into a single myth which was then the foundation upon which he built his own eschatological battle myth.

---

[26] D. S. Russell discusses the prophetic Day of the Lord and suggests that it gave rise to apocalyptic when it was developed and universalized (*Jewish Apocalyptic*, 92-95).

**(1) Ezekiel's Gog**

Ezekiel's vision of Gog and his vast armies falling by God's hand on the mountains of Israel is probably the oldest Divine Warrior story that can be taken as describing an age-ending battle. It is not fully apocalyptic, for it includes no angelic armies, no complete transformation of the earth, no resurrection of the dead. Still it provides a first taste of many apocalyptic images.

When Israel has returned from exile (Ezek 38:10-12), a monstrous alliance of nations will attack her from the north. Led by Gog of Magog (who is not otherwise known), this alliance will include many nations (38:5-6), perhaps even all nations (39:21). Gog is depicted as a sea monster to whom God says, "I will turn you about and put hooks into your jaws" (38:4), suggesting he is like Leviathan/Rahab, who is the symbolic representation of all evil.

When this monstrous army reaches the land of Israel, then God will appear as Israel's champion using as weapons earthquake, torrential rains and hailstones, fire and brimstone (38:19-22). Indeed God will appear in single combat against Gog, striking his weapons from his hands and so killing him and his armies on the mountains of Israel (39:3).[27] As in the Exodus, the Lord alone does the fighting. Following the divine victory, a new temple will appear on Mount Zion, with the dazzling glory of God coming from the east, entering the temple and filling it (43:1-6). God then proclaims that this is the divine home forever, the place from which God will rule the world (43:7). As a result of God's presence, a river of supernatural living water will flow from the temple, bringing life to vegetation where previously death reigned (47:1-12). Thus Ezekiel envisions a Divine Kingdom of Light and Life which transforms the earth.

**(2) Zechariah 14**

The second striking last battle vision in the Old Testament is Zechariah 14, the date of which is between 500 and 200 BC. In this story the prophet announces that "the day of the Lord is coming" (1). "All the nations" will at

---

[27] This is perhaps the direct antecedent to Paul's symbolic picture of Christ descending at the end to defeat all the powers (1 Cor 15:23-24), including the Man of Lawlessness (2 Thess 2:8).

first succeed in their attack against Jerusalem (2). "Then the Lord will go forth and fight against those nations...On that day his feet shall stand on the Mount of Olives...(which) shall be split in two from east to west by a very wide valley" (3-4). At the Lord's side will be "all the holy ones" (5), presumably the angelic armies.

When the battle is won, the Lord will bring a transformation of nature (6-8). In Jerusalem God will become king over all the earth (9), with the eternal light of day blessing the whole land. Then all those who survive the last battle will come up yearly to worship the Divine King in Jerusalem (16) as a new age of universal peace has dawned.

### (3) The Isaiah Apocalypse

The third major prophetic last battle vision is the first fully apocalyptic one, the story told in the "Isaiah Apocalypse" (Isaiah 24-27), which probably comes from the end of the third century BC.

When the whole earth has become polluted because of human sins, then God will come "to punish the inhabitants of the earth" (26:21). The Divine Warrior will bring low the high-flying oppressors, trampling them under the feet of the oppressed (26:5-6).[28] At the same time the Lord "will lay waste the earth and make it desolate" (24:1-6), for the foundations of the earth will tremble until it falls like a drunken man, never to rise again (24:18-20).

As the central image of this divine descent to conquer evil on the earth, the visionary says "the Lord with his hard and great and strong sword will punish Leviathan the fleeing serpent...he will slay the dragon that is in the sea" (27:1). Here Leviathan probably represents all evil, and its defeat signals the overthrow of the whole earthly order (that had become infected with chaos), and thus the creation of a new age.

As part of that conquest of all evil, "the Lord will punish the host of heaven in heaven and the kings of the earth, on the earth" (24:21). "The host of heaven" probably refers to the "sons of God," the members of the angelic council that had been given rule over the nations, but had rebelled against God and gone their own evil ways. So they will have to be defeated and punished (Ps

---

[28] This imagery may be the most direct antecedent of Paul's vision of the end of evil, when God will crush Satan under the feet of believers (Rom 16:20).

82:1–6).[29] Their worst evil was in corrupting the rulers of the nations of the earth, so those earthly rulers will have to be defeated and punished at the same time. Both the heavenly and the earthly criminals will be gathered in a pit, presumably under the earth, until the day of their punishment arrives (24:22).

As a significant part of the divine victory over evil, the Lord, will "swallow up death for ever" (25:8). Then God's own dead "shall live, their bodies shall rise" (26:19). Here the great transformation of the earth entails the defeat of death. The enemy that had previously swallowed up all God's people is itself swallowed up.[30]

When all oppressors are completely defeated, then the divine conqueror comes to reign in their place (26:13–14), on Mount Zion in dazzling light (glory). That divine Kingdom of Light will spread out to cover the whole earth, outshining all the heavenly bodies (24:23).

**(4) Daniel**

The Lord reigning in glory, the dazzling King of the Earth, also stands out as a central element of Daniel 7, one of the most influential of Hebraic visions of the End. First the fourth and last beast arises as the most monstrous and destructive of all the beasts (Dan 7:7–8). Since it comes "out of the sea" (2), it is presumably a new version of Leviathan, the sea dragon who represents and incarnates chaos, evil, death and destruction. Then the Ancient of Days on a fiery throne passes judgment so "the beast was slain, and its body destroyed and given over to be burned with fire" (11). No conqueror is mentioned, so the natural interpretation is that the stream of fire which issued from the divine throne (9–10) burst out and consumed the great enemy. Later, in the interpretation (15–27), the visionary does describe the last battle. The fourth beast's little horn "made war against the saints, and prevailed over them, until the Ancient of Days came and judgment was given for the saints of the Most High." Then they "received the kingdom," i.e. rule over the whole world (7:18,

---

[29] Kaiser says the host of heaven, literally the "army of the height," refers to "the astral angels of the nations which we meet in the Old Testament in Dan 8.3ff.; 10.13, 20f." (*Isaiah 13–39*, 194).

[30] In Paul's language, "the last enemy, death, is destroyed...death has been swallowed up in victory" (1 Cor 15:26, 54).

21–22). Probably these "saints" include both loyal angelic forces and suffering faithful humans.[31]

As part of this last battle, angelic armies fight each other, for the fourth beast is a supernatural monster and so fights heavenly battles. The visionary imagines that the little horn on the head of the beast "grew great, even to the host of heaven; and some of the host of the stars it cast down to the ground" (8:10). Probably the visionary imagined the fourth beast, which symbolizes the Greek Seleucid empire, as animated or guided by the Prince of Greece (Dan 10:20), the angelic spirit which lies behind, rules, and commands that empire.

The final symbolic version of the last battle in Daniel's visions comes in chapter 12. The first signs will be "a time of trouble" worse than the nation has ever experienced, when the little horn makes war on the saints and prevails over them (7:21, 25). But then the archangel Michael will descend, "the great prince who has charge of your nation," who will rescue from destruction all those whose names are in the book. Here Michael plays the role of the heaven-sent conquering savior that in the Daniel 7 vision was assigned to the Divine Judge whose throne shot out fire to destroy oppressors. After that victory, even death will be conquered (presumably by God, though no agent is named): some of the dead will be rescued, rising from the dust to receive everlasting life in glory, shining like the stars forever (12:1–3).

### (5) The Dead Sea Scrolls

After Daniel, all that is left to complete the Hebraic battle myth is for the enemy army to become the spear-head of a realm of evil commanded by the Angel of Darkness. That image finally appears in the Dead Sea Scrolls. There, the fullest pre-Christian Hebraic account of the last battle shines forth in the scroll named *The War of the Children of Light against the Children of Darkness*. In the Qumran vision, the world as a whole is a Kingdom of Darkness, ruled over by the Angel of Darkness, who is named Belial or Satan. Under this ruler, an army of angels of destruction and their human subordinates oppress human beings externally, while the spirit of falsehood or perversity works within all human beings to lead them astray.

The Scrolls see God as the one in control of history, for the conflict

---

[31] See H. Kvanvig, *Roots of Apocalyptic*, 571–583.

continues only as long as God allows it to. When God decides the End must come, then the final battle begins. Thus the day of that last battle is one "appointed [by God] from ancient times for the battle of destruction of the sons of darkness" (1QM i). In this angelic battle, God fights for the children of light, for the army includes, "the multitude of the Holy Ones...in heaven, and the host of the angels...the King of Glory is with us together with the holy ones" (1QM xii). Thus the battle will be both earthly, between the human children of light and darkness, and heavenly, between the angels of light and the angels of destruction (1QM i).

The Scrolls' myth seems to be that God will allow the two armies to fight for a while before he decisively enters the battle and wins the war. At first the battle will be even, with the children of light winning three rounds and the children of darkness winning three, so the fighting produces great suffering. But when the soldiers of God grow faint, then God will enter the battle to make the difference: "the mighty hand of God shall bring down [the army of Satan, and all] the angels of his kingdom, and all the members [of his company]" (1QM i). In this Divine victory the Exodus is the model, for the writer says that God will do to the armies of darkness as "You did to Pharaoh, and to the captains of his chariots at the Red Sea" (1QM xi).

As that Exodus victory brought an end to Israel's slavery, so the result of this final battle is the end of all evil, "everlasting destruction for all the company of Satan" (1QM i; see also 1QS iv). Of course that destruction includes the end of the Angel of Darkness: "This is the day appointed by God for the defeat and overthrow of the Prince of the kingdom of wickedness," which will produce "eternal succour to the company of His redeemed by the might of the princely Angel of the Kingdom of Michael" (1QM xvii). That will end the rule of darkness and usher in the rule of light. God's victory will produce for the survivors "every everlasting blessing and eternal joy in life without end, a crown of glory and a garment of majesty in unending light" (1QS iv). That hope seems dependent on Daniel 12, so it is likely that the Qumranians also believed in the resurrection promise given in Dan 12:3.

When the rule of light comes, God raises "up the kingdom of Michael in the midst of the gods, and the realm of Israel in the midst of all flesh" (1QM xvii). Thus Michael will rule all the angels, and Israel will rule the nations on earth, with God as eternal king over both realms, for "sovereignty shall be to the God of Israel" (1QM vi). The role of Michael as the commander of the angelic hosts which save Israel is traditional (Dan 12:1–3). However, the image of a kingdom of Michael, this angel as the ruler of the angels, is novel.

The prominence of this archangel overshadows the few Qumran references to an anointed King of Israel, "the Prince of the congregation" (1QM v), who will apparently take part in the last battle as the leader of the earthly armies. "The Blessing of the Prince of the Congregation" (1QSh v), describes this royal figure in Old Testament messianic terms, and blesses him that "he may establish the kingdom of his people for ever." As in Isaiah 11, this king will "bring death to the ungodly with the breath of (his) lips." As a result he will become the political ruler over the nations while the spiritual and religious leadership is given to others—the Messianic Priest and the Teacher of Righteousness.[32]

The contribution the Scrolls make to the Hebrew Last Battle tradition is threefold: they present the battle as the final conflict between two relatively equally matched kingdoms; secondly they make explicit that the battle is one in which both earthly and heavenly armies fight at the same time; thirdly, they proclaim that these armies are so equally matched that they each win three of the first six battles rounds of the war until the victory for the Light comes by God's hand in the seventh round.

## Last Battle Summary

The Hebrew Last Battle tradition as a whole, which Paul probably learned as a youth, was the combination of these various visions into a (probably unwritten) complete story.[33]

The end times arrive by God's ordination (EZS), when all the nations antagonistic to Israel make an unprovoked attack on Jerusalem (EZS). At the head of these armies is a single human ruler (Gog in Ezekiel, the little horn Antiochus in Daniel). These human armies are the earthly representatives of a cosmic kingdom of evil (D), led by Belial/Satan (S), which also includes an

---

[32] Ringgren, *Qumran*, 182.

[33] In this composite picture of the last battle, the sources of each element are indicated by these abbreviations: E = Ezekiel 38–39; Z = Zechariah 14; I = Isaiah 24–27; D = Daniel 7–12; S = The War Scroll.

army of angelic rebels led by the "princes" of the nations (ZDS). This Kingdom of Darkness is imagined as a monstrous beast (sometimes called Leviathan) rising up from the sea to destroy God's good creation (EID). In the beginning the battle goes badly for the people of Jerusalem led by their High Priest and Davidic King (S), for evil forces prevail for a while (ZDS). Indeed, even the loyal angelic armies on God's side (ZDS) are initially defeated in the battle against the forces of darkness (DS). This is the time of troubles, greater than the people of God have ever seen before, that is the sign of the fast approaching end (D).

Suddenly, God will appear and fight on the side of Israel (EZIDS) and the good angels led by Michael (DS). As God had conquered monstrous enemies before (S), so now, for the final time, God appears in single combat (EZD), to destroy forever the monstrous forces of evil.

The human role in the battle is disputed. Ezekiel pictures God alone (or with angelic forces) doing the fighting. The Scrolls say God fights hiddenly, in and through the human (and angelic) armies.

When God descends into the battle (Z), nature itself erupts as some of the divine weapons: earthquakes and flood (EI), fire and brimstone (E) appear, along with a devastating plague (Z), ending in one vision with the whole earth destroyed, never to rise again (I). Symbolizing this Divine Warrior's role in the victory is the picture of single combat, against the sea monster Leviathan, which God destroys with the heavenly sword (I), or with fire bursting out from the divine throne to destroy the fourth beast (D).

When the angelic rebels are defeated, and their earthly allies too, then the angelic and human leaders of the rebellion will be sent down to Sheol to await their final punishment (I), signalling the end of all the forces of evil, forever (EZIDS). On earth, when the foreign armies have been defeated, Israel will become the ruler of all the nations (DS), which will come to Jerusalem peacefully to worship the Lord (ZI). Michael will become the ruler of all the angels (S), subservient to God who becomes the Ruler of All (EZIDS). God's throne will be in a new temple (E) in Jerusalem, raised far above a transformed earth. God's glory will spread out from Jerusalem, completely outshining the sun (I).

As God's power creates this new earth, so also God will destroy the earth's most devastating evil—death. God will swallow up death forever, raising

from the dead those who had been faithful (ID). They will then shine forever
like the stars (D), a new angelic host worshipping God. But this shining army
will live on earth, centered in Jerusalem, where God will hold the feast to
welcome all nations into the eternal Divine Kingdom (I).

## Conclusion

In this chapter we have shown that the Hebrew tradition, from Exodus
to the War Scroll, gloried in the myth of God as the Heavenly Warrior, the
champion of his people Israel. This symbolism was not a mere minor regiment
in the story, but one of the central army corps, one of the major ways that the
Hebrew and Jewish writers understood God's relationship to humankind. Thus
it is not surprising that Paul took up this imagery and used it extensively.
Indeed, as we will show in the next five chapters, he seems to have used almost
all of the tradition, elaborating it by the good news that in Christ (rather than in
the Exodus) God's initial victory in the war to conquer all evil has already taken
place.

# III. THE ENEMY COMMANDER-IN-CHIEF

The god of this world has blinded the minds of unbelievers.
(2 Cor 4:4)
What fellowship is there between light and darkness? What
agreement does Christ have with Beliar? (2 Cor 6:14–15)
Hand this man over to Satan for the destruction of the
flesh... (1 Cor 5:5)
Take the shield of faith, with which you will be able to
quench all the flaming arrows of the Evil One. (Eph 6:16)
The God of Peace will soon crush Satan under your (the
Roman Christians') feet. (Rom 16:20)

## Introduction

When Paul speaks of "the god of this world" (2 Cor 4:4), he probably
is imagining Satan as Christ's chief enemy, the Ruler of the Kingdom of
Darkness, emperor over the principalities and powers, Commander-in-Chief of
the Army of Evil Spirits. His Satan is the chief of the enemy hierarchy. As
Russell asserted, "The Devil...stands at the center of the New Testament
teaching that the Kingdom of God is at war with, and is now at last defeating,
the Kingdom of the Devil."[1] Therefore in this chapter we will begin our

---

[1] Russell, *The Devil*, 222.

elaboration of Paul's picture of the forces of evil by seeking to discern as fully as we can how he understood and pictured the Ruler of the Kingdom of Darkness. As with all the other military pictures used theologically in the Bible, we believe Paul meant this one symbolically, not literally. Here we will simply elaborate the symbol, providing as detailed a version of Paul's myth as we can. Later, in chaper VIII, we will present arguments that Paul meant Satan symbolically, as a personification of the divine justice which has been corrupted by humans.

When we consider this antagonist in Paul's cosmic war myth, one of the striking facts is the variety of names and titles that the NT writers use for him. Paul gives him these names: Satan (seven times), Beliar (2 Cor 6:15), and the devil (Eph 4:27; 6:11). Another NT writer names him Beelzeboul (Mk 3:22). The descriptive titles Paul gives him include the god of this age (1 Cor 4:4), the satan (1 Thess 2:18, presumably meaning "the adversary" or "the enemy"), the tester/tempter (1 Thess 3:5), the evil one (2 Thess 3:3; Eph 6:16), and the ruler/prince of the power of the air (Eph 2:2). Other NT descriptive titles include: the prince/ruler of the demons (Mk 3:23), the enemy (Matt 13:25, in the parable of the wheat and the weeds), prince/ruler of this world (Jn 12:31), the accuser (Rev 12:10) pictured as a great red dragon in the sky (Rev 12:3), the ancient serpent (Rev 12:9), and the deceiver of the whole world (Rev 12:9). Just these titles alone give us a fairly full picture of the role of Satan in the mythology of the early Christians.

Satan's role in Paul's myth of the cosmos at war is quite like the picture given in the Scrolls. Satan is the Antagonist, the Great Enemy of God, Christ and the children of light. When using this military imagery, Paul portrays two kingdoms, of light and darkness, locked in a great battle until the End. In the Kingdom of Light (which God created through his initial victory in Christ's death and resurrection) Christ rules for God, providing protection for believers, who are the children of light. Outside, in the Kingdom of Darkness (2 Cor 6:14; Gal 1:4; Col 1:13), Satan rules, for he is the "god of this world" (2 Cor 4:4). The children of darkness (including the angelic principalities and powers) are his agents and instruments on earth. How exactly we should picture the relationship between these two kingdoms (and two ages) is not clear, so we will discuss it below (in chapter V) as we seek to develop Paul's picture as fully as we can.

In this chapter we will briefly summarize **A. The OT, Jewish and**

**Christian Background** to Paul's Satanology. Then we will consider Paul's most comprehensive title, **B. The God of This World**, which we will elaborate in light of Paul's references to the power of darkness and the present evil age. In **C. The Commander's Powers**, we will discuss the various ways that Paul speaks of Satan working in the world, coercing unbelievers, sending Death to rule all mortals, and probably even sending his spirit as the source of decay and death in Nature. **D. Elaborating Paul's Myth** will reconstruct Paul's fuller understanding of the history of Satan, suggesting that Paul, following the OT, probably saw Satan as originally given authority by God as an agent of justice.

## A. BACKGROUND

In our chapter "The Lord as a Man of War" we gave a detailed account of the OT and Jewish picture of Satan.[2] So here we will just summarize that before presenting briefly the Synoptic picture of Satan, which Paul could well have known as oral tradition.

### (1) OT and Judaism

From the OT Paul probably took over the image of Satan as God's judicial agent, one of the angelic sons of God (Job 1–2). This Satan spies on humans, accuses them, and tests them by bringing suffering. Thus he is the divinely-sent spirit roaming the earth who tempts people to go astray (1 Chr 21:1), and also the heavenly prosecutor and prison warden (Zech 3:1–5).

As we will argue below, Paul probably also identified Satan, God's punisher, with the angelic "destroyer" of the first-born at the Exodus (Exod 12:23, see *Jub.* 10:8–9) and with the death-dealing "angel of the Lord" bringing plagues as punishment (2 Sam 24:15–16; 2 Kgs 19:35). Perhaps Paul also saw Satan, or one of his subordinate demons, as the evil spirit sent by God into Saul (1 Sam 16:14) and the lying spirit sent by God to mislead Ahab (1 Kgs 22:23).

Further, it is plausible that Paul saw Daniel's Fourth Beast (Dan 7) as an image of Satan, or of one of his top subordinates, the Principality of Greece. Finally, Leviathan/Rahab, the great dragon of the deep, was probably taken by

---

[2] Pages 41–44 above.

Paul as another version of Daniel's Fourth Beast (which came out of the sea), the symbolic expression of Satan's presence on earth. Thus the stories of the destruction of Leviathan and the Fourth Beast were probably the immediate background to Paul's picture of Satan finally crushed by God (Rom 16:20).

The intertestamental writings, especially the Scrolls, suggest that the OT picture just summarized had become standard in the Jewish communities that thought in apocalyptic imagery. *Jubilees* names the Exodus Destroyer "Mastema," who is the OT Satan bringing punishment, but now by ruling a kingdom of evil spirits (*Jub.* 10:8-9; 49:2). Then in the Scrolls we get a clear picture of Satan/Beliar as the Angel of Darkness, the ruler of this whole world of darkness. Under him, as his supernatural subordinates, are angels of destruction and a spirit of deceit within people, while all the non-Qumranians are Satan's earthly army, the children of darkness.

### (2) Jesus' Teaching

Though we cannot know how much of the Synoptic tradition Paul knew, it is likely that he was familiar with its view of Satan, for it probably represents the imagery of the early oral tradition of the teaching of Jesus.

Perhaps the most interesting of the insights into the current myth of Satan that the Synoptics offer is the story in which some scribes from Jerusalem say that Jesus cast out demons because "he has Beelzebul, and by the ruler of the demons he casts out demons" (Mk 3:22). Jesus apparently adopted this imagery of a demonic hierarchy, for he spoke of Satan casting out Satan, of a kingdom divided against itself, both of which echo the picture of Satan as the ruler of a kingdom of demons. That imagery came originally from *Jubilees* and the *Testaments*, as we noted above, but by Jesus' day seems to have become standard. The emphasis in the imagery is upon Satan as the enemy, the ruler of an oppressive enemy kingdom. Not only does Satan oppress people by sending demons into them, but he also uses these demons to oppress them with physical ailments (Mt 9:32, 17:15, 18; Lk 13:16). No suggestion arises in these stories that demon-possession and demon-caused illness were forms of punishment.

Though the Synoptic Satan is clearly an oppressive enemy he still plays the judicial role which gave him his first entrance on the stage of Israelite myth (Job 1-2). Indeed, the chief Satan story in the gospels is the temptation story, where Satan plays precisely the role that the satan did in Job: providing tests for one of God's faithful, tempting him to fall so he could prove his faithfulness by rejecting the temptation. That same role is suggested when Jesus says to Peter "Get behind me Satan!" when Peter offers the tempting suggestion that avoiding the cross would be a good idea (Mk 8:33).

One final intriguing reference to Satan by the Synoptic Jesus is his saying on "the fall of Satan." When the seventy disciples report that the demons submit to them when they use Jesus' name, he replies: "I saw Satan fall like lightning from heaven. See I have given you authority to tread on snakes and scorpions and over all the power of the Enemy [*tou echthrou*]" (Lk 10:18–19). Just how we should take this "fall from heaven" is a much disputed point. Clearly it refers in some way to the diminishing of Satan's powers as exhibited in the disciples' successes in exorcism. Perhaps it is the explanation of why they have been successful. If that is the case, then this "fall" seems to be a recent event, not a primordial one or an eschatological one, which are the other two prominent interpretations of Jesus' meaning. Possibly this "fall from heaven" could be a symbolic expression of Jesus' victory in the temptation, just as his "binding the strong man and then plundering his goods" (Mk 3:27) seems to be a symbolic expression of his victory in the temptation.

From the teaching of Jesus we can see that Satan still played his judicial role from the OT, especially in the stories of Jesus' temptation/testing. Further, the Synoptics support the image of Satan as the ruler of the demons, the one who sends them out to oppress people, either by possessing them or by bringing physical ailments to them. No explicit picture of Satan as the enemy defeated at the Eschaton comes out in the Synoptic apocalypses, unlike in the Scrolls and (probably) in Paul's writings (see Rom 16:20). Instead, the intriguing images of the strong man bound and of Satan fallen from heaven at the time of Jesus' ministry provide the synoptic evidence for the conquest of Satan the enemy during Jesus' ministry. Perhaps the fall of the stars at the end (Mk 13:25) was an oblique reference to the story of Satan and his angelic army finally defeated.

## B. THE GOD OF THIS AGE

The most important Pauline title for seeing Satan as the great enemy is "the god of this age": "our gospel...is veiled to those who are perishing. In their case the god of this age [*aionos*] has blinded the minds of unbelievers, to

keep them from seeing the light of the gospel" (2 Cor 4:4).[3] Clearly this title
suggests that Satan (who almost certainly is the one referred to) rules over
unbelievers in some ways—by having the power to blind them, according to this
passage. Further, the title "god" suggests that Paul saw Satan as the ruler over
the present age of darkness. From the Scrolls' background we can reasonably
conclude that Paul too saw this enemy as the ruler of the Kingdom of Darkness.
As support for this conclusion we will now consider how Paul probably thought
the principalities and Satan were related.

### (1) Satan and the Principalities: Hierarchy or Anarchy?

Did Paul imagine Satan as the Commander-in-Chief of all the
principalities and powers, whom we will show in chapter IV are imagined as the
angelic national rulers of this present age? That is clearly the view of the Book
of Revelation, and that became standard in the Church in later centuries. Russell
expresses that view when he presents this summary of the NT picture of Satan:

> The Devil is a creature of God, the chief of the fallen
> angels...He is the lord of this world, chief of a vast multitude
> of powers spiritual and physical, angelic and human, that are
> arrayed against the Kingdom of God. Satan is not only the
> Lord's chief opponent; he has under his generalship *all*
> opposition to the Lord. Anyone who does not follow the Lord
> is under the control of Satan.[4]

This theory that the NT writers pictured a unified hierarchy of evil (as did the
writers of the War Scroll) has not been universally held by scholars. For
example, Noack argued the contrary, saying that the wide variety of names Paul
used for Satan and the powers indicates that he understood the supernatural
world to be in anarchy, composed of different powers in competition with each
other, as different nations in the world are.[5] This theory of anarchy among the
forces of darkness can be supported by the OT evidence. There (the) Satan plays

---

[3] Similar imagery is present in *The Martyrdom of Isaiah* 2:4, where Beliar
is called "the ruler of this world." Further, the Gospel of John (12:31) gives
him the title "the prince (*archon*) of this world." Thus Paul's title is not unique.

[4] J. B. Russell, *The Devil*, 247.

[5] *Satanas und Soteria*, 82.

a role as tester, accuser and punisher in God's court while the other sons of God, the princes of the nations, play their distinct roles as rulers of the nations on earth. In that system Satan is a secret agent of the United Nations while the principalities are national presidents.

The weaknesses of this "two systems of evil" solution to the puzzle of Pauline demonology are manifold. First, nowhere in intertestamental Judaism or the NT or afterward is this picture given overtly as the present nature of the system of evil. Instead, most of those sources picture Satan, under various names, as the chief of all evil powers. For example, in *1 Enoch* the "satans" and their chief Satan are at first distinct from the sons of God, the Watchers. However, later the sons of God were led astray by the satans, and so made themselves "subject to Satan" (*1 Enoch* 54:6). Most clearly the War Scroll pictures a single hierarchy ruled by Belial/Satan. Since the Jewish apocalyptic tradition has a unified view of the hierarchy of evil, we should assume that Paul had a similar view unless he made it quite clear that he saw anarchy in the ranks of the forces of darkness. He gives no such hint, and in fact implies the contrary.

Paul provides his first hint that he sees Satan and the principalities as a single system when he speaks of Christ's conquest of all evil, in 1 Corinthians 15: he speaks only of the conquest of the powers and of death, not of Satan, which suggests that he thought the conquest of Satan was implied in the conquest of the others. Perhaps Paul included Satan in his reference to the defeat of "every ruler [*archen*]" (24). Later he provides a second hint when he speaks of "the wiles of the devil," which he amplifies by the phrases "rulers...authorities...cosmic powers...spiritual forces of evil in heavenly places" (Eph 6:11–12). That clearly suggests that the devil is intimately connected with those subordinate angelic powers.

Thirdly, the fact that Paul called the gods of the nations "demons" (1 Cor 10:20) provides indirect evidence of his views on Satan. From both Jewish and Christian sources just before Paul wrote we discover that Satan was "the prince of demons" (*Jub.* 10:8–9; Mk 3:22), a title that we must assume Paul also knew. Therefore, when he calls the gods of the nations demons, he probably imagined them as under their Prince, Satan.

Fourth, Paul implies the rule of Satan over the gods of the nations when he makes his series of parallels in 2 Cor 6:14–15, where the following are associated: darkness, Beliar, unbelievers, idols. That suggests that Paul saw the worship of idols, i.e., of the gods of the nations, as part of the dominion of Beliar, which is another name for Satan. That implies that Satan is the ruler of the gods. Of course, when Paul uses the term idols (*eidolon*) here, he may be implying that the gods are really just statues. If that is the case, then the main spirit Paul pictures is Satan, with the gods of the nations as fictions (or just demons instead of gods) which are part of the blinding of unbelievers by Satan.

Finally, of course, the chief evidence that Paul thought of Satan as the ruler of all the forces of evil is that he gave him the title "the god [*ho theos*] of this age" (2 Cor 4:4). If he had said "a god," then we would rightly have seen him as one among equals. "The god," however, is most naturally taken to mean that when we consider "this age," this character is the absolute ruler of it.

Our conclusion is thus that in Paul's cosmic war myth Satan is the Commander-in-Chief over all the other spiritual forces, the ruler of the Kingdom of Darkness. Here is the starting-point of Paul's symbolic military picture, the font (presumably) of the darkness that blinds, oppresses, enslaves and seeks to destroy all the good in the creation.

### (3) The Nature of Satan's Kingdom of Darkness

When Paul calls Satan "the god of this age [*aionos*]" (2 Cor 4:4), the realm there mentioned is one he speaks of in a variety of other places, using a variety of names. In Gal 1:4 he calls it "this present evil age" from which Christ has set us free. In Col 1:13 he calls it "the power [*exousias*] of darkness" from which God has rescued us by transferring us "to the kingdom [*basileian*] of his beloved son." In Ephesians he calls it "this present darkness" (6:12). Then, finally, he speaks of this contrast between Christ's new kingdom and Satan's old one in 2 Cor 6:14–16:

> What fellowship is there between light and **darkness**?
> What agreement does Christ have with **Beliar**?
> What does a believer share with an **unbeliever**?
> What agreement has the temple of God with **idols**?
> For we are the temple of the living God.

From this variety of passages it is clear that when he was using his military symbolism Paul saw the world divided into two kingdoms: God's Kingdom of

Light in which Christ rules, and Satan's Kingdom of Darkness, which is the present evil realm in which people worship false gods, demons, the rulers of this present age. Christ's new kingdom is small, an island in a raging sea, threatened on every side. We can picture the sun breaking through a small hole in very heavy clouds, shining down on this island which becomes the area of light surrounded on all sides by darkness. A full exploration of this Kingdom of Light symbolism is in chapter V below on Christ's Initial Victory over the Forces of Evil.

The most immediate background for our understanding the Pauline symbolism of this world as an age of darkness comes from the Scrolls where this imagery is common. There the human world is divided into "the sons of light" (the Qumranians) and "the sons of darkness" (all outsiders), with hierarchies rising up from each of them. The darkness is ruled by "the Prince of the Dominion of Darkness" (1QM xvii) who is also called "Belial" and "Satan," so the present time of evil is called "so long as Belial continues to hold sway" (1QS ii). Even deeper background comes from Daniel's intertwining of these two realms of good and evil—God's saints surrounded by, and eventually victorious over, the forces of Antiochus and the Fourth Beast. Most noteworthy here is Daniel's image of the Fourth Monster dominating the children of light (7:21, 25) but finally being burned to ashes (7:22, 26). Satan in Paul's imagery is just such a monster who dominates this world of darkness, though the children of light remain spiritually free (in Christ's Kingdom of Light) from his depredations.

**Conclusion**

Satan, the god of this age, the Ruler of the Kingdom of Darkness, was apparently alive in Paul's imagination as the Commander-in-Chief of an evil empire that covered the whole of the earth, except for Christ's fortress island of light where Sin does not rule. The Scrolls, especially The War Scroll, provide apt background to this picture, for they present two realms of light and darkness which are visible in two groups of people in conflict.

## C. THE COMMANDER'S POWERS

Now that we have seen that Satan is pictured in Paul's myth as the

Ruler of all the Forces of Darkness, we need to present briefly Paul's understanding of the extent of Satan's powers in the world. Satan is powerful politically as **(1) Ruler of the Nations and Armies**. As such he is present in the angelic principalities and powers, while also using human rulers as his pawns. In addition, Satan is **(2) The Destroyer of Nature**, for he is a (or the) source of pain, probably is the Angel of Death and thus the source of the decay of all creation.

## (1) Ruler of the Nations and Armies

As the ruler of the Kingdom of Darkness, Paul's Satan has a central "political" role, the Emperor ruling over the national (angelic and human) princes. This role is implied, for Paul apparently saw Satan as the spirit behind and over all the principalities and powers, thrones and dominions, the rulers of this present age, who are probably also the elemental spirits of the universe.

### (a) Present in Principalities and Powers

In section B we argued for the view, held by most commentators on Paul, that the apostle, by calling Satan "the god of this age" pictured him as the Ruler of the Kingdom of Darkness, also called this present age, or this world. In that role Satan is presumably the Commander-in-Chief of all the principalities and powers, whom we will later show are the angel rulers of the nations (the gods and sons of god spoken of in the OT, e.g. Psalm 82). These rulers are spirits ordained by God to guide the nations into a just order, who allowed themselves to be worshipped and so became the false gods of the nations.

As the Emperor over all these princes of the nations, Satan was probably imagined by Paul as present and powerful to a significant extent in all nations. In particular Paul probably saw Satan as the dominant spirit in their political, economic and religious systems, all of which have been corrupted by Sin. In the next chapter, when we discuss Paul's references to those rulers of this present age, we will provide details of the ways in which Paul probably imagined them permeating the political, economic, cultural and religious realms of their nations. Paul probably imagined Satan's presence in those rulers on the model of Emperor and vassal kings, e.g., Alexander the Conqueror's rule through his generals over all the territory over which his armies had trampled.

In that kind of empire the power stems from the center, in the emperor's charisma, organization and control; but the power flows through the generals who are present and powerful because they control the armies which occupy the lands they have conquered. How much those generals stick to the letter of the emperor's decrees, and how much they act in self-serving ways, of course varied from place to place in the empire. Probably (so we will argue below) in the same way Paul imagined the rulers of this present age as varying in their allegiance to the Prince of Darkness, so in some places their rule was absolutely tyrannical (as under Antiochus IV), whereas in other places it was relatively benign.

## (b) Controller of Human Rulers

In Paul's myth, as in apocalyptic Judaism, those political angelic authorities exercise their power through human rulers of this present age. Thus Paul probably imagined that Satan's will and evil intentions are expressed in human rulers. For example, when Paul said that Christ was crucified by the rulers of this age (1 Cor 2:8) he was presumably thinking first of the Romans, and perhaps also of the Jewish leaders who had delivered Jesus to the Romans. However, his description of these rulers as now "passing away" (1 Cor 2:6) suggests that he was also thinking of the angelic princes who stand hiddenly behind the earthly rulers. Thus it is likely that Paul pictured the human rulers as agents of Satan too, as the next rung of the hierarchy that is topped by the Angel of Darkness and ends with the idol-worshipping children of darkness on the bottom.

One specific human agent in Paul's myth who is empowered by Satan is the eschatological Man of Lawlessness (2 Thess 2:9–10) who apparently will seem to many to be a savior. Though we will explore this vision in more detail as part of Paul's last battle imagery, at this point we will just emphasize that Paul saw Satan active within this figure, for he says:

> The coming of the Lawless One (is) by the working of Satan
> [*kat' energeian tou Satana*], who uses all power, signs, lying
> wonders, and every kind of wicked deception for those who
> are perishing because they refused to love the truth and be
> saved. (2 Thess 2:9–10)

Clearly this suggests that Satan can be the puppeteer behind human beings, in this case behind a tyrant modelled on Daniel's picture of Antiochus IV (for 2 Thess 2:4 alludes to Dan 11:36). That allusion suggests that Satan is modelled on Daniel's Fourth Monster. As Antiochus was the last agent of the Fourth Monster, so also apparently the Lawless One was the final agent of Satan. Indeed this Lawless One was perhaps even the full expression of Satan's power, because when this figure is destroyed all evil apparently disappears with it.

In the nations, therefore, wherever human rulers use their power for their own ends, following their natural impulses of self-interest, Paul sees Satan as the spirit at work. Almost certainly Paul believed all human rulers are slaves of Sin, so all national systems in his day were for him Satan's prisons (though with varying degrees of oppression).

### (c) Coercing Unbelievers

The Prince of Darkness in Paul's military myth apparently sends his unholy spirits all the way down to the bottom of the hierarchy. Though the principalities and human rulers are the most prominent of Satan's obedient officers, his most numerous servants, indeed slaves, are the infantry, the human children of darkness. All unbelievers are conscripts in the army of evil. Unlike believers, who are protected inside Christ's Fortress of Light, unbelievers are wholly unprotected from Satan's coercion. First of all Paul speaks of Satan blinding unbelievers (2 Cor 4:4); secondly he speaks of Sin (which we will argue in the next chapter is for Paul one of Satan's agents) as ruling unbelievers, an image he expresses in Ephesians by calling Satan "the spirit now at work within the sons of disobedience" (Eph 2:2).

One of Paul's images of the way the enemy works within people is by propaganda, fooling them, blinding them to the truth: "if our gospel is veiled, it is veiled only to those who are perishing. In their case the god of this age has *blinded the minds of unbelievers*, to keep them from seeing the light of the gospel" (2 Cor 4:3–4). The natural way that blinding takes place is by the community proclaiming, living and enforcing a viewpoint so thoroughly that those who are born into the community do not even recognize that they have been indoctrinated.

Paul was thinking here particularly of Jews who were indoctrinated in the Pharisaic view of living by the Mosaic Law (2 Cor 3:14–15). They believed in it so firmly that they could not see that their legalism conflicted with the OT spiritual emphasis on repentance, faith, trust, commitment, dependence on God, and love. Paul apparently believed that Satan was at work within the legalism in which he was brought up and which he saw still propagated in a semi-

Christian form by the "super apostles" who "disguise themselves as apostles of Christ" but really are Satan's ministers (2 Cor 11:5, 13–15). Apparently Paul saw Satan as a spirit at work within communities, urging them away from real dependence on God and into the (apparently) more powerful and attractive position of dependence on themselves (disguised as legalistic obedience to God). Such communities (both Jewish and Gentile) then oppressed the children of light, turning the spiritual war into a physical one.

A second image Paul offers, one that helps explain how the blinding works, is of Satan as the spirit at work within the passions of unbelievers, coercing them into obeying his commands as their commander-in-chief:

> You were dead through the trespasses and sins in which you once walked, following the Prince of the Power of the Air, the spirit that is now at work [*energountos*] in the sons of disobedience. Among these we all once lived in the passions [*epithumiais*] of our flesh, following the desires [*thelemata*] of body and mind... (Eph 2:1–3)

If Paul did not write this, it certainly does seem to express his view that Satan was a spirit at work within sinners, as we will see when we discuss the power Sin in Romans in the next chapter. How this prince is at work within unbelievers is suggested by the references to passions and desires (as also in Rom 7:5): Paul saw that natural human desires could become strengthened, then inflamed, and then burst beyond the control of the person. That inflammation he apparently pictured as the work of this spirit Satan within individuals. Of course this spirit has a collective aspect too, for the low standards of the Gentile community also played a role in allowing unbelievers to give sway to their passions (see Rom 1:24). In pagans this spirit often ruled, while in believers it was only a continuing temptation, because they resisted it.

In this section we have shown that Paul's myth of Satan included the picture of him as a spirit coercively at work within unbelievers, as the spirit of the Roman army ruled coercively over the spirits of Roman soldiers. In unbelievers Satan is a ruling power that coerces them into obedience, into sinning, unlike his role in Christian's lives where he can only tempt and seek to persuade. Satan seems to be an Unholy Spirit that blinds, inflames and oppresses those who are members of the Kingdom of Darkness. Perhaps Paul is thinking of the communal spirit of conformity that leads most of the members of any community to follow its ideological and religious party line, so they are blinded to the truth as they worship the gods of their community.

### (2) The Destroyer of Nature

Satan, in Paul's myth, not only rules the evil spirits but is also the Destroyer of Nature, the scourge that produces the corruption and death that permeates God's good creation. Clearly Paul believed that Satan could bring physical pain and disease (2 Cor 12:7). Probably Paul believed that Satan was the Angel of Death, the destroyer, the spirit that lies behind and within Death the great enemy (1 Cor 5:5; 10:10; 15:24–26). Thirdly, it is plausible that Paul believed that Satan was the source of, perhaps the spirit that produces, the corruption of the whole of nature, the spirit that brought about nature's "bondage to decay" (Rom 8:20–22). In all these ways Paul apparently pictured Satan as using nature as a weapon in his war against the light.

### (a) The Purveyor of Physical Pain

Clearly in Paul's myth Satan rules over nature to some extent, because, as in Job and the Synoptic story, he brings physical suffering, Paul's thorn in the flesh: "To keep me from being too elated by the abundance of revelations, a thorn [*skolops*] was given me in the flesh, a messenger [*angelos*] of Satan to harass me" (2 Cor 12:7–9). Paul does not identify what the thorn symbolizes, but it is clearly some form of chronic physical suffering. When Paul calls it an angel of Satan he suggests that Satan is the source of this physical suffering, that somehow Satan has power to produce physical suffering.[6] That is the traditional Hebraic picture. From as far back as the story of Job we find the satan bringing on the faithful Job "loathsome sores from the sole of his foot to the crown of his head" (Job 2:7). Similarly the Synoptic tradition has Jesus refer to a crippled woman as "bound by Satan" (Lk 13:16). Whether or not Paul and the early Christians thought that all physical diseases were the work of Satan is not clear,

---

[6] Clearly the purpose Paul refers to, keeping him from becoming too elated, is not Satan's, but God's, for it is a benefit, a blessing. Therefore Paul here speaks of a divine task that Satan undertakes, suggesting that Satan is here still God's agent. Perhaps Paul's view was that Satan is always eager to cause pain to believers, so is always willing to serve God in such cases.

but it is quite plausible. Thus Paul saw Satan wielding natural evil as a weapon in his war. Whenever the innocent are the victims of his attack, there the war bursts forth into view.

**(b) The Angel of Death**

Though Paul never explicitly connects Satan with death, we will argue in the next chapter that he implied that death is one of Satan's "agents" (as the author of Heb 2:14 believed). The passage in which Paul comes closest to connecting the two is when he says of the sinner in the Corinthian congregation: "You are to deliver this man to Satan for the destruction [*olethron*] of the flesh that his spirit may be saved in the day of the Lord Jesus" (1 Cor 5:5). The most natural interpretation of "the destruction of the flesh" is that it refers to physical death, for physical death is precisely what Paul pictures "the destroyer [*tou olothreutou*]" providing in 1 Cor 10:10. That destroyer, referring to the angel of death in the Exodus story (Exod 12:23), and to a plague from the Lord visited on the Israelites in a later story (Num 16:41-49), thus may well be a reference to Satan, though Paul does not say so explicitly.[7]

Further evidence for Satan as the ruler of death in Paul is the probability that when death the last enemy is finally conquered then Satan too is conquered (1 Cor 15:26, see Rom 16:20). Paul's silence on Satan's end in 1 Corinthians 15 suggests that Paul believed it was implied in the conquest of all the other powers.

Finally, it is quite natural for Paul to understand Satan as the angel of death, for this fits closely with two of the characteristics we have presented above: Satan's power to bring physical suffering suggests that he could bring pain to the uttermost, which would result in death (as the satan does in Job). Secondly, Satan's (probable) role as emperor of the rulers of this present age, the ones who killed Christ (1 Cor 2:6, 8) and control the sword which brings God's judgment (Rom 13:1-4), suggests that for Paul Satan is the spirit behind all the destructive power of governments. Thus as death is the chief weapon used by human armies, it would be no surprise for Paul to see Death as one of Satan's weapons. Indeed, Paul personifies Death, seeing it as "reigning" (Rom 5:21) and as an "enemy" (1 Cor 15:26). Therefore he probably pictured it as

---

[7] Since *Jubilees* (10:8-9; 49:2) spoke of the Exodus destroyer as Mastema (= Satan), it is quite plausible that Paul knew that interpretation too.

Satan's lieutenant, his right hand agent, possibly even his alter ego.

## (c) Source of the Decay of All Creation

Paul possibly also included in his myth the idea that Satan was (or controls) a spirit within creation that enslaved it to worthlessness and decay. Clearly, in Paul's myth Satan was a spirit that used Nature, in particular disease and death, so it is possible that Paul saw him as the source, or perhaps the controller, of all the natural evil in the world.

In Romans 1–11, his major theological exposition, Paul does not explicitly refer to Satan, so we have to read between the lines to know where he may have imagined Satan hidden in the darkness behind the evils he described. In particular, consider Paul's assertion that the creation is "under slavery to decay [*phthoras*]" because it has been "subjected [*hupetage*] to worthlessness [*mataioteti*]" (Rom 8:20–21). An argument that this slavery, decay and worthlessness point to Satan's rule includes the following points:

(i) Slavery was Paul's symbol used previously to describe the state of humans ruled by the power Sin (Rom 6:6, 16), who is Satan's agent (or so we will argue in the next chapter). Thus when Paul describes creation as under slavery, this may also hint that Satan is the slave-master.

(ii) The decay that Paul refers to is presumably the decay of living matter, the mortality, the life heading towards death that is common to all living things on earth. Since Satan is probably for Paul the angel of death, it is quite likely that Paul also sees Satan as (or as sending) the spirit at work within all the decay of creation.

(iii) Plausibly Paul's noun *mataiotes* (worthlessness, emptiness, vanity) alludes to pagan gods: Acts 14:15 has Paul urge the Lystrans to turn from "these worthless things [*ton mataion*]," by which he referred to their belief in Zeus and Hermes mentioned in the previous verse. In addition, Jer 2:5 says that the Hebrews had gone after "worthless things and so became worthless" (using *mataios* in the LXX), by which he apparently meant idol worship and its consequent moral decay. C. K. Barrett supports this worthlessness-means-gods suggestion by his translation of Rom 8:20: "For the creation was subjected to a vain life under inferior spiritual powers." His argument for this is that *mataiotes* and cognates in the LXX "sometimes refer to the gods of the heathen (e.g., Ps. xxxi.6)."[8]

(iv) Further, it is possible that Paul knew that a worthless person was sometimes called a *bene belial* in Hebrew (e.g., Dt 13:13; Judg 19:22 etc.), so his word worthlessness may have been an allusion to the name Belial/r which he used elsewhere for Satan (2 Cor 6:14).

(v) Finally, the satan in Job seems to have power over nature, using it to carry out destruction (1:16, 19; 2:7), so Paul may have inherited that story as part of his understanding of natural evil.

Thus it is plausible that Paul included in his cosmic war myth this plot line: as a result of human sinfulness God subjected all of the earthly creation to the rule of Satan who is thus the god of this whole world (natural as well as social). Satan tyrannically rules this world, as Antiochus IV ruled and oppressed the Jews in his day, and the Romans did in Paul's day. That absolute military rule includes first the imposition of mortality which produces the decay of all living matter, and second domination by the gods/principalities, Satan's subordinates, who are worthless for giving spiritual life.

Therefore we conclude that Paul pictured all the physical creation, insofar as it was in bondage to decay and death, as permeated by the spirit (of?) Satan. As God's Holy Spirit is the force providing life, order and freedom in the new creation, so Satan was probably in Paul's imagination the unholy spirit providing oppression, disorder and death in the old creation. Since the present condition of the earth includes both life and death, both order and disorder, both freedom and oppression, Paul may have pictured Satan as locked in an armed conflict with God's Spirit everywhere throughout creation. The war will be fought to a conclusion, for either light or darkness will eventually rule completely.

## Conclusion: Paul's Character Satan

In Paul's cosmic war myth the character Satan, the god of this age, has extraordinary powers: first, Paul apparently pictured Satan as the commander of the principalities and powers, who are the angelic rulers behind each nation. Through the principalities Satan then rules over all the human rulers of this age and so over all the earthly political, economic and religious realms outside

---

[8] *Romans*, 165–166.

Christ's Kingdom of Light. The second level of Satan's power is his coercive
rule within all unbelievers, all the children of darkness. In them Satan rules via
the slave-master Sin, forcing them to give in to their impulses, forcing them via
community pressure to worship the so-called gods (the principalities). Finally,
the broadest extent of Satan's power in Paul's story is his role as the destroyer
at work in nature: he sends physical disease as his messenger, permeates the
whole of living matter with decay, and thus sends Death as his ultimate agent,
the final enemy.

## D. ELABORATING PAUL'S MYTH

In order to understand this Pauline myth of the Ruler of Darkness more
fully we need to consider how Paul probably imagined him to have reached this
high position, and why he became God's enemy after starting off as God's
obedient servant.

The basic data that is the foundation for our reconstruction of Paul's
myth includes the following, which then raises the questions we will seek to
answer:

(1) In the Hebraic tradition (which we presume Paul accepted) Satan is
a heavenly spirit, a son of God, who began as God's obedient agent sent to test,
accuse and punish humans. In the beginning Satan had some power over Nature
as part of his weaponry but otherwise he acted alone, without subordinates.[9]

(2) In the tradition also, God appointed 70 angelic princes of the 70
nations (also called gods and sons of god), the hidden spirits that were ordained
to provide law, order and justice through their guidance of the human ruler of
their nation. In the OT story these princes had no direct connection with Satan,
except that like him they were also sons of God and so were directly under the
authority of God.[10]

(3) In Daniel (as earlier in Psalm 82), the angelic princes had become
God's enemies, fighting against God's heavenly army, parallel to the way their
nations became the enemies of God's people.

(4) In 1 *Enoch* 54 the visionary reports that by means of temptation

---

[9] See pages 41–44 above.
[10] See pages 37–41 above.

Satan came to rule over the sons of God (called Watchers).

(5) In Paul's myth, the princes, called the rulers of this present age and other names, seem to be under the authority of Satan, subordinate commanders in the army of darkness.

(6) Further, Paul's picture includes an enslaving spirit Sin which oppresses all unbelievers. This spirit probably is an agent of Satan (as we will show in the next chapter), so Satan's darkness snuffs out the light within every unbeliever.

(7) Paul's complete picture includes Satan as God's chief enemy, at the top of the evil hierarchy. As the Ruler of the Kingdom of Darkness, he has the princes of the nations under his command, Sin and Death spread into every person on the earth, and all unbelievers as slaves in the army fighting under him.

The two questions we seek to answer are these:

(1) How did Paul imagine that the satan God's agent (in Job) became Satan God's enemy (in Paul's myth)?

(2) Is Paul's Satan wholly God's enemy? Or does Paul still hold to the OT picture in which Satan works as God's willing agent when he tests, accuses and punishes human beings?

We seek to answer these questions because our full understanding of Paul's military symbolism depends on seeing beneath the surface of Paul's explicit teaching to the myth he assumed. Support for this procedure, our further exploring Paul's assumed biography of Satan, comes from Forsyth who notes that "the very brevity of the allusions to Satan...is revealing," for it implies that some episodes in the Satan story are, "familiar to one's readers. The developed adversary of Jewish and Christian apocalyptic is a familiar figure to Paul and his audiences, and he is familiar as the agent in a story they all know."[11] If we are going to see beneath the tips of the iceberg, which is all we have in Paul's brief mentions of Satan, then we must explore the hints he offers, using the background he presumably knew.

## (1) Agent Become Enemy: Three Possible Myths

In order to answer our questions and thus construct Paul's assumed

---

[11] *The Combat Myth*, 271.

history of Satan, we need to consider three proposed myths. The first is the famous miltonian one in which Satan rebelled before the creation, and so came into the human world as an **Invader**, one who usurps power for he has no divinely given authority at all. The second is the story that Satan was appointed God's **Regent over the Earth**, but rebelled at his subordinate role and so became God's enemy, though he retained his power over the earth. The third myth is that Satan, beginning as God's tester and **Prison Warden**, was so successful that he got all humankind and all the angelic Princes in his prison, thereby becoming de facto ruler of the whole earth; along the way, by his rigid application of the rules of justice, he rebelled against God's gift of mercy, thus becoming God's enemy even while continuing to be God's tester, accuser and prison warden. As an enemy he seeks his own advancement, being eager to increase his own power, rather than seeking simply to serve God.

**(a) Invader: Usurper of God's Authority**

One of the best-known accounts is Milton's, in which Satan rebelled against God before the creation of the earth and was therefore banished from heaven to Sheol. As revenge for his banishment he decided to corrupt the earth, so he invaded it. Thenceforth by deception, temptation, and oppression he gradually accumulated enough power until he became the Great Enemy of God, the god of this world. This myth goes back perhaps as far as Irenaeus in the second century, whose views are summarized by Russell this way: "The Devil apostasized and fell from heaven...he is only a usurper of authority that legitimately and ultimately belongs to God...The Devil fell from grace because he envied God, wishing to be adored like his maker."[12]

This myth is the least likely of the three we are considering to be what Paul assumed. Its mortal defect is that it contradicts the OT picture of Satan as originally God's obedient agent, one of the members of the heavenly council of sons of God during Israel's history. Since Paul still gave Satan judicial functions it is very likely that he took as authoritative the OT picture of Satan as originally God's obedient servant.

Secondly, this pre-mundane rebellion myth was probably not Paul's because there is no support for it in the tradition prior to Paul. The one story that comes close is in *The Books of Adam and Eve* which may have been written

---

[12] Russell, *Satan*, 81.

by Paul's day, and may have been known to him, but probably was not authoritative to him. In this story, when Satan was called on to worship Adam as God's image, Satan refused on the grounds that Adam was his inferior. Thus Satan rebelled and then tried to set his throne equal to God's, which resulted in him being banished from heaven (reflecting Isaiah 14). So in revenge he corrupted Eve.[13]

Like Milton's myth this account does suggest that Satan had no God-given authority on earth. However, unlike the miltonian version this account does not place the rebellion before God created humankind, because the conflict comes over an already-created Adam. Thus no extant book from Paul's day depicted a pre-mundane rebellion of Satan.

Thirdly, the miltonian myth was not likely to be Paul's because its pre-creation fall image first appears in the time of Irenaeus, ca. AD 175. Indeed Origen, writing even later, in the third century, was the one who developed the myth fully. He based his myth on allegorizing interpretations of Isaiah 14 and Ezekiel 28, making them both apply to Satan who is not mentioned in either.[14]

For these reasons, this myth of Satan's pre-mundane rebellion, his expulsion from heaven, and his subsequent coming from Sheol to invade earth and usurp God's power is not very likely to be the story Paul assumed. The chief objection to this theory is that it has no room for the clear OT story of (the) Satan as an agent of God's judicial will, originally not God's enemy at all.

**(b) Appointed God's Regent**

The second possible theory to explain how in Paul's myth Satan became the ruler of this world is that God appointed him to that role. This could have happened at the beginning of the world, or at the time when God appointed the 70 sons of God as the Princes of the nations. The chief argument for it is that no creature could become the ruler over the whole of this world without God granting the authority.

Green points to NT titles as possibly suggesting this myth, not only "the god of this world" but also John's "ruler of this world" (Jn 12:31): "is it possible that he was assigned some special task of oversight of the world by God

---

[13] *The Books of Adam and Eve* xii–vii. A similar but much briefer version is given in *2 Enoch* 29:4–5.

[14] Russell, *Satan*, 131.

in the beginning before his fall?...God's angelic administrator of our earth?"[15] Though he sees this as speculation, Green suggests that it would account for Satan's power over the earth.[16]

The chief argument for this myth perhaps is this: we may assume that no spirit could become ruler over the whole of the earth  except by the will of God; Satan appears to be such a ruler, for Paul calls him "the god of this present age"; therefore God must have willed Satan's rule, appointing him to that role. Presumably the appointment took place at or near the beginning of human history.

The chief objection to this theory is that no evidence can be found in the Bible that directly supports this myth of Satan as earth's original ruler by divine decree. Indeed, the OT references to (the) Satan show a very limited role, with God alone as the ruler over the whole earth. The closest we come in the Bible to such a regent on earth is in the pictures of the unnamed chief angelic warriors found in Josh 5:13-15 and Dan 10:5-13. Both these warriors could be taken as God's ruler over the earth. However, their warrior role makes it more likely that they were simply generals, limited to making war, rather than rulers who are in charge both in peace and in war. More important, however, these angels are wholly God's servants, the antagonist (in Daniel at least) to the fallen angelic princes, so the Prince of Darkness was a quite different character.

Our conclusion then is that there is no evidence in the Bible or pre-Christian Judaism to suggest that God had ever appointed an angel as regent over the whole earth, and certainly no evidence that that particular angel had become Satan. Indeed the OT Satan is clearly not such a figure but has quite limited authority.

### (c) Appointed Prison Warden

The third possible myth that Paul could have assumed on how Satan became the god of this world starts with the OT story of (the) Satan as God's judicial agent. This story suggests that (i) God appointed Satan to a limited role

---

[15] Green, *I Believe in Satan's Downfall*, 47.

[16] Another writer who uses this myth is C. S. Lewis in his fantasy *Out of the Silent Planet*. There the Dark Eldil, the ruler of earth, was appointed to that role by God at the same time other eldils were appointed to rule over the other planets. Even when he later rebelled against God he retained his earthly power (120-121).

on earth, as tester, accuser, prison warden and hangman. However (ii) humans failed the test by committing themselves to idolatry, to this present evil age. Thereby Satan's agent Sin gained power over them and all humans became inmates in the prison, subjects of Satan, slaves in the Kingdom of Darkness. At the same time (iii) Satan gained rule over the princes of the nations because they too fell into sin, by allowing themselves to be worshipped as gods; so as their punishment they became prisoners under the prison warden of Earth. Finally, (iv) Satan became God's enemy along the way in this process because (as in Zech 3:1-5) Satan demands that justice be fully done, but God often offers mercy, against which Satan rebels. Thus Satan finally sets himself up as god of the earth, seeking his own advancement in power and prestige, instead of God's.

In the beginning then, in this myth that may have been the one Paul imagined, Satan was a single agent on earth, without any subordinates (Job 1-2). His authority was his mandate from God to test human beings, to accuse those who fail the test, and then to punish them as their prison warden and executioner. Though he had no spirit subordinates, he did have power over Nature, for he was able to use wind, storm, earthquake and plague to bring destruction on humankind. This is the OT picture which Paul probably accepted.

Secondly, as we will show in the next chapter, Paul saw Adam and Eve's sinning as the first step into slavery to Sin (Romans 5-7), by which he probably meant membership in Satan's Kingdom of Darkness. Paul pictured all people as following in Adam's footsteps, succumbing to temptation (Rom 5:12-21). As Satan succeeded (through his agent Sin) in getting humans to fall, one prisoner at a time, so he succeeded in building up his kingdom. This Kingdom of Darkness lies behind Paul's reference to the way that all are "imprisoned...under the power of sin" (Gal 3:22), "imprisoned and guarded under the law" (Gal 3:23).

Thirdly, in this proposed myth, the principalities and powers were originally ordained as God's attempt at damage control when sinning had become widespread as people formed nations. As a bulwark against that widespread sinning, God ordained the angelic princes to provide justice, law, order and punishment in each of their nations (see Rom 13:1-4). Clearly for Paul those princes of the nations eventually became enemies of God. Our hypothesis is that he probably saw the origin of this enmity in the way they allowed themselves to be worshipped as gods (see Rom 1:19-23; 1 Cor

10:19–20).

Fourth, the princes are now subordinate to Satan, in his prison too. When they allowed themselves to be worshipped, they too fell, so they too came under Satan's punitive control. Though no OT text speaks of Satan as the punisher of angels, his role as punisher of humans makes it natural to imagine that God had also given him the angelic realm to police. In addition, the immediate background for this development is given in *1 Enoch* 54 which reports that the sons of God (called Watchers) were led astray and so became subject to Satan. Later, the Scrolls' picture of Satan having subordinate angels of destruction supports this picture as the standard Jewish apocalyptic one which Paul probably learned and adopted.

Finally, in this myth of The Rise of Satan from God's secret agent to God's chief enemy some reason for his enmity to God needs to be offered. The most likely imagery that Paul adopted is that Satan rebelled against God's mercy, God's refusal to allow Satan to punish humans as fully as they deserved, for that is the picture given in Zech 3:1–5 which is the oldest representation of conflict between God and Satan. Wink hints at this as the NT myth, saying: "Satan...seems to have evolved from a trustworthy intelligence-gatherer into a virtually autonomous and invisible suzereign within a world ruled by God." Referring to the story in Jude 8–9, Wink adds: "Satan is characterized by an excessive zeal for strict, merciless justice...he is a legalist."[17]

In this version of the myth (suggested by combining Job 1–2, Zech 3:1–5 and Rev 12:1–12) the heavenly prosecutor's problem (apparently) arises when he goes too far, demanding justice when God seeks mercy.[18] From the beginning, in Job, the satan sees God as too soft, for God gives Job all the good things in life and the satan seeks to take them away, believing they are undeserved. Even more striking is the vision in Zechariah, for there Satan is the accuser, the one who wants to punish Joshua, but God resists, offering mercy and redemption instead. Then after Paul's day the same conflict of mercy and

---

[17] Wink, *Unmasking the Powers*, 22–23, 21.

[18] Van der Hart reflects this same picture when he writes: "So absorbed is Satan in his task of accusing, tempting and punishing, that it has become an obsession with him. He cannot do anything else and he cannot even consider the possibility that man could be treated in a different way" (*The Theology of Angels and Devils*, 49).

justice is suggested in the fall-of-the-dragon myth in Rev 12:1–12, especially in vv. 10–11. Naturally, the agent of justice, whose kingdom grows with every sinner sent under his rule, will resist when God (apparently arbitrarily) mercifully plucks some sinners out of prison and takes them into his own house as free people. Thus Satan is a true believer in justice taken to the extreme, justice completely without mercy, because that would make him the ruler of all humankind inside his prison of darkness. This suggests that the rebel Satan's highest purpose is self-advancement.

This picture of Satan the extreme legalist is the one that Caird presents in *Principalities and Powers* (37) where he writes:

> Satan, the servant of God, entrusted with the maintenance of divine justice, becomes the Devil, the enemy of man and God...throughout his tragic history his zeal for justice remains unimpaired. He is a martinet, who demands that men shall be dealt with according to the rigour of the law, and will go to any lengths to secure a verdict. His tragedy consists precisely in this, that law is not the ultimate truth about God, so that, in defending the honour of God's law, Satan becomes the enemy of God's true purpose.

Paul probably found this myth to be valuable because it helped explain the contrast between his gospel and the law preached by the Pharisees and the Judaizers. These opponents greatly objected to Paul bringing Gentiles into God's Kingdom when they had not obeyed the law fully. His gospel is that God comes in mercy, that mercy is supreme; by contrast Satan blinds the advocates of the law (2 Cor 4:4) into believing that justice is supreme, that only those who obey the law fully can become right with God. Thus the anger and enmity of the Judaizers against Paul is aptly expressed in the myth of the anger and enmity of Satan against God over the same issue.

## Conclusion

We cannot be certain that Paul did in fact entertain a detailed myth of the rise of Satan from his servant role in Job to his position as the Ruler of the Kingdom of Darkness. However, it is likely that he and his readers did have some account of this change as the background against which to read his brief references to Satan. Of the three myths we have presented, clearly the third is the one that fits best with Paul's own imagery as well as with the tradition which he inherited. The miltonian myth of Satan the Invader conflicts with the story in the OT that Satan began as God's obedient judicial agent. The second myth of Satan as God's Regent over the earth suffers from the complete silence of the tradition, though it does not conflict with that tradition. The strength of the third myth is that it integrates all of the evidence into a plausible account. Thus we propose this third myth as the account that Paul probably assumed as part of his military version of the gospel.

### (2) Conscript or Volunteer?

One particularly disputed subject is whether Paul's myth of Satan includes the adversary as willingly continuing as God's agent of justice, or as wholly God's implacable enemy, one forced to act for God's justice by the over-riding providence of God. Clearly the myth we are advocating as probably Paul's—the legalist who rebels against God's mercy—presents Satan as eager to do God's justice, indeed over-eager. The alternative viewpoint is that Satan seeks to do only evil, and so must be forced by God to be the continuing agent of justice. Thus this debate provides the central conflict between our theory of Paul's myth and the popular miltonian alternative (the invader myth).

### (a) Conscript?

The post-biblical, later miltonian, myth pictures Satan as wholly God's enemy, motivated solely by hatred of God and desire for revenge. For example, describing the patristic picture in general, Russell speaks of Satan as,

> a cosmic power...that *wills and urges evil for its own sake* and hates good for its own sake...The evil in him procedes...from his free choice of hatred...The Devil, whose will is wholly given to hatred, wishes to distort the cosmos as much as he can.[19]

Similarly Wright's interpretation in *The Satan Syndrome* is that Satan, even in the Bible, "is an enemy who, against his will, finds himself doing the work of a servant...the illegitimate and invalid authority of Satan is even so taken up by God and through God's creative sovereignty alone made to serve the purposes

---

[19] Russell, *Satan*, 222 (italics added).

of God" (50). Further, Wright rejects the view that Satan is still God's willing agent to some extent, saying that this confuses Satan with God, so "evil ceases to be evil and becomes partly good" (49). Wright then reinterprets the OT passages such as Job 1–2: though the satan appears to be God's willing and obedient agent, that obedience is disguise, sham, deceit. Instead Satan is really God's implacable enemy whose hatred of all good is used by God for his own good purposes.

The defect in this myth is that it proposes a character that is inconceivable to us: an intelligence and will that is wholly evil. For two reasons such a purely evil spirit is hardly conceivable: (i) no rational agent can be wholly evil because evil is always parasitic on good; (ii) Even when an author (e.g. Milton) tries to create a purely evil Satan, he fails to do so because the motivations of his Satan are desires for good things, in particular to advance his own (supposed) good.

(i) First it seems clear that no rational agent can be purely evil. (An irrational, insane, human is an example of natural evil not moral evil.) A forceful rebuttal of the purely-evil-Satan myth comes in C. S. Lewis's argument against an eternal moral dualism:

> If Dualism is true, then the bad Power must be a being who likes badness for its own sake. But *in reality we have no experience of anyone liking badness just because it is bad*. The nearest we get to it is cruelty. But in real life people are cruel for one of two reasons—either because they are sadists, that is, because they have a sexual perversion which makes cruelty a cause of sensual pleasure to them, or else for the sake of something they are going to get out of it—money, or power, or safety. But pleasure, money, power, and safety are all, as far as they go, good things...*wickedness...turns out to be the pursuit of something good in the wrong way*...badness is only spoiled goodness.[20]

Thus it is plausible to conclude that all moral evil, that which is willed by a rational spirit, is parasitic on good. Our own experience provides extensive evidence of this conclusion: No spirit can produce moral evil unless it exists

---

[20] Lewis, *Mere Christianity*, 49 (italics added).

(which is good), has rationality (which is good), knows the difference between good and evil (which is good), has power to exert its will (which is good), and is motivated by seeking some gain (which is usually some personal good). Moral evil only exists as a parasite feeding on good. Perhaps that is part of what Paul implied by saying that Satan appears as an angel of light (2 Cor 11:14), i.e. he offers a lesser good as the bait for his evil.

(ii) When authors try to create a totally evil character Satan, they end up with an incoherent picture, showing that the idea of a totally evil rational spirit is self-contradictory. For example, Milton's Satan on the surface is described as wholly evil, but is clearly motivated by various penultimate goods. Satan proclaims "ever to do ill our sole delight." Indeed he takes up the possibility that God will coerce good from them, saying: "If then his Providence out of our evil seek to bring forth good, our labour must be to pervert that end, and out of good still to find means to evil."[21] Such words show that Milton wanted to describe his Satan as wholly evil.

When, however, we listen to Satan's purposes and motivations, and those of his colleagues, we find a variety of goods essential to their characters. *Hope*: for example, Satan knows that the suffering in Hell is bad, and so he lives by "hope" that they can "overcome this dire Calamity" (11). Hope for future good is a great good, one of the powerful motivations God has given to rational creatures. *Community*: further Satan applauds the lack of strife among his legions, the "union, and firm Faith, and firm accord," all of which are goods by which they strive to attain their hoped for end (33). *Justice*: indeed that end is "our just inheritance" showing that Satan is one who sees justice as a good standard on which they can depend (33). *Good*: indeed to summarize the purposes of Satan and his minions, we can profitably take this purpose: "*seek our own good from our own selves*" (39). That indeed is a general truth about evil-doers as we experience them: they do seek good, but it is their own (perceived, and often mistaken) good, which they put before the good of everyone else.

Thus the myth of the pre-mundane rebel Satan, who from the beginning of the creation of earth has sought solely to do evil, is literarily and psychologically incoherent. A rational creature who seeks evil for evil's sake is

---

[21] Milton, *Paradise Lost*, 11.

not conceivable in practice, given what we experience of the necessary mixture of good in the evil within all evil-doers on earth. Thus the theory that Satan seeks solely to do evil, and so must be forced by God to do the good of justice, is unlikely.

## (b) Continuing Volunteer

The view that seems to accord best with Paul's other imagery thus is that Satan continues to be a willing agent of justice even after he becomes God's enemy. In Paul's account of Satan's judicial role it seems clear that God's interests and Satan's interests coincide. God wants people to be tested, wants to have sinners accused, wants to have justice done, wants unrepentant sinners to fall deeper and deeper into slavery to sin. Satan the Enemy wants all those things too. Thus God's work and Satan's willing work coincide at these points. The difference arises over their ultimate purposes: By having people tested, accused and punished God seeks to chasten, i.e., to lead sinners to repent and be reconciled to him. By contrast, Satan the Enemy tests, accuses and punishes in order to consolidate his Kingdom of Darkness, to advance his own power.

In this picture of Satan the Enemy still serving as God's willing agent of justice, we have a continuation of the central OT picture of God as the ruler of the imperial powers of earth: there God used Assyria, Babylon, Persia and Greece as his agents of justice, bringing punishment to his own people and often to other nations. In none of these cases did God need to coerce the oppressor nations, for they were eager to attack, eager to conquer, eager to absorb the weaker Israelites into their own growing kingdoms. That is the picture that Paul probably adopted: God's purpose of wrath coincides with the enemies' purpose of punishing this small nation for its impudence in standing up to their empire's demand for submission. Thus it is likely that in Paul's myth Satan is God's willing servant, but Satan's motivation is not obedience but power, quite like that of the OT empires, seeking to build up his own kingdom.

## Conclusion: Paul's Full Myth of Satan

In this chapter we have described Paul's myth of Satan by exploring the iceberg that lies beneath the tips that come out explicitly in his references. The central strands of his myth probably include the following points: (i) Paul probably pictured Satan as originating as God's good agent of testing, accusing and punishing on earth, as described in the OT. (ii) As this minister of justice he became the ruler of all sinners, for God gave sinners over to slavery to Sin (Satan's agent) to be punished. (iii) Presumably, when the angelic princes of the nations allowed themselves to be worshipped (the root of all human sin), they too became Satan's slaves. (iv) By that means (the sin of rational creatures) Satan became the god of this world, the ruler of the present age of darkness.

(v) Presumably Paul pictured Satan at some point rebelling against God, refusing simply to be God's agent but seeking to be an independent power, and so he became God's enemy. (vi) The most likely motivation for that rebellion is that Satan (the minister of justice) is a legalist and self-righteous as the Judaizers were, so God's grace superseding justice led him to rebel against God. Satan (in Paul's myth) probably saw his realm of justice, law, order and punishment as the most important in all of creation; therefore when God proclaimed mercy, especially through the death of Christ, Satan rejected it, seeing it as God going astray from his own eternal standard. So in his rebellion Satan sought to return to the original good, by making his way of justice (i.e., punishment which drives people deeper into sin) supreme. (vii) Though he is God's enemy, he willingly continues to test, accuse and punish as God created him to do; but now his purpose is to build up his own Kingdom of Darkness, not to serve God.

(viii) In Paul's imagination this great enemy is now the Commander-in-Chief of all the forces of darkness, which includes all the angelic princes of the nations, all the human rulers and institutional powers of the nations, and all the humans who are enslaved to Sin. Thus Satan is manifest in the tyranny of governments and religions, especially in their legalism and their oppression by which they advance their own causes.

# IV.  THE  ARMY  OF

# THE  KINGDOM  OF  DARKNESS

## Introduction

In a military story, i.e. one in which the conflict results in combat, fighting, destruction and death, the central actors are opposing kingdoms and their armies. In this chapter we will describe one of those kingdoms, Satan's Kingdom of Darkness, in order to suggest how Paul pictured the forces of evil that Christ came to conquer. Naturally, since this concerns one of Paul's symbol systems, the pictures were meant symbolically by Paul. In this chapter we will simply elaborate the pictures, trying to see the whole that Paul simply touched on occasionally. Our argument for Paul's angels as symbolic expressions of God's present power, not literal spirits, is in chapter VIII.

On one side in the Pauline combat myth is the Kingdom of Light—God, Christ, the angelic host (1 Thess 4:16; 2 Thess 2:7) led by the archangel (presumably Michael), and the human children of light (1 Thess 5:5; Eph 5:8) on earth, who are empowered and purified by God's Spirit. Together they stand for and defend goodness, holiness, mercy and justice. In the next chapter we will elaborate Paul's myth of the way God created this kingdom through his victory in Christ on the cross.

On the other side of the war front stands the Kingdom of Darkness (2

Cor 6:14; Col 1:13; Eph 6:12), the rebel army dominated by **The Commander-in-Chief, Satan**, the "god of this present age" (2 Cor 4:4). That character, the chief antagonist in Paul's story, we have described in the previous chapter. In this chapter we will describe the rest of the hierarchy of the army of darkness. Immediately under Satan's command are **A. Satan's Generals: The Angelic Rulers of the Nations** known of old as the princes of particular nations, for example the Prince of Persia and the Prince of Greece (Dan 11:3, 20). In Paul's letters they appear under many names—e.g. principalities and powers, rulers of this present age, and elemental spirits of the universe. At the bottom of the Satanic army hierarchy are **B. The Infantry Hordes: The Children of Darkness** (cf Eph 5:8), those human beings who do not believe in Christ and so live in the darkness of this age (cf Rom 2:19; 1 Thess 5:4; 2 Cor 6:14).

Hidden inside the Satanic hierarchy, within the children of darkness, is a pervasive, invasive, unholy spirit under the Angel of Darkness' control. **C. The Saboteur Spirit: Sin** is the invasive spirit which Satan sent throughout the human race, enslaving all human beings, as demons possessed some people in the gospel story (cf Rom 3:9; 5:12; 6:6, 12, 16; 7:8).

The saboteur, Sin, is even more destructive in the activity of its subordinate, **D. The Last Enemy: Death** which is the second Satanic spirit, one that enters in wherever Sin goes (Rom 5:12; 6:23; 7:9). Indeed Death goes far beyond Sin, for it has permeated all of nature (Rom 8:20–21) and will be the last enemy defeated (1 Cor 15:26).

### A. SATAN'S GENERALS: The Angelic Rulers of the Nations

> Among the mature we do speak wisdom, though it is not a wisdom of this age, or of the rulers of this age [*ton archonton tou aionos*] who are passing away [*ton katargoumenon*]. (1 Cor 2:6)
> Formerly, when you [Gentiles] did not know God, you were enslaved to beings who by nature were not gods [*tois phusei me ousi theois*]...how can you turn back again to the weak and beggarly elemental spirits [*stoicheia*]...(and become) enslaved to them again. (Gal 4:8–10)

As we suggested in the previous chapter, Paul probably entertained in his imagination a cosmic myth in which Satan, "the god of this present age," was the supreme commander over an angelic and human army of darkness. The second level of angels in his myth, Satan's immediate subordinates, are the ones Paul calls by many different names, but most aptly "the rulers of this age" (1 Cor 2:6).[1] Paul's picture of these angelic rulers was probably based on the OT imagery of the princes of the nations mentioned in Daniel 10. These princes were probably seen by Jews as the 70 angels called sons of God who were ordained by God to provide justice to each of the 70 nations (Deut 32:8-9; *1 Enoch* 89:59-60). They worked by providing guidance to the human rulers of the nations in the administration of justice. However, as human rulers of the nations became oppressors, so also (in the Jewish picture) the national angels became oppressors, so God condemned them for their injustice and threatened future punishment for them (Ps 82:1-6; *1 Enoch* 90:25).

In this section we will not argue for all the debatable points in this reconstruction, but simply focus on a few of the most important. **(1) The Angelic Rulers as God's Judicial Agents**: though a common later theory in the patristic period was that these rulers usurped rule over the nations, it seems more likely that Paul saw them, as the Jews apparently did, as ordained by God to provide justice to the nations. **(2) The Stoicheia as Oppressive Angels, Even Over the Jews**: though *stoicheia* can be also translated "elementary principles" or "basic elements," the contexts in Galatians and Colossians suggest that Paul uses this term (as did later Christians, Jews and Greeks) to refer to the oppressor angels, who even have power over Jews through the Mosaic law. **(3) The Powers of the Angelic Rulers** are political-religious and supernatural. Unlike Satan who is at work in individuals and nature as well as in social groups, Paul's rulers of this present age seem to work mainly through political

---

[1] Among the many names Paul apparently used for the angelic rulers are these: princes (*archas*; Rom 8:38; 1 Cor 15:24), authorities (*exousiai*; 1 Cor 15:24; Col 1:16), powers (*dunameis*; Rom 8:38; Eph 1:21), angels (*angeloi*; 1 Cor 6:3; Gal 3:19; Rom 8:38), elemental spirits of the universe (*stoicheia tou kosmou*; Gal 4:3; Col 2:20), rulers (*archonta*) of this present age (1 Cor 2:8), thrones (*thronoi*; Col 1:16) and dominions (*kuriotetes*; Col 1:16; Eph 1:21), so-called gods (*legomenoi theoi*; 1 Cor 8:5) and demons (*demonioi*) to whom the pagans offer sacrifices (1 Cor 10:20). By this variety he includes many LXX names for national angels, names also used in Hellenistic writings about their gods. Thus he provides a bridge between the two cultures.

and religious groups, though their power transcends those groups and can only be successfully opposed on a supernatural level.

## (1) The Angelic Rulers as God's Judicial Agents

In his *Principalities and Powers*, Caird asserts that, "Paul's belief in angelic beings who stand behind the political institutions of paganism is too well attested in other passages [other than Romans 13:1–7] to be in dispute" (23). While not many may dispute the point, we need to bring out the evidence for it in order to emphasize that in Paul's myth these national rulers were judicial agents, just as Satan was, not usurpers of authority who are simply evil. First of all we will present the OT and Jewish evidence and then show how Paul implicitly presents the rulers as God's agents of justice to some extent, seeing them of course as agents who became enemies.

The Old Testament does not explicitly describe the angelic princes of the nations as God's agents, but implies it, as we argued in detail in chapter II. Russell summarizes this theory of the way the Jews came to postulate evil angels by saying:

> There gradually grew up...the notion that the angels to whom god had given authority over the nations...had outstripped their rightful authority and taken power into their own hands. No longer were they simply God's envoys to whom he gave charge of punishing those who denied his rule; they themselves became part of the rebellious family and took upon themselves the right to reign.[2]

As the inheritor of this tradition, Paul probably assumed it in his cosmic myth. He does not explicitly call the angelic rulers God's agents, but he implies it as we can see by considering various passages.

(i) Paul clearly believed that human rulers were God's agents of justice, for he writes:

> Let every person be subject to the governing authorities; for there is no authority [*exousia*] except from God, and those

---

[2] Russell, *Jewish Apocalyptic*, 237–238.

authorities that exist have been instituted by God...the
authority does not bear the sword in vain! It is the servant of
God to execute wrath on the wrongdoer. (Rom 13:1, 4)

Even though those human rulers were also oppressors at times, and stood at the
top of a system that allowed the strong to grind down the weak (e.g. slaves and
colonial subjects), still they were God's agents because they produced a certain
amount of justice.

(ii) When Paul spoke of the pagan rulers as "authorities" (*exousiai*) he
used a word that he also used for angelic forces, in particular when he said that
at the end Christ would defeat "every ruler and every authority [*pasan exousian*]
and power" (1 Cor 15:24). Thus it is likely that when he spoke of earthly
authorities he also had in mind the angelic authorities who lurked invisibly
behind them. Thus Cullmann, following Dibelius and others, argued that in
Romans 13, when he spoke of authorities as God's servants, Paul was thinking
both of human and angelic rulers.[3]

(iii) That combination of human and angelic authorities quite plausibly
was on Paul's mind when he spoke of Christ's execution in 1 Cor 2:6, 8 where
he says:

we do speak wisdom, though it is not the wisdom of this age
or of the rulers [*ton archonton*] of this age, who are passing
away [*ton katargoumenon*]...None of the rulers of this age
understood this; for if they had, they would not have crucified
the Lord of glory.

Almost certainly Paul had in mind the human rulers of Rome, and perhaps of
the Jews, when he spoke of those who crucified Christ. However, when he said
the rulers "are passing away" that does not apply very well to the human
(especially Roman) rulers of his day, for they were just as much in control as
they had ever been. Thus it is likely, as most commentators observe, that he was
thinking here also of the angelic rulers, for his gospel was that Christ had
already defeated those angelic rulers (Col 2:15), so they were in the process of
passing away. Arrington supports this interpretation when he writes:

---

[3] Cullmann, *Christ and Time*, 194–195.

> Paul's reliance on the apocalyptic tradition makes it probable
> that [1 Cor] 2:6 refers to a heavenly as well as an earthly
> battle. Christ's victory has cosmic significance. The old aeon
> with its powers has been rendered ineffective, and Christ is
> now Lord of the world...exalted above all other gods and
> lords (8:5, 6).[4]

Thus it is likely that Paul thought of human and angelic rulers of this
present age together, as partners; therefore, since the human rulers are God's
agents of justice, Paul probably also thought of the angelic rulers as God's
agents, the ones who taught justice, law and order to the nations.

(iv) Paul apparently believed that the angelic rulers were created, just
as the human ones were (Col 1:16). Since they were created by God, God
presumably had a purpose for them, and that seems to be as the mediators of
divine justice on earth.

Our conclusion then is that Paul probably followed his Hebraic tradition
in picturing angelic rulers standing hiddenly behind each of the nations. Each of
these angels, according to the tradition, had been ordained by God to bring law,
order and justice to the nation to which it was assigned.

### (2) The *Stoicheia* as Oppressive Angels: Even Over the Jews

In Galatians Paul speaks of both Gentiles and Jews as slaves to the
*stoicheia tou kosmou*, which can be translated either "basic principles," or
"elemental spirits," of the universe. Our view is that it is more likely that he
meant elemental spirits, and by that referred to the angelic rulers of the nations.
The new insight Paul offers in this passage is that the tyranny of the angelic
princes extends even over the Jews.

First, speaking apparently to the Gentile Christians he says:

> Formerly, when you did not know God, you were enslaved to
> beings that by nature are not gods...how can you turn back
> again to the weak and beggarly *stoicheia*...You are observing
> special days, and months and seasons and years. (Gal 4:8–9)

---

[4] Arrington, *Paul's Aeon Theology in I Corinthians*, 137.

When Paul describes the *stoicheia* as "by nature not gods" that suggests that the people had previously thought that they were gods, i.e. supernatural spirits to whom they should bow. Paul, however, saw the pagan gods as demons, evil angels, the national princes who had wrongly allowed themselves to be worshipped as gods; thus it is likely that here he was thinking of the *stoicheia* as such fallen angels. Further, the reference to observing special days suggests a connection with the stars, which many Gentiles saw as supernatural spirits, for astrology was very popular in Paul's day. Thus it is quite likely that when Paul spoke of *stoicheia* he was referring to the angelic spirits which he pictured as ruling the nations, and which the Gentiles pictured as acting through the stars.

Other interpreters taking this view include Schlier, who concludes that the *stoicheia* in Galatians, "are probably stars under whose influence the Galatians had felt bound to observe certain sidereal festivals. The principalities which dominate the stars make them as it were 'gods.'"[5] In the following centuries both Greek and Jewish writers used this term to refer to astral spirits, as shown by Arnold in *Powers of Darkness* (54).

That view that Paul thought of the Gentiles as slaves to their national angelic princes is not at all surprising, for that was probably what the Jewish tradition in general taught. What is surprising is that Paul speaks of himself and his fellow Jews as similarly enslaved: "Now before faith came, we [Jews] were imprisoned and guarded under the law until faith would be revealed...while we were minors, we were enslaved to the *stoicheia tou kosmou*" (Gal 3:23; 4:3). Here Paul was probably assuming his prior comment that the law had been "ordained through angels" (Gal 3:19), by which he probably meant that God did not hand on the law personally but delegated angels to do the job. Paul suggests here that the law is the work of angels, and that the result of that work is imprisonment, slavery, oppression. The connection with the Gentiles' enslavement to the elemental spirits is that in both cases these angels were probably ordained by God to provide law, and by that means they came to oppress the humans under their power. In addition, Paul may well have seen a further parallel, that both the angelic rulers and the law were good servants but became evil masters when the people worshipped them. As M. Barth asserts, "Only because some powers, including the law, are idolized by man have they

---

[5] Schlier, *Principalities and Powers in the New Testament*, 23.

become evil."[6]

The problem with saying Paul pictured the Jews as suffering under the oppression of angels of the law is that Deut 32:9 says that God put the Gentiles under the sons of God but kept Israel for himself to rule directly. However, the later apocalyptic tradition presented Israel as under the angel Michael, for Dan 10:21 calls him "Michael, your prince." Thus it is plausible that the Jews in general did think of angels as mediating in some way between God and Israel (a view explicitly asserted by Philo), though these were presumably always good angels. The new idea in Paul's myth is that the angels do not simply do good, just as the law is not good in all its effects. Thus Paul's negative judgment on the effects of the law (Romans 7) is aptly reflected in his picture of Jews as victims of angelic oppression, slaves of the elemental spirits of the universe.

If this interpretation of the *stoicheia tou kosmou* as angels is correct, then it provides further support for the thesis of the previous section: Paul saw the national angelic rulers as God's agents of justice who had gone on to practice injustice also. Though their activities in providing justice, law and order were supposed to provide freedom and security, they in fact practiced injustice as well and so brought slavery and sometimes unjust death.

**Conclusion**

Driver summarized Paul's view of the power and pervasiveness of the angelic powers well when he wrote:

> Since the religious, social and political spheres of ancient life were all intimately interrelated, these beings [the angelic rulers] were the controlling forces behind the values, ideologies and social and political structures which held societies together.[7]

The Pauline military myth that we are seeking to reconstruct thus has angelic rulers of the nations as Satan's immediate subordinates—the generals in the Army of Darkness. As Satan was originally God's agent of justice over humanity generally, so also the rulers of this present age were all ordained by

---

[6] M. Barth, *Ephesians chs 1-3*, 181.

[7] Driver, *Understanding the Atonement for the Mission of the Church*, 78-79.

God to provide justice, law and order in their particular nations. Just as Satan eventually went astray and became God's enemy, so also the rulers departed from their assigned task, bringing injustice to their nations, the violent domination of the many who are weak by the few who are strong.[8]

## B. THE INFANTRY HORDES: The Children of Darkness

> You, beloved, are not in darkness, for the day to surprise you like a thief; you are all children of light and children of the day; we are not of the night or of darkness. (1 Thess 5:4-5)

In Paul's military symbolism, believers are the children of light and **(1) Unbelievers are the Children of Darkness**, the workers of evil. As members of the kingdom of darkness **(2) Unbelievers are Satan's Infantry**, humans doing Satan's work of tempting and persecuting believers, seeking to destroy the Kingdom of Light.

### (1) Unbelievers are the Children of Darkness

Paul calls Christians "children of light [*huioi photos*]," not "of the darkness" (1 Thess 5:5; see also Eph 5:8). Therefore he understands non-believers to be children of darkness, though he never explicitly calls them that. Those who have not accepted God's revelation find "their senseless minds were darkened" (Rom 1:21), so they become "those who live in darkness" (Rom 2:19) and do "the works of darkness" (Rom 13:12). That unbelievers are the

---

[8] Perhaps we should note here that one scholar has asserted that Paul did not believe in evil angels at all. Carr, in his *Angels and Principalities*, argued that all Paul's references to angels were to good angels who are praising God, so there is no hostile angelic army under Satan's command. This theory is thoroughly analyzed and criticized by C. E. Arnold in "The 'Exorcism' of Ephesians 6:12 in Recent Research: A Critique of Wesley Carr's View of the Role of Evil Powers in First-Century AD Belief." The central objections Arnold raises are that Carr arbitrarily rejects Eph 6:12 as a secondary addition to the text, does not mention 2 Cor 12:7 with its reference to "an angel of Satan," and ignores all the evidence of a hostile angelic/demonic army presented by the gospels. Arnold concludes: "Carr has misunderstood first-century belief about the 'powers' as well as Paul's view of the *archai kai exousiai*" (84).

ones characterized by darkness, and under the rule of the Dark Prince, is clear in Paul's admonition: "Do not be mismated with unbelievers. For what partnership have righteousness and iniquity? Or what fellowship has light with darkness? What accord has Christ with Belial?" (2 Cor 6:14–15).

That use of the name Belial, and connecting it with darkness, provides the closest parallel in Paul's writings to the Qumran language where Belial/Satan is the ruler of the human children of darkness. The War Scroll refers to "the attack of the sons of light against the company of the sons of darkness, the army of Satan" (1QM i). In Qumran the phrase "sons of darkness" may have referred to all the forces of evil, human and angelic, but they are most obvious in the human armies that the sectarians will fight against. The Scrolls further describe this group as those who are governed by "the spirit of falsehood" so they are "the children of falsehood (who) are ruled by the Angel of Darkness and walk in the ways of darkness" (1QS iii). In picturing the children of darkness coming to battle the children of light, the War Scroll essentially elaborates the older tradition of foreign nations coming up to fight against Israel at the end (Gog in Ezekiel 38, all the nations in Zechariah 14, the fourth beast in Daniel 7).

The Old Testament does not use the phrase "children of darkness," but it clearly is the source for the contrast between light (from God) and darkness (from God's enemies). For example, Isa 60:2–3 reads: "For darkness shall cover the earth, and thick darkness the peoples; but the Lord will arise upon you and his glory will appear over you. Nations shall come to your light."[9] Thus the Qumran and NT imagery of God's enemies as children of darkness is rooted in these and other OT passages.

For Paul then, the children of darkness are all who do not believe in Christ, who are ignorant of God's revelation, worship idols, live in vice, and thereby show themselves to be servants of Belial.

## (2) Unbelievers as Satan's Infantry

By calling unbelievers the infantry in Satan's army we mean to suggest that Paul did not see them as simply adherents of a different religion. Rather he pictured them as fighting against believers, doing them harm, and doing it as agents of Satan. Indeed, he probably believed that all unbelievers were active in

---

[9]See also Isa 8:21–22; 9:2–4 and Ps 143:3.

the army of darkness.

**False Apostles.** The most obvious example of such agents of Satan who oppose the gospel is seen in Paul's criticism of the "false apostles" (*pseudapostoloi*, 2 Cor 11:13) who had tempted the Corinthian believers away from the gospel that Paul had preached. Paul calls those preachers Satan's "servants who disguise themselves as servants of righteousness," just as "Satan disguises himself as an angel of light" (2 Cor 11:13-14). Clearly Paul here is thinking of Satan as really the angel of darkness, and so his disguised servants are also really messengers of darkness. This is one of the clearest expressions of his view that some humans are Satan's subordinates, the infantry in Satan's army as it seeks to conquer the world, to bring it all under darkness.

**Persecutors.** Further, Paul probably looks upon all persecutors of Christians as the forces of darkness, the agents of Satan. For example, the Thessalonians had suffered persecution from their own countrymen (1 Thess 2:14) and Paul was concerned that in their suffering "the tempter had tempted you" (1 Thess 3:5) so that his labor would have been in vain. Clearly, here, those humans who were persecuting Christians are seen by Paul as working for Satan, providing the situation that tempts believers to fall away. So the persecutors are Satan's agents, the army of the children of darkness fighting against the light.

**Pagan Worshippers.** Thirdly, in his category of the children of darkness who harm believers Paul probably includes all the Gentiles who worship their national angelic rulers, the weak and beggarly elemental spirits (Gal 4:8-9). Those pagan worshippers, living in darkness out of which the Gentile believers had been rescued, remain tempters, tempting the Galatian Christians to return to the slavery of the elemental spirits (Gal 4:9).

Finally we return to 2 Cor 6:14-15, in which Paul connects unbelievers, iniquity, darkness and Belial and warns his readers that uniting with those forces will be disastrous for them. The parallelism suggests that in Paul's thinking all unbelievers are workers of iniquity, living in darkness and serving Belial (whether they know it or not). In the specific cases discussed above Paul makes that connection explicit, describing some specific unbelievers as soldiers of Satan. However, it is plausible that Paul saw all those who were unbelievers as the active soldiers in Satan's Kingdom of Darkness, just as the Qumranians proclaimed.

Though these children of darkness have worldly power, physically enforced political and religious authority, Paul saw them as ultimately weak. They can physically harm and socially coerce the children of light, but they cannot reach into their hearts and minds to force them to reject Christ. Thus, while these human enemies seemed to Christians to be the most immediate, and therefore the most dangerous, of their foes, Paul thought otherwise. The really dangerous enemies were the spiritual ones, those that could go beyond physical and social coercion. The chief of these dangerous powers was the demon-like Sin which tempted believers, indeed invaded them if they opened themselves to such invasion.

## C. THE SABOTEUR SPIRIT, SIN

I see another rule in my members *making war* against the rule of my mind, and *making me captive* to the rule of Sin in my members. (Rom 7:23)

In his military symbolism, Paul pictures Sin as a demonic spirit which makes war against individuals, fighting within them, indeed capturing them and so making them prisoners of war (Rom 7:23). Sin invades the lives of individuals, making them slaves who cannot do the good even when they will it (Rom 7:15–20). In Paul's concrete and picturesque language, Sin enters, Sin reigns, Sin enslaves, Sin kills (Rom 5:12, 21; 6:6; 7:9). In this insidious form, the power of darkness (emanating from its ruler) takes over human lives and turns the humans into children of darkness. Paul knew that the more obvious expressions of Satan's oppression in history are external, the political and economic slavery Israel knew at the hands of Egypt, Assyria, Babylon, the Seleucids and the Romans. For Paul, however, following Jesus' lead, the chief battleground had shifted inward. He apparently saw Satan's war against God as centered within people, where Satan sends this spirit of darkness called Sin.

First of all, under **(1) Sin the Demon** we will present evidence and arguments for the conclusion that Paul did imagine a demon Sin as Satan's agent oppressing people. Then in **(2) Pure Aggression or Initial Free Choice?**, we will discuss one of the central puzzles of Paul's military symbolism: Does he suggest that human beings are simply victims of evil forces? Or does he suggest that to a certain extent people are responsible for their slavery under Sin?

Finally we will explore **(3) The History of Sin's Invasion**.

## (1) Sin the Demon

Our hypothesis in this section is this: Sin (in Paul's military myth) is pictured as the evil correlate of God's Holy Spirit: Sin is Satan's secret agent, a saboteur spirit, a demon at work in individuals turning them into Satan's slave soldiers.

### (a) Evidence and Arguments

The evidence for this thesis of Sin (in Paul's military symbolism) as a demon, Satan's unholy spirit, can be found in the following six points.

(i) Sin, for Paul, is sometimes imagined as an evil spiritual force, not just a human act or state. Paul speaks of Sin [*(he) hamartia*, singular] in Romans 5–8 as an agent of a variety of actions. By contrast, in this context he uses the terms "transgressions" and "sins" when he refers to human evil actions. Perhaps the most significant description depicts Sin "making war against [*antistrateuomenon*]" the inner law (Rom 7:23), showing that Paul saw Sin as a military figure; "Sin entered the world" (Rom 5:12); "Sin reigned in death" (5:21); Sin previously "reigned in their mortal bodies" (6:12); the readers could "present their members as weapons [*hopla*] of unrighteousness to Sin" (6:13). Clearly Paul here imagines Sin as an efficient agent, an evil spirit (perhaps even a personal one) to which people can be enslaved when it is at work within them.[10]

(ii) Since Satan is the traditional source of temptation to sin, it is likely that Paul saw this evil as Satan's own (or even Satan in disguise). Specific evidence for this interpretation comes from Paul's silence about Satan when the demon Sin is in view: in Romans 5–8, where Sin is the major actor representing the Kingdom of Darkness, Paul never mentions Satan, though elsewhere Satan plays an active role in human sinfulness (e.g. 1 Cor 7:5; 2 Cor 2:11; Eph 2:2). Thus in Romans 5–8 Paul probably spoke of Satan's activity under the name Sin. If that is so, then Sin is probably here imagined as a demon, the power of Satan at work in individuals, as the Holy Spirit is the power of God at work in

---

[10] Leivestad remarks: "Just as a demon may possess a body, sin has made our flesh its abode so that the limbs have to obey the directions of sin" (*Christ the Conqueror*, 116).

individuals.[11]

(iii) Sin as the opposite of God's Spirit seems to be the picture in Paul's imagination, because of the following parallels: just as (a) the Holy Spirit (b) comes from outside (from God), (c) enters into believers, and (d) leads them into goodness, so also (a) the unholy spirit Sin (b) comes from outside (presumably from Satan), (c) enters into unbelievers, and (d) leads them into evil. This parallel and contrast seems to appear overtly in at least one passage: "For the law of the Spirit of life in Christ Jesus has set me free from the law of Sin and Death" (Rom 8:2). The parallel suggests that the forces on each side are similar. As the Spirit of Christ in a person is the bringer of life, so also Sin is the bringer of death (Rom 6:23). Thus this parallel suggests that Sin is the immanent agent of Satan as the Holy Spirit is the immanent agent of God.

(iv) Further evidence for that agency is the fact that some of the powers Paul attributes to Sin are among those which he also attributes to Satan. First of all, both use law to lead people astray (Rom 7:11 for Sin; 2 Cor 3:15–16 and 4:4 for Satan). Second, both have the power of bringing death: "The gift of God [i.e., the gift given by God] is eternal life" stands in parallel to "the wages of Sin is death" (Rom 6:23); therefore the latter will be most appropriately interpreted as "the wages paid by Sin to those who have served it." Thus Sin is the bringer of death, as Satan also is in Paul's military symbolism (see 1 Cor 5:5). Since Sin exercises Satan's powers, Paul probably imagined Sin as Satan's agent (or even as Satan himself) at work in individuals.

(v) Background support for Paul probably seeing Sin as Satan's saboteur in individuals is the fact that in the Scrolls Satan sends out a single "spirit of perversity" which dominates individuals from within, causing them to sin. That power is quite like Paul's power Sin, for it too controls people, forcing them to sin. Given the many parallels between the Scrolls and Paul's military symbolism, we are probably justified in concluding that Paul, like the authors of the Scrolls, thought that Satan was the source of the power Sin.[12] The

---

[11] Leivestad supports this by saying, "In Romans 6–7 *he hamartia* often functions as a substitute for Satan himself" (115).

[12] For detailed discussion of the spirit of perversity/deceit in the Scrolls see K. G. Kuhn, "New Light on Temptation, Sin and Flesh in the New Testament," and J. Gnilka, "2 Cor 6:14–7:1 in the Light of the Qumran texts and *The Testaments of the Twelve Patriarchs*."

difference between the evil spirits in these two sources is this: in Qumran the spirit of perversity is natural, given to all at birth; Sin for Paul, however, is an invasive spirit that springs to life in the individual when the law arrives (Rom 7:8). Further, Paul blames the law for the rise of Sin's power, whereas in Qumran the law is the way to escape the hold of the spirit of perversity.[13]

(vi) In that characteristic of being a foreign invader, Paul's power Sin is more like *The Testaments of the Twelve Patriarchs'* spirits of deceit (*T. Naph.* 3:3). They are also referred to as "Satan and his spirits" (*T. Dan* 6:1), and as "spirits of Beliar" (*T. Iss.* 7:7). The similarity with Sin in Paul's myth is that these are also pictured as external forces that invade the human spirit, e.g. the spirit of anger, the spirit of hatred and many others. These "spirits of deceit" are the agents Satan sends into people which cause them to sin, just as Sin according to Paul deceives people (Rom 7:11) and causes them to sin (e.g. *T. Sim* 2:7 and *T. Jud* 19:4). Thus it is likely (given the extensive parallels between Paul and the Testaments) that Paul, too, thought of Sin as Satan's agent invading the lives of human beings to drag them into the kingdom of darkness.[14]

Our conclusion is that Sin (in Paul's military symbolism) is a demonic agent sent out by Satan to infiltrate the hearts and spirits of all human beings, thereby making them slaves of Sin, children of darkness, coerced soldiers in the army of the Prince of Darkness. Just as the demon-possessed people in the gospel stories could not control their own bodies or minds (e.g. Mk 5:1–5 on the Gerasene demoniac), so also Paul pictured the Sin-possessed (all unbelievers) as under the control of this sabotaging inner spirit.

## (b) Objections Answered

This view of Paul's power Sin is not new, for it was suggested long ago by Dibelius when he wrote: "Sin has its position in men: 'possession' (by demons) as it is described in the gospels is the analogy to it. Thus we can describe Sin as a demon which has entered into man."[15] This is similar to the earlier theory of Kabisch who looked upon Sin in Romans 7 as "a hypostasis of

---

[13] For a full discussion of the similarities and differences between Sin in Paul and the "spirit of perversity" in the Scrolls, see Macky, *The Problem of Sin in Romans*, ch. 8, "The Spirit of Perversity."

[14] For more details on the *Testaments'* spirits of deceit, see Macky, *The Problem of Sin in Romans*, chap. 9, "The Spirits of Deceit."

[15] Dibelius, *Die Geisterwelt im Glauben des Paulus*, 122.

Satan."[16] More recently de Boer described Paul's language in Rom 5:12–21 as personifying Sin as "an alien intruder" and as a "reigning cosmological power" because it enters human life and reigns there.[17] In none of these works, however, did the authors provide a detailed argument for this conclusion that Paul pictures Sin as Satan's agent, a demon possessing all the children of darkness. Secondly, none of these authors presented our theory that this picture is an essential component in Paul's military symbolism.

One opponent of this Sin-as-demon interpretation is Gunter Roehser in his book on Paul's symbolism for sin entitled *Metaphorik und Personification der Sund: Antike Sundenvorstellungen und paulinische Hamartia*. In speaking of Rom 6:13, where Sin and God are the two Lords to whom people can yield, Roehser says:

> as to sin, I take it as decided, that one recognizes its character as abstract-personification and avoids any suggestions of Satanology. Devil and demons plainly play no role in the present context; only where the devil is named specifically can we bring him in. Otherwise one abolishes the deed-character [*Tatcharacter*] of *hamartia* and undermines thereby the foundation of ancient Judaism as of the Pauline reflection. (163)

Here Roehser raises three objections to our view of Sin as Satan's agent, a demon within: (i) For Paul sin is always a deed. (ii) In Romans 5–7 Paul does not mention Satan, so we cannot legitimately bring in demonology to interpret his picture of Sin. (iii) Sin, along with Law and Death are "abstract-personifications," which entails that "a mythological background is explicitly denied" (143).

Our replies to these objections are relatively simple:

(i) Roehser does not recognize that Paul uses multiple symbol systems to speak of sin, so Roehser conflates them (as has traditionally been done by theologians seeking Paul's "doctrine of sin"). When Paul is using his military symbolism he does NOT picture sin as a deed, but instead as a power at work

---

[16] *Die Eschatologie des Paulus*, 165.
[17] De Boer, *The Defeat of Death*, 147.

within people. This demon, of course, produces deeds, but the whole emphasis of this military imagery is that people are **victims** of Sin, ones forced to act contrary to their wills. Of course elsewhere, in the judicial and personal symbol systems, he emphasizes sins as deeds (of transgression or rebellion). But from this military perspective (which dominates Romans 6–7) Sin is a power, a force, an evil spirit, not a deed.

(ii) The fact that Paul does not specifically mention Satan in Romans 5–7 does not prevent him from alluding to him. In particular, when Paul says that "Sin, finding opportunity in the commandment, worked in me all kinds of covetousness" (Rom 7:8) it is quite likely that he was alluding to the Garden of Eden story, and to the snake which the tradition identified as Satan's agent (concerning which, see 2 Cor 11:3, 13–15): "Sin [like the snake, Satan's agent], finding opportunity in the commandment [like the forbidden fruit commandment], worked in me all kinds of covetousness [as the snake aroused desire for the fruit in Eve]." Further, we have argued above that the parallels between Satan's activity and Sin's (deceiving, using the law, bringing death) make it highly likely that Paul saw Sin as Satan's agent, the means by which Satan carried out his plans.

(iii) Roehser's "abstract-personification" view of Sin, one that rules out seeing mythological imagery, is unconvincing. Authors personify in order to make abstractions, or mysteries, concrete; in Romans 5–8 the concrete image Paul evokes is of a demon, an unholy spirit, parallel to the Holy Spirit. Thus Roehser's attempt to rule out using mythology (in particular demonology) in elaborating Paul's imagery seems to be arbitrary at best. Roehser's fear is that if we see Sin as a demon, then we will dogmatically conclude that people are not responsible for their sinning. Paul has no such problem because he pictures sinners not only as victims (military symbolism), but also as rebels (personal symbolism) and criminals (judicial symbolism). Therefore, we conclude, we will not distort Paul's total views by taking the Sin imagery mythologically. Indeed, doing so will enable the military picture to play its fully effective role in depicting one significant aspect of the human problem: sinners are indeed (to some extent) victims of evil forces beyond their control.

## (2) Pure Aggression or Initial Free Choice?

One important issue that our Sin-as-demon interpretation raises is whether Paul considers people to be completely victims of Sin's invasion, the way (apparently) that the demon-possessed were viewed according to the Gospels.

Paul's picture of Sin's oppression in Romans 7 is vivid, and extreme (by Biblical standards): he seems (at first reading) to depict this oppression as the result of pure demonic aggression, because he makes no clear mention of human choice. He says that when the law against coveting came, he then knew what coveting was and as a consequence: "Sin...produced [*kateirgasato*, brought about, created] in me all kinds of covetousness [*epithumian*, desire]" (Rom 7:8). The picture he paints here is quite like the standard view of demon possession: when the opportunity arises, the demon invades a person's life quite apart from any deserving. As the evil empires (Assyria, Babylon, Greece, Rome) aggressively invaded innocent nations, so also (it seems that Paul imagines) Satan's evil empire invades the lives of innocent people. Thus when he is telling about the evil spirit Sin, in this military symbolism, Paul seems to depict it as simply an enemy agent, one that possesses innocent people against their will. His surface picture in Romans 5–7 presents Sin breaking through the gate in their castle, overpowering them by force.[18]

While on first reading Paul's words in Romans 7 seem to picture such an act of aggression, an invasion of the innocent castle, on second look Paul provides hints that the inside-dweller opened the gate in the castle wall, however slightly.

First of all, in Romans 6 Paul spoke of choice as significant in the story when he said:

> Do you not know that if you present [*paristanete*] yourselves
> to anyone as obedient slaves, you are slaves of the one whom
> you obey, either of Sin, which leads to death, or of obedience,
> which leads to righteousness...**you once presented**
> [*parestesate*] **your members as slaves** to impurity and to
> greater and greater iniquity. (Rom 6:16, 19)

Paul certainly here suggests that the beginning of Sin's rule over sinners came when they actively "presented," or "handed over" themselves to Sin, by

---

[18] See de Boer (166) who adopts this purely invasive picture.

choosing the life of impurity which led them on a downward spiral into complete slavery. Later, Paul underlines this point when he implies that all people were once "alive, apart from the law" (Rom 7:9); he probably pictured all people as, once upon a time, when they were young, yielding their members to Sin.

Secondly, when Paul says that the coming of the law provided opportunity for Sin to deceive, that suggests a choice also—though an uninformed choice, one made in ignorance of the consequences. He writes: "Sin, finding opportunity in the commandment, deceived [*exepatese*] me and through it killed me" (Rom 7:11). Thus Paul apparently pictured Sin as working its evil way initially by deception, presumably making its victims think they were still free when in fact they were putting their feet in the chains. The basic idea Paul seems to depend on here is this: when we deceive a person, we seek to get them to choose what we want them to choose, though it is against their best interests. Thus when Paul says "Sin deceives" he seems to suggest that people open the castlegate to Sin, once its smooth talking has deceived them into thinking that it will do them no harm.

In the third place Paul seems to emphasize choice and responsibility in his judicial and personal symbol systems, which suggests that he intended his readers to assume it here. We can appropriately fit these various symbol systems together if we understand the present oppression by Sin to be due in some way to a previous choice that human beings made. The most plausible place for choice in this story is this: when Sin entered weak human flesh, it stirred up human passions (Rom 7:5, 8), which people then chose to allow to run free. In this interpretation we agree with Beker who says that for Paul,

> Sin commences its road to power by appearing as a free choice in the context of the command. "You shall not covet" (Rom 7:7)...Once a person has transgressed, the option to obey or disobey ceases. Sin, so to speak, grows over a person's head and traps him into bondage.[19]

---

[19] *Triumph*, 215. Among the many books on sin, one of the most interesting in describing Paul's slavery story is McCormick's *Sin as Addiction*. McCormick stresses both the initial choice and the ultimate slavery which are the two main parts of Paul's military plot. The weakness of this book is that it does not connect this imagery with Paul's military symbolism.

That story is the heart of the history of Sin's invasion, its deceit leading to sabotage and slavery, to which we now turn.

### (3) The History of Sin's Invasion

This hypothesis that Paul pictured a demon Sin as Satan's agent will help us clarify some passages in Paul's letters. In addition, it will enable us to paint a somewhat fuller portrait of the sabotaging demon than we have already. Since Paul (in his military symbolism) pictured Sin as a demon, a saboteur spirit which invades human lives when they open the castlegate, we can understand more adequately his enigmatic account of the history of that invasion.

Paul describes the beginning of Sin's reign this way: "Sin entered [*eiselthe*] the world through one man" (Rom 5:12). Clearly Paul is here alluding to the story of Adam (and Eve), suggesting that Sin has had a hold on human beings (for "the world" presumably means the human world, not the natural world) from the very beginning of the race. Paul does not specifically say why or how Sin entered through that one man (Adam), but from the allusion to Genesis 3 we can draw this conclusion: Adam's disobedience, transgression, choice of the immediately pleasant, was the opening through which Sin entered. In Paul's language, Adam chose "to live according to the flesh" (Rom 8:5), thereby allowing Sin to enter. This suggests that in Paul's military myth, Sin existed as Satan's agent before humans sinned. Lying in wait (as God warned Cain in Gen 4:7) Sin was unable to enter the human heart until the first persons rejected God's way, and so (presumably) lost God's protection. Thus Sin, the powerful, insidious spirit deployed by Satan, secretly slipped into the castle of human inner life through the first sinning by human beings, through Adam and Eve. Like an *agent provocateur* entering a peaceful, walled city and turning it into a snakepit, so Sin sneaked into human hearts.

Next, Paul apparently pictured Sin's possession of Adam as leading eventually to its possession of all Adam's children (by some means not here mentioned), for "all sinned" (Rom 5:12). It seems likely that Paul pictured Sin spreading out throughout all Adam's descendants. The evidence for this interpretation is that he says (a) "Death [entered the human world] through Sin" (Rom 5:12b), and (b) "Death spread [*dielthen*] to all people" (12c). Together those statements suggest that "Sin spread to all people" as the means.

How Sin passed on to Adam's children Paul does not specifically say, but our discussion above provides a plausible story. The main clue to Paul's plot comes in Romans 7 when law seems to be the key Sin uses to open the gate into the fortress of the human heart. Paul says: "Apart from the law Sin lies dead. I was alive once apart from the law, but when the commandment came, then Sin sprang to life and I died" (Rom 7:9). Though this statement is highly metaphorical, we propose the following elaboration as an approximation of what he was imagining:

(a) Apparently Paul pictures young children, those who have not yet been given any rules to obey, as initially free from Sin's rule; that is the probable meaning of his metaphor "I was alive once apart from the law."

(b) Thus the occasion for Sin possessing Adam's children seems to be when they are given rules to obey, when the law is laid down to them, presumably at a young age, "when the commandment came."

(c) "Apart from the law sin lies dead" suggests that Sin already lurks at the door to the child's heart but is powerless to enter.

(d) "Sin sprang to life" suggests that when the child has rules imposed, then Sin, which has been lurking beside or even in the child, gains power over the child.

(e) By saying "I [the child] died," Paul probably means (s)he died spiritually, i.e. was ruled, indeed possessed, by the spirit (Sin) that brings death (see Rom 6:13), for elsewhere he speaks of being "enslaved to Sin" (Rom 6:6).

That scenario of Sin taking over suggests that Paul imagined the story this way: Sin is a spirit lying at the door of the innocent human heart, waiting for an opportunity to enter. (Perhaps Paul pictured Sin as hiding, inactive, within all infants, like a dormant plague bacillus. Alternately, perhaps Paul pictured Sin as travelling hiddenly in every family, waiting for the moment to invade every new addition.) The coming of the law then provides a test, the opportunity for choice. Invariably the person chooses to disobey, to live according to the flesh, which allows Sin to set sinful passions running free; by that means Sin takes over. All "present themselves as obedient slaves...of Sin," which then forces them "to obey the passions of their mortal bodies" (Rom 6:16, 12). Then the person is no longer spiritually alive and free but has become a conscript dragooned into the Army of Darkness. From that slavery, Paul proclaimed, no humans could rescue themselves.

**Conclusion**

Sin, when Paul is thinking in military terms, is Satan's evil spirit sent out from the darkness of enemy headquarters to infiltrate the heart of every person on earth. By deception it persuades people to open the castlegate and allow it in. Once inside, it works as a spy, hiddenly easing its way into the decision-making center of the person. Once there it becomes a counselor depended on for guidance, and so can lead its victims deeper and deeper into the darkness which is the Enemy's favorite hiding place. Like a saboteur destroying defenses secretly from within the fortress, Sin works insidiously, taking control and overcoming the defenses against evil. Only when it is exposed as an enemy, then rejected by its victim, and driven out by God's more powerful Spirit, can people be free from its hidden slavery.

### D.  THE LAST ENEMY: DEATH AS A COSMIC POWER

The last enemy [*echthros*] to be destroyed [*katargeitai*] is death. (1 Cor 15:26)

When Paul refers to Death as "the last enemy," he clearly shows that he sometimes pictures it as a cosmic power, parallel to, if not superior to, the rulers and authorities he mentions in the same sentence (1 Cor 15:24–26). That military imagery for Death surfaces in various other passages too, most notably in Rom 5:12–8:39 where its subordination to the ruling power Sin is a striking feature.

In these various passages Paul has provided us with a small array of still pictures that represent a dramatic narrative: the unspoken narrative is his myth in which action and reaction, attack and retreat, conquest and destruction, are events that fill the imagination. Thus our task here, as throughout this exploring of Paul's military symbolism, is to reconstruct Paul's myth from the still pictures he has left us. In this endeavor, our knowing the Jewish apocalyptic background that Paul probably assumed provides a wealth of possibilities we will consider.[20]

---

[20] Our picture is similar to de Boer's in *The Defeat of Death* where he says Death for Paul is "an inimical, murderous, quasi-angelic power that has held all Adamic humanity in subjection and enslavement...Paul cosmologizes or

## (1) Paul's Snapshots of the Enemy King Death

The most interesting of Paul's suggestions on Death's role and power comes from its connection with Sin. In Paul's myth, Sin first enters the world (Rom 5:12), attacking Adam, and (presumably) through his acquiescence gaining entry into the previously Sin-free castle of human and earthly life. Death follows (Rom 5:12), then goes its own way. Death spreads to all humankind, at first following Sin (Rom 5:12), but Death also spreads to the whole biological world, for Paul probably alluded to Death's stranglehold when he spoke of nature's "bondage to decay" (Rom 8:21). Still, because Sin is the superior, the leader, Paul also sees Sin reigning *in* (i.e. through, by means of) Death (Rom 5:21), for Sin was the power which led Death to its role as tyrant. We will now discuss these main metaphorical references to the enemy agent Death, especially in its role as follower in the foot-steps of the demon Sin.

(a) Paul's myth of Death opens in Eden where Sin first attacks and breaks through the castle wall of human innocence. Then Death follows in its footsteps: "Sin came into the world through one man and Death (came) through Sin" (Rom 5:12). Since Paul apparently looked on Sin as an invisible agent of Satan, we can appropriately take its "entering" as an act of aggression. Thus Paul could well have imagined Sin entering as a conqueror like Antiochus IV sending his army to break through the walls of Jerusalem and plunder the temple (1 Macc 1:30–31). Then Death, coming right in its footsteps, could be imagined as the consequent, continuing oppression that the conquering army practices over the conquered city (1 Macc 1:33–35).

(b) Paul says of this tyrant: "So Death spread to all human beings because all sinned" (Rom 5:13). Apparently Paul saw Sin leading the way, moving from the conquest of one city (Adam) out and beyond to all the cities and towns and villages of the realm of humankind. When Sin spread, as conquerors always tend to do until they are stopped, so did its follower, its agent of permanent oppression, its executioner, Death.

(c) That universal oppression by Death Paul expresses in clearly

---

'mythologizes' death for his readers in both 1 Corinthians 15 and Romans 5" (183). Others who support this view are Kasemann in *Romans* and Beker in *Triumph*.

political terms by saying: "Death reigned [*ebasileusen*] from Adam to Moses, even over those not sinning [*me hamartesantas*] in a way like the transgression of Adam" (Rom 5:14). That reference to sinning in a way unlike Adam's transgression probably means sinning caused by the reign of Sin even in the absence of law, which latter is required before one can transgress (cross the line laid down by the law). Here Paul apparently stresses his military imagery, Sin and Death as tyrants. This stands in clear contrast to his judicial/legal imagery in which sinning *is* a transgression (perhaps of an unwritten law) and death is punishment for the transgression.[21]

Paul pictured Death as following Satan's demon Sin into every corner of the human realm leaving no descendant of Adam outside its kingdom. In that universal sway it is much worse than the Roman Empire which could only extend its oppression a certain distance from Rome before its lines of supply became weaknesses. Death, by contrast, spreads its oppression throughout the whole human race, for "in Adam all die" (1 Cor 15:22).

(d) That reign of Death probably extended in Paul's imagination beyond humankind, on through the whole biological realm, and perhaps into the non-living realms of nature as well, for he promises: "the creation itself will be set free from its bondage to decay" (Rom 8:21). While Paul does not mention Death explicitly here, it is almost certain that the term "decay" (*tes phthoras*) includes a reference to the process by which Death eventually destroys all living things. By using the term "bondage" or "slavery" (*tes douleias*) he alludes to his earlier assertions that Sin enslaves people (Rom 6:6), and of course Death is a confederate in that slavery (Rom 5:21; 6:9, 8:2).

(e) Another interesting image Paul offers of the connection between Sin and Death is this: "Sin reigned [*ebasileusen*] in Death" (Rom 5:21). The implication here is that Death is the more apparent of the two, the one humans cannot miss because Death strikes every community continually. Thus Death's reign is present and local, obvious and inescapable; by contrast, Sin perhaps remains hidden, for people do not always recognize that their sinful behavior is (in Paul's military symbolism) the product of the tyrannical rule of Sin. So Paul emphasizes that Sin is influential everywhere by saying that Sin reigns in Death: everywhere that Death holds its sword over the creatures there the greater tyrant

---

[21]See De Boer, *Defeat*, 166.

is Sin.

(f) One further metaphorical saying that offers us a hint of Sin as the greater threat is Paul's statement that "the sting [*to kentron*] of Death is Sin" (1 Cor 15:56). Here Paul's symbol pictures Death as a creature which can only do harm through its sting. It is "a venomous creature, a scorpion or a hornet, which is rendered harmless, when it is deprived of its sting. The serpent has lost its poison-fang."[22] Paul therefore suggests that Death cannot do a person any ultimate harm unless Sin is also present and active. If a person becomes free from Sin, as Paul says believers do (Rom 6:17–18), then Death may scare and threaten, but it cannot bring the ultimate destruction of eternal exclusion from God's presence.

(g) Though we will consider it in more detail in a later chapter, we must glance briefly at Paul's most obviously military metaphor concerning Death: "The last enemy [*echthros*] to be destroyed [*katargeitai*] is Death" (1 Cor 15:56). The previous enemies mentioned were "every principality and rule and every power," referring to the angelic rulers of the nations which we described earlier in this chapter. Since Paul's character Death is in this class, we can clearly see that he imagined it as an angelic power too, an invisible spirit that influences life on earth.

Since Death will be the *last* enemy, it is in some respects more powerful than all the other angelic spirits. Presumably that power is seen in the way it spreads its wings over the whole human race, indeed over the whole of the living biological realm, possibly even over the whole of creation, as we discussed above. In particular Paul implies here that Death is more pervasive, in some respects a more enduring enemy to humankind, than Sin is. Sin will be defeated earlier; Death goes on and on, fighting and killing to the very End.

## (2) Death as Satan's Spirit

One further aspect of Paul's personified enemy Death is the connection

---

[22] Robertson and Plummer, *First Corinthians*, 378. Beker takes this hornet and its sting imagery a bit too far when he says "death can also be the agent and sin its instrument (1 Cor 15:56)" (*Triumph*, 190). Death probably has no control over Sin in Paul's imagery, so Sin is more appropriately pictured as the superior power at work.

between Death and Satan. Earlier we argued that in Paul's myth Sin was imagined as a demon, an invisible spirit sent out by the Prince of Darkness to rule in the lives of all his subjects/slaves. Since in the myth Death goes wherever Sin goes, even beyond, we can reasonably conclude that Paul imagined Death as Satan's agent also.

This connection between Satan and Death was common in Paul's Jewish tradition. First of all the Book of Job pictures the satan as having the power to bring death to Job's servants and children (Job 1:14–19). Later Wis 2:24 says, "Through the devil's envy death entered the world, and those who belong to his company experience it." Similarly the Jewish-Christian Epistle to the Hebrews reflects this view by calling the devil "him who has the power of death" (Heb 2:14). Finally, "In the Talmud, Satan is also the 'Angel of Death' (Baba Bathra 16a; Jer. Sabb. 2, 6 etc.)."[23]

This background provides adequate reasons for us to believe that Paul too thought of Death as an agent of Satan, perhaps even an aspect of Satan, but there is further evidence for it in his own statements.

(a) The Destroyer [*tou olothreutou*], the angel who destroyed [*apolonto*] sinners, whom Paul mentions in 1 Cor 10:10, plays a role quite like the one assigned to Satan earlier (*olethron tes sarkos*, 5:5). This similarity of role and similarity of wording suggests that Paul connected the two names, probably seeing them as two expressions of a single figure.

(b) In 1 Cor 15:24–26, when Paul speaks of Death as the last enemy, the earlier enemies are the angelic powers, so it is likely that Paul was here imagining Death by using the symbol of an angelic spirit also.

(c) In 1 Corinthians 15 Paul never mentions the end of Satan, so he presumably subsumed it under something else, and the most likely place is in the destruction of the last enemy, Death. Thus Paul probably saw Death as a mask that Satan wore, or a spirit that was at his core. Since the destruction of Death is the end (1 Cor 15:26), and the crushing of Satan is the end (so we interpret Rom 16:20 below), the two enemies are in some ways one in Paul's myth. Perhaps we should think of Sin-Death as the spirit of Satan, so when they are destroyed Satan is too.

Thus we conclude that Paul probably pictured Death the last enemy as

---

[23] Kluger, *Satan in the Old Testament*, 159, n.26.

the spirit of Satan, the last facade of Satan, the final expression of that angelic power. Probably Paul pictured Death ruling over all who died, like a shepherd in control of a flock (Ps 49:14), a warden ruling a prison, a slave-master tyrannizing a plantation. How exactly this spirit is related to Satan Paul does not say, but we perhaps will not be far off if we say the spirit of Death is of the essence of Satan, parallel to the way that the Spirit of Life (Rom 8:2) is of the essence of God (see 1 Cor 1:10–11).

## (3) The Kingdom of Death

While Paul is not explicit on the matter, our view is that his battle myth probably included the following plot elements: (a) Before the coming of Christ, as is commonly suggested in the OT, all the dead were imprisoned in Sheol, the realm of the dead, which was commonly pictured as in the Underworld. (b) Christ therefore descended to that realm when he died, but God conquered Death by "raising him from the dead" so that he no longer is under the slavery to Death that all others experience (Rom 6:9). (c) In the present, those who are "in Christ" have been rescued from the eternal threat of Death (Rom 8:2), but are still subject to its physical threat (1 Cor 15:22). (d) Thus believers, those in Christ, do die physically. Then they are "asleep" (1 Thess 4:13), "dead in Christ" (16), which presumably refers to an unconscious but protected state. (e) In the end dead believers will be raised at the beginning of the Last Battle (1 Thess 4:16; 1 Cor 15:23) and will then receive the gift of eternal life (Rom 2:7). (f) Dead sinners probably are never raised but continue on separated from God forever, though the final defeat of Death can be taken (as in universalism) to imply that all people are finally freed from its hold.

The interpretations in (b) through (f) are topics of discussion in later chapters, so all we will present here is an argument for (a), the theory that Paul saw Death, before the coming of Christ, as the tyrant ruling over all the dead, who were gathered in Sheol, probably called Hades by Paul. The Greek mythological picture of Hades, the place and the ruler (called Pluto by the Romans) who was King of the Underworld, was probably not far from Paul's picture of this mysterious reality. Possibly he believed, as did the Greeks and Romans and some Jews (see *1 Enoch*), that there were divisions in Hades-Sheol, so that those who were faithful Israelites were separated from those who are the great oppressors and other evil-doers. Our hypothesis is that Paul believed that all the dead are in Hades-Sheol

(a) The one piece of semi-direct evidence in Paul's writing concerning the state of the dead prior to Christ's resurrection is this statement: "Christ, being raised [*egertheis*] from the dead [*ek nekron*] will never die again. Death no longer has dominion [*kurieuei*, rules] over him" (Rom 6:9). The spatial image of being raised, lifted up from a lower place, was probably meant symbolically by Paul's day. Still the picture evoked is of a realm under the ground, which is called "the dead," metonymy for "the gatheringplace of the dead." Presumably the image in Paul's mind was the old Hebraic one, also found in the Greek and Roman myths, that the dead are all gathered under the earth, in the Underworld.

(b) The ancient Hebrew picture, found throughout the OT, is that all the dead go down into the grave, return to the dust, are gathered to their fathers, descend into Sheol the place of gloom where God is not present. The most vivid picture of Sheol is given in Isaiah 14 in which the King of Babylon descends to Sheol where he finds himself as weak, dishonored and powerless as everyone else there (9–11). Later, when hope in resurrection arose, the image offered is this: "Many of those who sleep in the dust of the earth shall awake..." (Dan 12:2). This clearly suggests the image of people asleep under the surface of the earth (see Ps 13:3; Jer 51:39; 1 Kgs 1:21, 2:10 etc.).

(c) The standard Hebraic image of the dead gathered in the Underworld was also standard in Greek and Roman mythology with which Paul was probably familiar. The stories of living heroes (Odysseus, Orpheus, Aeneas) descending into the Kingdom of Hades are some of the most striking of all the myths of Paul's world. Perhaps the myth of Orpheus descending to rescue his beloved Eurydice is the one that seems the clearest foreshadowing of Paul's gospel of Christ's victory over death, though it is very different in many ways. What we can assume Paul found useful as imagery are these points: the picture of Hades' Kingdom as under the earth; death and burial as the normal way to enter that kingdom; the rule of King Hades, who may in Paul's mind have been an apt expression of King Death. One issue that this contemporary mythology raises is whether Paul would have found the division of Hades into the pleasant Elysian Fields and the punitive Tartarus[24] to be an acceptable picture.

---

[24] Virgil, *Aeneid*, Bk. 6.

(d) Before Paul's time some Jewish writers had pictured a similar division of the Afterworld, for in *1 Enoch* 22 the visionary pictures three hollow places, which provide holding pens for the three groups of dead people: one for the righteous (22:9), a second for sinners who did not receive punishment on earth (22:10–11), and the third for sinners who have already suffered their punishment on earth (22:12–13). A related division provides the setting for Luke's parable of "The Rich Man and Lazarus" (Lk 16:19–31), for the (apparently innocent) oppressed Lazarus ends up in the pleasant place with Abraham while the sinful rich man ends up in punishment, with a great gulf separating them. Finally, in the post-Pauline Jewish work 2 Esdras, the view is clearly stated that right after death punishment will start for those who have sinned, while rest will start for the righteous (7:75–101). Thus in Judaism we seem to have a progression of views: (i) in the OT all are in Sheol together; (ii) in *1 Enoch* (2nd century BC) divisions arise in Sheol; (iii) in Luke (ca AD 85) and 2 Esdras (ca AD 100), immediate rewards and punishments are promised.

(e) But what did Paul think? Since he grew up in the Greek world it is plausible that he learned the story of the division of the Underworld into places of reward and punishment. Further he probably found nothing in his Jewish upbringing to make him object to it. Justice seems to demand such a division and clearly Jewish thinkers had already adopted it, as we showed above in discussing *1 Enoch*. However, Paul offers two hints that he did not see rewards and punishment starting right after death (at least not before the coming of Christ). The first is his proclamation that punishment will come on "the day of wrath" (Rom 2:5) by which he presumably refers to the Last Day, the Day of Judgment. If final punishment does not come until then, he probably did not think of sinners already in Tartarus being punished the way his contemporary Virgil did. Secondly, since even believers are "asleep" (1 Thess 4:14), that is unconscious (as we will argue in chapter V), presumably unable to experience either good or bad, it is likely that he thought of all the dead as asleep and unconscious, so it probably made no difference where they were gathered.[25]

---

[25] In chapter V below we will examine the two passages which have often been interpreted as referring to the immediate rewarding of believers upon their deaths (Phil 1:24 and 2 Cor 5:1–10). We will argue that neither of them should be taken to mean that Paul adopted the Virgilian picture of immediate rewards after death. Instead they should at most be taken to refer to the Enochian picture

**Conclusion**

Our conclusion is that Paul probably thought of all the dead prior to the coming of Christ as held in Sheol under the prison warden Death. Death rules not only over the living, making them eventually die, but even more over the dead, keeping them from conscious life. Possibly Paul pictured the faithful Israelites and righteous Gentiles (see Rom 2:15) as separated from the rest of the dead, but it is unlikely that he believed that rewards and punishments had already begun. Especially in his battle myth, when he imagined the world prior to Christ's coming as ruled by the Prince of Darkness, he probably pictured all the dead as gathered together in the prison of darkness under the earth. Thus a central task for Christ was to enter that prison and bring freedom to Death's slaves, the way Cyrus, God's earlier anointed one, entered Babylon and freed the Jewish slaves there (Isa 45:1-4).

**(4) Sin and Death as Confederates**

When Paul personified Sin and Death, speaking of them both as reigning, like an emperor and his regent over a kingdom, he probably imagined some relationship between the two. However, he never makes that relationship explicit, so we must explore possibilities in order to see deeper into his myth.

The main characteristics of Sin and Death that Paul suggests in his myth as we have described it in the previous section, are these:

(a) Sin is the leader, the power that attacks first, while Death follows after it, going wherever Sin has first of all broken through the castlegate (Rom 5:12).

(b) The two are evil confederates, working together for the harm of humankind. No conflict between the two ever appears in Paul's myth, so they are enemies of humanity acting wholly in harmony with each others.

(c) Sin not only enters first but is also the superior, the one which reigns through Death (Rom 5:21) which is thus its subordinate in this imagery.

(d) Still Death is the immediate king over humankind, the one (presumably) whom humans immediately recognize as their ruler (Rom 5:14).

---

of an immediate division between the faithful and sinners, so that the faithful while dead, asleep, are still "dead in Christ" (1 Thess 4:16), i.e. protected by him from all harm.

(e) In that role as the immediate ruler Death goes beyond the realm where Sin first conquered: Death (apparently) spreads from the human realm to the whole biological realm, for the "bondage of decay" (Rom 8:21) is probably another way Paul imagines that death reigns. Perhaps Death even reigns in the non-living world, as the power that causes decay even in objects of stone and iron.

(f) In the human realm, where both Sin and Death reign, the condition of the victims is worse than elsewhere: Sin is Death's "sting," that which makes Death eternally "deadly."

(g) Part of that may be due to the fact that when Sin enters a human person via the law (Rom 7:8–9), the result is (spiritual) death—"I died." In this state humans are worse off than the sub-human world which cannot die before it dies.

(h) Both Sin and Death are to some extent God's servants, for they both express God's wrath against sinners (see Rom 1:24–25, 32, 3:9), just as Satan and the angelic powers do.

(i) In some respects Death is the more powerful of these two confederates, at least more tenacious, for it is the last enemy, the one that successfully resists all God's counterattacks until all God's forces are mustered against it at the very end. Further evidence for this Death-is-stronger-than-Sin image is Paul's suggestion that believers are free from Sin's rule (Rom 6:17–18) but not free from Death's until the End.

## Sin/Death: Empire/Procurator

This array of characteristics of the relationship between Sin and Death suggests a social/political symbol that will provide an apt image of the two reigning: the (widespread) Roman Empire and its local procurator (e.g. in Judah). The empire symbolizes Sin, while the procurator (and his armed guard) symbolize Death.

Using this model we can discover parallels to each of the points we made about the relationship of Sin and Death in the previous section. For example, as Sin comes first and Death follows so also the empire arrived in new colonies first, as an army conquering, destroying, overthrowing national rulers. Then, when the war was ended, the procurator was sent as the ruler, the one through whom the empire maintained its hold. Wherever the empire attacked and conquered, the procurator (in some places a proconsul) and government followed. Further, as Death is the last enemy and so in some respects stronger and more tenacious than Sin, so also the local procurator's tyranny is in some respects stronger than the empire's.   If the empire was conquered by a successful attack on Rome, still the far-flung armed contingents led by procurators would still have to be conquered one by one by one by one.

By these and many other parallels between Sin/Death's reign and the empire/procurator's reign we see a model that may well have lain in the back of Paul's imagination. The imagery of enemies, of a destructive conquest, and of reigning, all suggest that Paul had a political model in mind as he wrote. Even if he never explicitly made the Sin/empire, Death/procurator parallels, his understanding of the empire's rule probably lay behind his imagery, for the empire was the power that reigned over him throughout his whole lifetime.

Of course this empire-procurator model has its limitations. For example, in some places colonized people eventually freed themselves by local uprisings, but Death is far too powerful for any humans to defeat. Still this imagery does provide help in thinking of Paul's picture of Satan's underlings, the confederates Sin and Death. By speaking of Death as a subordinate through whom Sin (Satan's agent) rules, Paul suggested **Death is the spearpoint driven home by the whole Kingdom of Darkness**. Death as experienced, the universal end to the lives of biological creatures, is bad enough when seen by itself as a natural phenomenon. However, Paul pictured it as the visible enemy behind which lies hidden all evil in the universe. The human procurator is bad enough when considered just for his own qualities—one who kills any disturbers of the peace. But when he is seen as the visible single soldier representing a huge evil army, then he is much worse.

## Conclusion

In this chapter we have blown up, and painted in details on, Paul's snapshots of the supernatural enemies under Satan that he pictured threatening and oppressing humankind: the Rulers of this Present Age, the Children of Darkness, Sin and Death. By picturing these enemies, Paul suggests that humans are (to some extent) victims, that they are in need of (and perhaps deserve) the rescue that God alone can provide, and indeed has provided in the initial victory in the life, death and resurrection of Christ.

# V. GOD'S INITIAL VICTORY

Through Christ God Established
the Kingdom of Light

## Introduction

In the previous two chapters we have developed in detail Paul's military version of the world's problem: when imagining God's relationship to the creation by means of this cosmic war symbolism he pictures this age as a Kingdom of Darkness, ruled by God's great enemy the god of this present age. This Prince of Darkness has a hierarchy of subordinate enemies at his command, the Angelic Princes of the Nations, who rule the human children of darkness through their political and religious structures. Further, Satan has sent out the demon Sin to possess and oppress the whole of humankind, leading its subordinate Death to spread its bondage to decay throughout the whole biological creation (and perhaps beyond). Thus in Paul's military myth, prior to Christ's victory, the Army of Darkness holds the whole human race under its tyrannical oppression, symbolized by the way the Egyptians, the Babylonians and the Seleucids had oppressed Israel in the past. Thus, as we will show in this chapter, in his battle myth Paul pictures God's salvation as a victory over these enemies. As a result of the victory God translates his people into the new Kingdom of Light, freeing them permanently from the oppression practiced by the forces of darkness.

Imagining such creation-wide oppression by the forces of darkness, Paul knew the victory could only be won by a divine conquest that renewed but went far beyond **A. God's Ancient Victories**, over Egypt, Babylon and the Seleucids, when he previously freed his people from tyranny. Such a military/political victory was the symbol Paul used to imagine God's spiritual victory in Christ. In Christ, God's light has invaded the world, and through his life, death and resurrection God has liberated one region, thus **B. Through Christ God Created the Kingdom of Light**, which is the first glimmer of the new age that is coming. As part of the creating that new kingdom, **C. God Disarmed the Principalities and Powers**, so now there is a realm, a safe fortress, into which those angelic enemies cannot enter. In order to create that realm Christ died to Sin, and thereby **D. Sin the Demon was Conquered**, rescuing believers from its slavery, so they need no longer serve it. Finally, by Christ's death, resurrection and ascension **E. God (Partially) Defeated Death**, so that all who have joined his Army of Light need no longer fear its eternal threat.

## A. GOD'S ANCIENT VICTORIES AS PAUL'S MODEL

In his military version of the gospel Paul was updating (and spiritualizing) the traditional Hebrew military story which we summarized in Chapter II: God is the warrior who conquers Israel's enemies and brings his people to safety by making of them a kingdom within a fortified realm of light. In particular Paul was probably influenced by the three most famous stories of God's victories, at the Exodus, over Babylon, and through the Maccabees.

### (1) Exodus Conquest

The Song of Moses celebrates the Exodus as God's great victory, for it depicts the Lord as a man of war throwing the Egyptian army into the sea (Exod 15:4). The result of this victory is the creation of Yahweh's people (Exod 15:16), the eventual forming of the Kingdom of Israel, and the establishing of the sacred place (17) where God will reign forever (18).[1]

Clearly that Exodus victory was a significant part of Paul's treasury of

---

[1] See Forsyth, *The Old Enemy*, 95.

traditional stories, for he uses it as the prototype of God's victory in Christ (1 Corinthians 10). Indeed he suggests that Christ was there in that ancient victory, showing his own power and grace (10:4). Thus the creation of Israel in its own kingdom under God in Canaan probably for Paul symbolized (and perhaps foreshadowed) the new Kingdom of Light that God creates in Christ.

### (2) Victory over Babylon

Even more significant for Pauline use is the way that Second Isaiah takes up the Rahab mythology and uses it to foreshadow a future Exodus-like victory of God (Isa 51:9–11). As we will show in the next section, Paul quotes from Second Isaiah and probably was dependent on it for his light imagery and for his picture of God rescuing his people from slavery and transferring them to a new, free, kingdom. Thus while Paul never directly mentions the conquest of Rahab, it probably is significant background for Paul's own imagery of the divine conquest of the forces of evil.

The return from Babylon, after God had conquered the Babylonians through Cyrus the Persian (Isa 45:13), was one of the great victory stories in the Hebrew tradition. When some of the people returned to Jerusalem and eventually rebuilt the Temple, they regained their religious independence once more (Haggai, Zechariah), though still remaining under the political rule of the Persians. This religious freedom (amidst continuing subordination) was an earthly prototype of the spiritual freedom (with continuing physical oppression) that Paul saw believers gained by entering Christ's Kingdom of Light.

### (3) The Conquest of the Fourth Beast

The third and perhaps most dramatic of the divine rescues that Paul probably had in his memory was the story of the rescue of Judea from the Seleucid tyranny. The divine rescue came through the Maccabees, who fought in God's name (1 Macc 3:18–22) and drove the Seleucid oppressors away. They recovered Jerusalem, cleansed the temple, fortified the city with high walls and strong towers, and turned the lights on again (1 Maccabees 4). Thus the Maccabees created a new, independent, Kingdom of God's people, centered in the city of lights, thereby holding back the darkness of evil which still surrounded it. That story probably served as a model for Paul's gospel of the Kingdom of Light shining freely amidst the still-powerful Kingdom of Darkness.

That same Maccabean victory was symbolized in Daniel's great vision in which God takes dominion from the Fourth Monster and gives it to his people again (Dan 7). This monstrous adversary symbolizes yet transcends the aggressive Seleucid empire, just as Paul saw the Kingdom of Darkness transcending its human foot-soldiers. That monster suggests the supernatural (angelic) aspect of the oppressors, the invisible principality that lies hidden behind the visible Seleucid tyrant. Further, God's victory is overwhelming, since simply the coming of fire from God destroys this enemy (Dan 7:10–11), foreshadowing Paul's picture of the coming of Christ as God's light driving back the darkness.

This brief survey shows that Paul's victory-through-Christ symbolism stands in front of a substantial Hebraic background which we presented in detail in Chapter II. This background will provide significant help in elucidating and elaborating his picture. According to the ancient stories God several times conquered the enemies of his people and thus brought them to live safely in God's own kingdom centered in Jerusalem. Often those enemies were symbolized as forces of darkness, so God's victory is the invasion of the light in their midst, which is just what Paul pictured as having happened in Christ.

## B. THROUGH CHRIST GOD ESTABLISHED
## THE KINGDOM OF LIGHT

> The Father, who has enabled you to share in the inheritance of the saints in the light, has rescued us from the power of darkness and transferred us into the kingdom of his beloved Son. (Col 1:13)
> The Lord Jesus Christ...gave himself for our sins to set us free from the present evil age. (Gal 1:4)

Our hypothesis is this: an essential element in Paul's military version of the gospel is his picture of God in Christ defeating and so driving back all the forces of darkness and thereby establishing the Kingdom of Light. This new spiritual kingdom can aptly be imagined as a fortress on a high hill, with the light from heaven shining brightly on it, while all the world around remains in darkness. Inside the high-walled fortress Christ rules over and protects all those who have joined his army. Paul's image seems to be that this is a heavenly kingdom which has shone down, invading the earth and driving back the darkness. Thereby it becomes a small (at first), invisible (in the present age, to unbelievers), realm into which believers are taken by God and protected (spiritually) from the re-intrusion of darkness. We can aptly picture it as a fortified beachhead (since it will continue advancing), one into which believers enter and are kept spiritually safe from their enemies in the outside Kingdom of Darkness.[2]

## (1) Traditional Background to the Kingdom of Light

As specific background to Paul's Kingdom of Light image, no source is more striking than the Book of Isaiah. This book is filled with images of the coming victory of God's light which provided the background for Qumran and the early Christians to speak of the Messiah's victory as the coming of light into darkness.

First, Isaiah foresaw the coming of God's peaceful kingdom on a supernaturally-elevated Mt. Zion and urged his people to "walk in the light of the Lord" (Isa 2:5). This suggests that God's light would shine on that mountain sanctuary. Later Isaiah specified how this new day would dawn, proclaiming: "the people who walked in darkness have seen a great light; those who lived in a land of deep darkness—on them light has shined" (9:2), in the child born to be king (9:6). Of course the coming of the light brings victory, indeed God himself sometimes is the victor in Isaiah's visions, for he says: "The light of Israel will become a fire, and his Holy One a flame; it will burn and devour (the Assyrian's) thorns and briers in one day" (Isa 10:17).

Even more central for understanding the NT imagery of victorious divine light is the victory-of-light imagery in Second and Third Isaiah. The Babylonian prophet speaks of the Servant of the Lord as given by God as "a light to the Gentiles" (Isa 42:6; 49:6). Paul echoes this image by calling Jews "a light to those who are in darkness" (Rom 2:19). Further, Second Isaiah says the Lord himself "goes forth like a soldier, like a warrior," proclaiming, "I will

---

[2] As we will note later, living believers still must venture out into the darkness where they are still vulnerable to the physical attacks of the forces of darkness.

turn the darkness before them into light" (42:13, 16). Thus the victory over Babylon, and the rescue of the people from that forced exile, is the coming of the light which drives back the darkness of oppression (see Isa 51:4), just as in Paul.

Most striking of all is the picture in Isaiah 60, for it could have been composed by Paul himself, since it so accurately seems to foreshadow his picture of what God did in Christ:

> Arise, shine; for your light has come,
>   and the glory of the Lord has risen upon you.
> For darkness shall cover the earth,
>   and thick darkness the peoples;
> But the Lord will arise upon you,
>   and his glory will appear over you.
> Gentiles shall come to your light,
>   and kings to the brightness of your dawn. (1–3)

Paul too saw the world as covered with darkness; he too saw the Lord (in his case Christ) coming, bringing the glory of the Lord into their midst; he too saw this light establishing a place where the divine light shines out to the whole world; and especially he emphasized the divine welcome to Gentiles.

Finally, we may briefly note how central this imagery of the victory of the light over the darkness was in the Qumran community. For example, in the War Scroll the battle is between the children of light and the Angel of Light on the one hand and the children of darkness and the Angel of Darkness on the other. This is the hope of victory: "Thou hast decreed for us a destiny of Light according to Thy truth. And the Prince of Light Thou hast appointed from ancient times to come to our support...But Satan, the Angel of Malevolence, Thou hast created for the Pit" (1QM xiii). Thus when the victory takes place God will apparently create an eternal Kingdom of Light on earth. Especially striking in anticipation of Paul's picture is a Qumran psalmist's fortress imagery, which echoes the ancient Hebrew psalmists': "I shall be as one who enters a fortified city, as one who seeks refuge behind a high wall" (1QH vi). Thus in Paul's day the hope that God will protect his followers in a spiritual fortress was still used and available for Paul's myth.[3]

## (2) Paul's References to the Kingdom of Light

In several passages Paul speaks clearly of the Risen Christ ruling over believers, showing that he pictured a new kingdom, a safe realm, as the new creation God brought forth in the resurrection.

### (a) The New Kingdom (Col 1:13)

Perhaps the most revealing Pauline passage concerning the new Kingdom of Light is his statement in Colossians:

> The Father, who has enabled you to share in the inheritance of the saints in the light, has rescued [*herrusato*] us from the authority [*exousias*] of darkness and transferred [*metestesen*] us into the kingdom [*ten basileian*] of his beloved Son. (Col 1:13)

Here Paul pictures God as the victor over the Kingdom of Darkness, for he has rescued believers from it and transported them (as in the Exodus and return from exile) into a kingdom of their own Lord, a kingdom of light and no darkness.

The "authority of darkness" clearly is a reference to the present evil age (Gal 1:4), the rule of the god of this age (2 Cor 4:4), the darkness that is associated with Beliar (2 Cor 6:14). Since its opposite is the Kingdom of Christ, we should naturally see Paul as understanding it as a Kingdom of Darkness, a tyranny in which all human beings found themselves before Christ came, as we described it in the previous two chapters. Secondly, since Paul speaks of darkness as the prison from which they are rescued, he was thinking of light as the condition of the realm into which they were going. That interpretation is clear because the saints, those who are rescued, end up "in the light" (Col 1:13). Therefore the Kingdom of God's beloved Son is a Kingdom of Light, the place where the light Christ brought has conquered the darkness permanently.[4] In Christ God has once again commanded that light shine in darkness, and that

---

[3] For further discussion of the Scrolls see above II.C (4) and II.D (5), and Forsyth, *The Old Enemy*, 199-207.

[4] See Arnold, *Powers*, 111-112.

light seems to be the glory of God which appeared in Christ (2 Cor 4:6).[5]

God's "rescue" of the saints by "transferring" them from the Kingdom of Darkness to the Kingdom of Light reminds us not only of the Exodus, but also of the hope of Second Isaiah: he saw his people in the darkness of Babylon and hoped for God's light to rescue them and transfer them to God's own land in Judah (Isa 42:16) where they would be the light to the Gentiles (Isa 49:6). That new kingdom would be universal, for God promises: "To me every knee shall bow, every tongue shall swear" (45:23). Since that is the promise that Paul quotes in speaking of God's exaltation of Christ in Philippians 2, it is very likely that Paul knew this prophet's hope of God's new kingdom for his people. Thus Christ's rescue of believers, bringing them into the Kingdom of Light, may well be modelled on God's rescue of the exiles and returning them to Jerusalem and his Temple.

### (b) Christ's Death as the Means (Gal 1:4)

Clearly Paul understood the death and resurrection of Christ as the decisive events in the creation of this new Kingdom of Light. He speaks of Christ's death as decisive in the rescue from the Kingdom of Darkness, when he says: "The Lord Jesus Christ...gave himself for our sins to set us free [*exeletai*] from the present evil age, [*ek tou aionos tou enestotos ponerou*] according to the will of our God and Father" (Gal 1:4). "The present evil age" is one of his many ways of speaking of the Age or Kingdom of Darkness within which all sinners are bound. It is parallel to "the authority of darkness" (Col 1:13), and "this age" of which Satan is god (2 Cor 4:4), to which believers are not to conform (Rom 12:2), and which has ignorant rulers over it (1 Cor 2:8).[6] Paul understands it as a prison camp, an exile from which the prisoners are unable to free themselves, a gloomy underworld in which evildoers thrive, since

---

[5] Segal emphasizes the connection between Christ and the glory of God, saying it is central to Paul's Christology: "Paul's phrase the Glory of the Lord must be taken both as a reference to Christ and as a technical term for the *Kavod*, the human form of God appearing in biblical visions" (Segal, *Paul the Convert*, 60). Thus the light of the Heavenly Creator became present on earth in the risen, glorious Christ known to believers. In addition, "as an heir of Christ, the believer shares the Glory of Christ (Rom. 8:17)" (Segal, 10) by entering his glorious Kingdom of Light.

[6] Burton, *Galatians*, 13.

evil always loves the darkness.

When he says Christ gave himself (i.e. by his death) to "set them free," he uses the verb *exaireo*, which most basically means to take up out of, or to lift out. When used in the NT in the middle it means to rescue, usually referring to God coming down into the darkness of human difficulty and lifting someone out of it before they are killed. It is used in stories of Joseph (Acts 7:10), Israel under the Egyptians (Acts 7:34), Peter in prison (Acts 12:11) and Paul when he was about to be killed by a mob (Acts 23:27). Thus when Paul uses it here he presumably has that kind of picture in mind. Here, however, it is not an individual whom God lifts up out of danger but (potentially) the whole human race. This is the greater Exodus, for that original rescue from an evil kingdom took place as God says, when "I bore you on eagles' wings and brought you to myself" (Exod 19:4), at Sinai, the mountain of God. When God lifts a person out of mortal danger he then puts him or her into a new realm, one in which that danger is gone. For Paul that permanent new realm is the Kingdom of Light over which Christ rules, the new mountain of God. Like the psalmists of Qumran, Paul probably imagined this safe new realm in OT imagery as "a fortified city" where the faithful find "refuge behind a high wall" (1QH vi).

### (c) Christ Exalted to Kingship (Phil 2:9–11)

That rule of Christ in the present is clearly referred to in the phrase "the kingdom of his beloved son" (Col 1:13), but it is suggested elsewhere also. In Philippians 2, in which Paul praises Christ for his descent into the human condition, even to the depths of death on the cross, the end of the story is that his resurrection is (or leads to) his exaltation, which apparently is the beginning of the new reign of Christ: "Therefore God also highly exalted him, and gave him the name that is above every name, so that at the name of Jesus every knee should bow, in heaven and on earth and under the earth, and every tongue confess that Jesus Christ is Lord" (Phil 2:9–11). In the present, only believers confess that Christ is Lord, so this universal worship can only happen in the future. Clearly, however, this passage shows that Paul saw Christ as already exalted, already given the highest name, already the king.

Other passages in which Paul alludes to the picture of Christ already reigning offer further insight into his cosmic victory myth. First of all, he says to the Corinthians that Christ, the first fruits of the resurrection, is now reigning and will continue to reign until the victory over the forces of evil is complete:

"For he (Christ) must reign [*dei...basileuein*] until he has put all his enemies under his feet" (1 Cor 15:25). As we will argue in the chapter on the Last Battle, in Paul's myth this reign is present, not millenial, for Paul clearly sees Christ as already having defeated the powers, though their final destruction is yet to occur.[7]

Secondly, he alludes to the heavenly kingdom of Christ when he says to the Philippians: "Our commonwealth [*to politeuma*] is in heaven, from which we await our Savior, the Lord Jesus Christ" (Phil 3:20). *Politeuma* means state (which is a kingdom when it has a king), and was sometimes used by colonists to refer to their homeland.[8] Thus Paul here suggests that Christ's kingdom is a heavenly one, and that believers are colonists out in the wilderness awaiting the coming of their king to turn their colony into a new homeland.

Thirdly, Paul pictures this present reign of Christ as including believers when he says to the Colossians: "If you have been raised with Christ, seek the things that are above, where Christ is, seated at the right hand of God...for you have died and your life is hidden with Christ in God" (Col 3:1, 3). Christ's seat at God's right hand implies that he is God's regent over the earth, the king over this kingdom. Even more important is the image of believers symbolically present with Christ in his heavenly reign, thus alluding to the benefits that have already come to them (see also Eph 2:4–6).[9]

Thus in all these passages Paul pictures a kingdom of Christ, of which believers in some way are already subjects. With one foot they stand (spiritually) in the Kingdom of Light. In addition, since believers are still on earth, still physically, economically, politically and socially involved in worldy affairs, they

---

[7] See Ridderbos, *Paul*, 559. Markus Barth asserts that for Paul "the subjugation of the powers is still in progress" (*Ephesians chs 1–3*, 170).

[8] Arndt and Gingrich, *Greek-English Lexicon*, 692.

[9] Another passage that may suggest Paul's picture is his reference to the heavenly Jerusalem (Gal 4:26). Perhaps he pictured that as the seat of Christ's present reign, and used the OT hopes for an exalted Jerusalem as the basis for his picture (e.g. Isa 2:1–4). Lincoln argues that that is essentially Paul's view: "By faith the Galatians are already members of the heavenly Jerusalem...(which) stands for the new order of salvation bound up with the new age which is accessible now to faith." Therefore "the believer is to live as the free citizen of a free city." (Lincoln, *Paradise Now and Not Yet*, 22, 26.)

still have the other foot in the Kingdom of Darkness.

**(d) Christ as God's Light**

Among Paul's many references to the connection between Christ and the light, one that deserves special mention is this: "For it is God who said 'Let light shine out of darkness,' who has shone in our hearts to give the light of the knowledge of the glory of God in the face of Jesus Christ" (2 Cor 4:6). The context for this statement is the picture of Satan as the god of this world who has brought darkness by blinding all unbelievers, keeping them "from seeing the light of the gospel of the glory of Christ who is the image of God" (4:4).

While we cannot plumb the depths of Paul's mysterious vision here, we can say the following with confidence:

(i) Here Paul sees Christ as the light (or glory) of God which comes into the world to confront and defeat the darkness which is Satan's tyranny.[10]

(ii) The victory comes by God's light in Christ shining into the hearts of believers, thereby presumably making them children of light (1 Thess 5:5).

(iii) The reference to God's original creation of light suggests that Paul was here thinking about a new creation (see 2 Cor 5:17). Apparently Paul saw in the victory of Christ a new event of the shining of God's light to overcome the darkness and create a new world, which elsewhere he calls the Kingdom of Christ.

(iv) Christ's face shines with the glory of God, the dazzling light of God's presence, because Christ is the image of God, the one who symbolizes God and so makes him present.

Thus Paul apparently pictured Christ as the light of God's own presence which shone into, invaded, the world of darkness. Thereby God defeated the darkness, driving it back and so creating a new Kingdom of Light in its midst.

**(e) Beachhead**

How then did Paul imagine Christ's present hidden kingship, since God has made him the Lord over the whole world (Phil 2:9–11)? Beker suggests that the safe, Spirit-ruled fortress of light is "the avant-garde of the new creation in a hostile world, creating beachheads in this world of God's dawning new

---

[10] Segal writes of Paul's imagery here: "Paul's conversion experience involved his identification of Jesus as the image and Glory of God, as the human figure in heaven" (*Paul the Convert*, 61).

world."[11] Further support for this military picture of Christ's new kingdom comes from Paul picturing the enemy as building up its own fortresses (2 Cor 10:3-5). Since he pictured the enemy lying behind fortified walls, he very likely pictured believers inside their safe haven in the same way.

Thus Paul may well have pictured the present world on analogy with a rebellious province which the emperor's son came to set free. He succeeded in creating a beachhead upon which he built up strong fortifications. Though the emperor's son represents the legitimate ruler over the whole empire, in this rebellious province he only holds power in the small area he has retaken so far. As time goes on he continues to drive back the darkness, to expand the beachhead, until all the province is retaken for the emperor (1 Cor 15:25).

Further, since the frontier, the beachhead, in Paul's imagery lay between the earthly and the heavenly realms, this new liberated realm could well be pictured as light from heaven shining down right in the middle of the old realm of darkness. Earlier, the Maccabean victory resulted in the new people freed, their temple lighted once more, but still they remained surrounded by the evil empires. Perhaps Paul likewise pictured Christ's heavenly Jerusalem of light surrounded by the darkness. He may have imagined a fortress-like heavenly Jerusalem (Gal 4:26) descending into the middle of this age of darkness (an image used later in Revelation 21), becoming the city of light set on a hill which beckoned all the nations to its gates (Isa 2:2-4). Inside the impregnable walls of this eternal Jerusalem, Christ is the light which shines upon all, bringing their new life of freedom from the powers (2 Cor 4:6), as long as they remain inside the fortress. His task, however, is to send his troops out from that safety, pushing forward the frontiers until the whole of the rebellious province has been retaken—a task that we will consider in the next chapter on "The Ongoing War."

### C. HOW GOD DISARMED THE PRINCIPALITIES AND POWERS

> (God) disarmed the principalities and powers and made a public example of them, triumphing over them in (Christ's cross). (Col 2:15)
> While we were minors, we were enslaved to the elemental

---

[11] *Triumph*, 155.

spirits of the universe. But when the fullness of time had
come, God sent his Son...to rescue those who are under the
law...So you are no longer a slave but a child. (Gal 4:3-5, 7)

In Paul's military myth of God's victory in Christ, one central battle is
apparently against angelic rulers of the nations, whom God defeated at the cross.
The background for this victory comes in earlier stories of divine conquest of
supernatural powers. Stories of God's conquest of Rahab or Leviathan the sea
monster point to the divine warrior's supernatural victories in the past (Isa
51:9-11; Ps 74:13-14). The Isaiah Apocalypse pictures the eventual punishment
of the host of heaven (Isa 24:21) and the defeat of Leviathan by God's sword
(Isa 27:1). Daniel pictures God conquering the Fourth Monster, and Michael
defeating the Princes of Persia and Greece. This same supernatural victory
symbolism also bursts forth in later Jewish apocalyptic writings (*1 En* 10:4-88;
1QM i).

In chapter IV we presented a reconstruction of Paul's picture of the
angelic powers, based on his hints and the assumption that he followed the
traditions of his people. An angelic prince (a principality, or ruler of this present
age) stands invisibly behind each nation, ordained as God's agent of justice in
that nation. When these rulers allowed themselves to be worshipped as gods,
that promoted injustice and oppression, as well as idolatry. Not just the Gentiles
but also the Jews, in Paul's picture, suffered under this angelic oppression. The
*stoicheia* who handed down the law were such rebellious angelic rulers who kept
the Jews in slavery.

These angelic enemies Paul pictured as defeated by God in Christ. Thus
now, any who die with Christ thereby also die to the angelic powers (Col 2:20),
i.e. are no longer spiritually subject to them. The coming of Christ rescued them
from slavery to the princes (Gal 4:3-4, 7), making them now free members of
Christ's kingdom instead. Now none of the angelic rulers can spiritually or
eternally harm believers (Rom 8:38-30).

## (1) Disarming the Principalities (Col 2:15)

Paul's most direct use of the symbolism of the defeat of the angelic
rulers comes in his saying that through the cross of Christ, "He [God] disarmed
[*apekdusamenos*] the principalities and powers and made a public example
[*edeigmatisen in parresia*] of them, triumphing [*thriambeusas*] over them in him

[Christ]" (Col 2:15). Considerable debate has surrounded the proper translation and interpretation of the main words, but in the light of our previous discussion of Paul's military symbolism we take the verse to suggest the following story:

(a) In Christ (particularly through his death on the cross which is referred to in v.14) God fought and triumphed over the angelic powers, with the resurrection and ascension as the triumphal procession.[12]

(b) The major step in that fight was God "making a public example" of them, i.e. showing the so-called gods up as pretenders, only creatures, indeed as evil creatures, thus exposing their demands to be worshipped as false.[13]

(c) How the Cross showed up the princes as pretenders Paul does not say, but the following may well fit his thinking: the injustice of the powers was exposed when they killed an innocent man; their foolishness was made evident when they tried to defeat a spiritual power by physical means (see 1 Cor 2:6-8 discussed below); and their supposed divine power was shown to be mere sham when God showed himself to be superior to them by far, through the resurrection.

(d) When God exposed their pretensions, that diminished their influence, indeed "stripped" off their arms and insignia and so "disarmed" them of much of their misused power.

(e) The triumph imagery is vividly expressed by Caird when he writes: "Like a Roman emperor, entering the capital in triumphal procession with a train of discredited enemies behind the chariot, Christ has made an exhibition of the powers, celebrating a public triumph over them."[14]

(f) A few verses later, in Col 2:20, Paul gives a further hint of the way this victory was won. In Christ's death and resurrection, the powers lost all influence over Christ, for he "died to the elemental spirits of the universe" (Col 2:20). That seems to mean that he escaped permanently from the realm in which

---

[12] We take God as the actor because "God" is the subject in verse 13 and presumably is the "he" mentioned in verse 14.

[13] Arnold, *Powers*, 80.

[14] *Principalities*, 86. By contrast Roy Yates presents a quite different view, arguing that the principalities and powers are Christ's supporters, not his enemies. ("Colossians 2.15: Christ Triumphant," 579–580). In this interpretation Yates follows in the footsteps of Wesley Carr who denies the presence of evil angels in Paul's myth, a view we have shown above is quite unlikely.

they rule, because he now rules in the Kingdom of Light which has driven out the darkness from this new beachhead.

(g) That same freedom from the angelic powers is now available to believers, for they "with Christ died to the elemental spirits" (Col 2:20); that same new life comes by Christians "stripping off [*apekdusamenoi*] the old nature [*ton palaion anthropon*]" (Col 3:9) and thereby entering Christ's new Kingdom of Light (Col 1:13).

(h) Thus we come full circle, back to God's victory as the setting up of the new Kingdom of Light. Christ, by his obedient death, escaped from the hold of the powers, and then by his resurrection became the ruler of the spiritual Kingdom of Light, which is free from the tyranny of the powers. The defeat of the powers provides the foundation for that picture: in his death Christ drives back the powers from the beachhead and thereby establishes the new kingdom into which the powers of darkness cannot enter.

## (2) Why the Cross is God's Secret Wisdom and Power (1 Cor 2:6–8)

Paul's gospel proclamation is that the earthly conflict between Christ and the forces of evil ends with an ironic twist: the powers (both human and angelic) appeared to have won the victory by crucifying him; however, his obedience even to death provided the way for God to defeat them and create the new Kingdom of Light. He speaks of the twist in this passage:

> Among the mature we do speak wisdom, though it is not a wisdom of this age or of the rulers of this age, who are perishing. But we speak God's wisdom, secret and hidden, which God decreed before the ages for our glory. None of the rulers of this age understood this; for if they had, they would not have crucified the Lord of glory. (1 Cor 2:6–8)

As we argued in the previous chapter, "the rulers" probably refers both to human rulers and to angelic ones, because in Paul's myth only the angelic ones are in the process of perishing, i.e. having their realm constantly diminished.

Paul never directly explains what in particular God had decreed that the powers were ignorant of. However, the rest of 1 Corinthians 1–2 makes it very likely that he is thinking of the principle of divine working through weakness: God requires an empty vessel in order to bring his divine power fully to bear in that person or community. As evidence of this principle we hear God say to Paul, "My power is made perfect in weakness," which Paul affirms by saying "whenever I am weak [humanly speaking] then I am strong [in the power of Christ]" (2 Cor 12:9-10). That seems to summarize Paul's message in 1 Corinthians 1-2 in which he stresses that God's wisdom chooses nobodies (in the worldly sense) and makes them somebodies (1 Cor 1:26-29). This divine wisdom and strategy was made most evident in the cross, for there Christ used no worldy wisdom, wealth, or power, but simply was obedient and humble.

The angelic and human rulers naturally believed that in their conflict with Christ they were the ones who held the decisive power. They had the world's wisdom, wealth, and power, both judicial and military, while Christ had nothing, in comparison. However, the powers did not know that when the humble, obedient, Sin-free Christ died (as an unjustly condemned victim of their oppression), his death would open the way to a resurrection; in the resurrection God would create a new Sin-free, Death-free and thus powers-free Kingdom of Light into which believers could enter even while still in the flesh. Apparently Paul's story here is that the angelic and human rulers saw Christ as an earthly threat, so they used their earthly power—judicial authority exercised through physical force—to rid themselves of him. That apparent victory was in fact real defeat, for they provided exactly the means by which God in Christ could defeat them.

Thus the secret, hidden wisdom of God, which was revealed in the Cross, is that human weakness provides room for divine strength; human foolishness opens the way for divine wisdom; human self-sacrifice, self-emptying, is the necessary step towards divine exaltation. The powers thought that worldly strength is supreme, but by using that strength to kill Christ they ushered in their own eventual destruction, as Saul did when he drove David into exile.

### (3) The Law, the Powers' Chain, was Broken (Galatians 4)

In the previous chapter we argued that in Gal 3:19-4:11 Paul pictured Jews as well as Gentiles as slaves to the angelic powers, there called elemental spirits of the universe. His myth of the angelic rulers apparently depicted them as controlling the law, both political and religious. Thereby they oppressed the people under them, treating them as slaves. Though the law (whether Jewish or

Gentile) is not evil in itself, it is the chain that the angelic rulers use to form a chain gang of all those under them. Thus Paul's military gospel proclaims that God sent Christ into that slavery (Gal 4:4), taking the chain on himself, then breaking it and thereby freeing all the slaves who would follow him to freedom.

Though the Mosaic Law is a good thing (Rom 7:12), Paul seems to suggest that it had become a chain around the necks of his people. Perhaps that had happened because they had put it in the place of God, as the Gentiles did with their ruling (thus law-enforcing) angels. Dunn emphasizes this interpretation:

> Paul's argument is to the effect that Israel's overevaluation of the law had interposed the law between God and Israel and, far from distinguishing Israel from the other nations, had simply made Israel like the other nations, as being under a heavenly power.[15]

Therefore when Christ broke the hold of the law, that ended the tyranny of the heavenly powers because it disarmed them, taking away the weapon they used.

Paul seems to suggest in Gal 3:19-4:11 that it was essentially the coming of Christ into the world that brought about the end of the powers' tyranny through the law. Before Christ came, they all, both Jews and Gentiles, "were imprisoned and guarded under the law...enslaved to the elemental spirits of the universe" (Gal 3:23; 4:3). As minors they were no better off than slaves as they awaited the coming of their adulthood (4:1-2). But when God decided the time was ripe, he sent Christ into their slavery, "born under the law, in order to redeem those who are under the law" (4:4-5). In Christ's coming the owner of the estate declared that the time of their slavery under the law was over, that they were henceforth the adult heirs of the estate. The chain was broken by Christ's coming, death and resurrection, so the tyrants who used it were deposed forever.

Thus when believers were freed from the law, they were at the same time freed from the hold of the powers: "Formerly" they were "enslaved to

---

[15] Dunn, "Echoes of Intra-Jewish Polemic in Paul's Letter to the Galatians," 473. See also Duncan, *Galatians*, 134-136.

beings that by nature are not gods" (4:8), but now they are free. Of course in their freedom they still could return to the darkness, i.e. they could choose to "turn back to the weak and beggarly elemental spirits" (4:8–9), by "observing special days and months and seasons and years" (4:9–10). Clearly, for Paul, those who had been transferred (Gal 1:4) into Christ's new kingdom were freed from the rule of all angelic powers, and so would be foolish to return to the chain gang from which they had been rescued.

### D. SIN THE DEMON CONQUERED

> We know that our old self was crucified with him so the body of Sin might be destroyed, and we might be no longer enslaved to Sin. For whoever has died is freed from Sin. (Rom 6:6–7)
> God...sending his own Son in the likeness of Sin-dominated flesh, in order to oppose Sin...conquered Sin in the flesh. (Rom 8:3)

In chapter IV we showed that Paul, when thinking in military terms, pictured Sin as a demon, an agent of Satan, the opposite of God's Holy Spirit in believers. By personifying and mythologizing Sin he presented a powerful symbol that expressed his insight into the overwhelming power of human sinfulness, a state from which humans cannot free themselves. From the darkness of enemy headquarters Satan's demonic subordinate Sin sets out to infiltrate the heart and will of every person on earth. Beginning with Adam and Eve, it uses the law as its camouflage, its secret way of approach to the human will. Through the law it attacks where humans are weakest, in their passions and desires. By deception Sin persuades every person to open the gate into their inner castle and allow it to come in. Then, like a saboteur destroying defenses secretly from within the castle, Sin works insidiously, taking control and overcoming the defenses against evil. Quickly the person becomes enslaved to Sin, completely unable to break free, indeed at times forced to do evil even when wanting to do good. The result is that the whole human race, all who are born in Adam (Christ excepted), are chained together as slaves by the unifying evil spirit Sin. Together they form the army of the children of darkness, Satan's enslaved infantry, the Body of Sin.[16]

In this section we will present Paul's story of the divine conquest of the demon Sin which Paul points to in Romans 6–8. **(1) God in Christ Conquered Sin (Rom 8:3)**, for Christ's Sin-free life and obedient death overcame the power of Sin. **(2) Christ Died To Sin (Rom 6:10)**, which freed him forever from the realm in which Sin rules. By his resurrection he was elevated above the Sin-enslaved world of darkness, thereby enabling God to create the new Sin-excluded Kingdom of Light into which believers can enter. By faith and baptism **(3) We Died to Sin (Rom 6:2)** when we were crucified with Christ (Rom 6:6) and now **The Spirit Frees Believers from Sin (Rom 8:2)**. When they enter his Kingdom of Light, the Spirit takes the place in them that Sin took when they were still children of darkness. Thus **(4) The Body of Sin was Defeated (Rom 6:6)**, for in the Kingdom of Light the whole Adamic body possessed by Sin has been split in two with believers now freed from Sin. Of course the final destruction awaits the End.

### (1) God in Christ Conquered Sin (Rom 8:3)

The strongest Pauline suggestion of the importance of Christ's Sin-free life for God's victory over Sin comes in Rom 8:3 in which he says: "God...sending his own Son in the likeness of Sin-dominated flesh [*sarkos hamartias*] flesh, and to deal with [*peri*] Sin, conquered [*katakrine*] Sin in the flesh." We will now justify this translation and interpretation of the key images. Of course the solid foundation for this approach comes in our argument that Paul imagined Sin as a demon (in Romans 5–8), which we gave in detail in the previous chapter.

### (a) Entering the Battlefield: Likeness of Sin-Oppressed Flesh

The qualification "likeness of" presumably means this: Christ was "in

---

[16] Clearly this is only one symbolic depiction of the human problem, complementary to his other symbols of humans as guilty transgressors (judicial), as alienated children (personal), and as members of a wild and fruitless tree (organic). The value of the demon Sin as a symbol is that it expresses the tyranny of evil, the experience of humans unable to change themselves by their own wills because they are locked in the great system of evil that pervades the whole of humankind.

the flesh" in the sense of being a full human being living in this world, this age, but did not experience the "Sin-oppressed" life that is characteristic of all other human beings. Nygren expresses this common interpretation when he writes: "He (Christ) shared all our conditions. He was under the same powers of destruction. Out of 'the flesh' arose for Him the same temptations as for us. But in all this He was master of sin."[17]

We translate *hamartias* as Sin-dominated, Sin-oppressed, Sin-occupied, because of the previous context. The whole of Romans 6–7 emphasized the imagery of Sin as an active agent that possesses unbelievers and thereby oppresses them, indeed kills them. "Sin-dominated flesh" does not mean that the material body, rather than the human inner person, is the place where Sin has its slavery. Clearly for Paul Sin rules in the inner person, for knowledge of the law and the inner, spiritual sin of coveting are both stressed in Romans 7. Thus in 8:3, "Sin-possessed flesh" refers to the whole human condition of living under the tyranny of the enemy hierarchy. By this symbolism Paul emphasizes that sinners have lost their freedom, and so are prisoners (of war), slaves, who can only be freed when the enemy who has conquered them is itself conquered.

For Paul it was important that Christ was born into ordinary human life, for that was where the battle took place. That significance of Christ's coming in the flesh is brought out by Leivestad when he says: "The flesh is the territory that is to be liberated from the occupation of sin. The incarnation of Christ means an invasion on territory occupied by the enemy."[18] He stresses that the defeat of Sin must be in "the" flesh, not in "his" flesh,

> because the flesh of Jesus is representative of all flesh. If sin
> is conquered in the flesh of Jesus it implies that the dominion
> of sin over flesh is broken. From that moment it is no longer
> sin that is master, but Christ. (118)

Thus in his battle myth Paul pictured Christ entering the realm of the flesh, the realm of darkness, by his incarnation. Only by coming onto the battlefield itself could Christ confront and then conquer the enemy army. While on the battlefield, Christ suffered the life-long attack of Sin, being tempted as

---

[17] *Romans*, 315.
[18] *Christ the Conqueror*, 118.

all human beings are. Sin's rule, however, requires human acquiescence (Rom 6:12), and Christ refused to give his. Thus, against him the attack was unsuccessful, in contrast to its success with all other humans. That point is made explicit when Paul writes: "For our sake God made him who knew no sin [*ton me gnonta hamartian*] to be sin, so that in him we might become the righteousness of God" (2 Cor 5:21). The implication is that Christ's freedom from slavery to Sin was essential to his ability to rescue others from it. He alone could march onto this battlefield and fight successfully; so he alone could rescue others who had always before been killed by this deadly enemy Sin (Rom 7:9).[19]

### (b) Sin Conquered

We translate *katekrine* in Rom 8:3 as "conquered," evoking the picture of the divine warrior coming into battle and overwhelming the enemy army (e.g. Isa 63:1-6). The alternative translation "condemned" is unlikely because here Paul was apparently thinking of Sin as the demon sent out by Satan to tyrannize the whole world. Therefore, ending its hold means conquering it, in order that people will be "set free" from it (Rom 8:2). A few verses earlier Paul emphasized this victim-of-oppression imagery, for he had cried out as a man oppressed, "O wretched man that I am, who will rescue [*hrusetai*] me...?" (Rom 7:24). Therefore, when the victory comes it must be a rescue, which requires the defeat of the tyrant, as God defeated the Seleucids in his most recent physical victory over a tyrant.

Murray in *Romans* adds two more arguments for seeing Paul as speaking here of Sin as conquered. The first is that *katakrino* "is used in the New Testament in the sense of consigning to destruction as well as of pronouncing the sentence of condemnation (*cf.* I Cor. 11:32; II Pet. 2:6)."[20] For example, 2 Pet 2:6 says: "by turning Sodom and Gomorrah to ashes he (God) condemned [*katekrinen*] them." Here the verb clearly refers not to simply a declaration, but to the action in which the tyrant is destroyed. Secondly Murray notes that law could condemn Sin, i.e. declare Sin's sinfulness, just as well as God could, but Paul expressly states that law could not do the job that

---

[19] What exactly Paul was imagining when he said that God "made him to be sin" is not at all clear.

[20] Murray, *Romans v. 1*, 278.

was needed to rescue people from Sin (Rom 8:3). Therefore, Murray concludes, what God does here goes beyond the declarative activity of condemning to embrace the victorious activity: "God executed this judgment and overthrew the power of sin" (278). Just as the Ancient of Days burned up the Fourth Beast (Dan 7:11), so God in Christ burned Sin out of the lives of believers.

Thus in Rom 8:3 Paul was imagining Sin as an oppressive power which coerces people against their wills, as he had described it in chapter 7. Therefore, God's action in Christ was much more than simply a declaration of the evil of Sin, but was a victory over it. Though the odds seemed all against him, and his weapons seemed puny, Christ defeated Sin just as the faithful David defeated Goliath and the rag-tag band of Maccabees defeated the Seleucid empire. DeBoer is thus accurate in his description of the heart of Paul's battle myth when he says: "(Christ's) death marks God's triumphant invasion of the world under the power of sin to liberate human beings…from its destructive and death-dealing power."[21]

### (2) Escape From Sin's Kingdom: He Died To Sin (Rom 6:10)

Paul's picture of how Christ, and following him Christians, are freed from the tyranny of the demon Sin is suggested in this passage:

> Our old man was crucified with him, in order to destroy the body of Sin [our corporate, Sin-dominated, life in the Army of Darkness], so we might be no longer enslaved to Sin. For the one who has died is freed from Sin….The death he (Christ) died he died to Sin [*te hamartia apethanen*], once for all. (Rom 6:6–7, 10)

Paul's symbolic story of Christ's death here seems to be that by his faithful death he escaped Sin's realm, the Kingdom of Darkness, forever. Then, as we will show below, that enabled all who enter his Kingdom of Light with him to enjoy the same freedom.

Saying he "died to Sin" is parallel to saying he "died to the elemental

---

[21] *The Defeat of Death*, 156. See also Beker, who writes: "The death of Christ addresses itself to sin as a cosmic power and slavemaster, that is to the human condition 'under the power of sin'" (*Triumph*, 191).

spirits" (Col 2:20): both imply that in his death he escaped from this world of darkness where Sin and the angelic powers reign. The basic imagery seems to be that in this age, living in the flesh, Christ was subject to the physical oppression of the Kingdom of Darkness, which included the temptation of Sin. When he died (and was raised), however, he departed from this age, this world, this Kingdom of Darkness. Therefore, the forces of darkness had no more power over him, just as the Egyptians had no more power over the Israelites once they escaped from the Kingdom of Egyptian Darkness (by the symbolic death of passing "through the Red Sea" as Paul suggests in 1 Cor 10:1-2).

Before Christ, when people died and escaped from this temporal world of darkness, they entered the eternal world of darkness. In Christ's case, however, God rescued him by raising him from the dead (Rom 6:4). Paul pictures this as God transporting him into the Kingdom of Light which God created through him, and over which Christ rules. In that kingdom (probably pictured as heavenly light shining on earth) Christ is forever free from Sin's knocking at the gate of his heart, for the Kingdom of Light is totally Sin-free. Here is the spiritualized fulfillment of Ezekiel's visionary hope for the new Jerusalem, the new Temple where the Lord will rule forever in purity (Ezekiel 40-48).

The "once for all" (Rom 6:10) quality of Christ's death suggests that in Paul's myth his death to Sin was not his alone. Somehow it was also a representative action, one incorporating all others who will become members of his kingdom, for they "were crucified with him" (Rom 6:6). Like the champion going into battle for all his people, e.g. David fighting as the representative of Israel against Goliath, so Christ entered the battle in the world of the flesh. He was the champion sent by God to conquer the forces of evil on behalf of all humankind. In his Sin-free life and death, Sin was conquered, and in his resurrection the new realm of Sin-free light opened up for all who join him in dying to Sin. The "once" is the creation of the new Kingdom of Light; but it is "for all" because now all who believe in Christ can die with him (as we will now show) and so enter the new sin-free kingdom.

## (3) Rescue for Believers: We Died to Sin (Rom 6:2)

As Christ died to Sin, once for all, thereby escaping from the Kingdom of Darkness in which Sin ruled, so this same divine rescue has been given to all believers, all those baptized into Christ: "we died [*apethanomen*] to Sin...whosoever was baptized into Christ Jesus was baptized into his death...our old man was crucified with him" (Rom 6:2–3, 6). Just as Christ by death defeated Sin by escaping from the realm of Sin's rule, so also all believers are rescued spiritually from the realm of Sin's rule when they too in Christ die to Sin. What happened to Christ happened to them, for they are united in Christ, so they are co-crucified with him. As Murray suggests: "If we view sin as a realm or sphere then the believer no longer lives in that realm or sphere...The believer died to sin once and he has been translated to another realm"[22] The realm of Sin's rule is the Kingdom of Darkness, while the new, Sin-free realm is Christ's Kingdom of Light into which believers are transported when they die to Sin. The means of that death seems to be that in baptism they identify themselves with Christ and his crucifixion, so his death becomes theirs too: "one has died for all, therefore all have died" (2 Cor 5:14). Just as Christ fought Sin and died, so also believers take up arms against Sin and "die" to it.

Paul's general principle here is that "anyone who has died is freed [*dedikaiotai*] from (the slavery imposed by) Sin" (Rom 6:7). As we noted above when speaking of Christ dying to Sin, Paul's basic image seems to be that when people die they escape from this present age of darkness in which Sin rules. That, of course, applies to physical death, but he uses the same principle as one that makes sense of spiritual death, when people die with Christ. That death rescues them from the prisoner-of-war camp which is the Kingdom of Darkness and transports them into the Kingdom of Light, where Sin no longer enslaves them.[23]

As further amplification of Paul's symbolic picture of Christ's death to Sin effectively conquering Sin for believers, he says: "The rule [*ho nomos*] of the Spirit of life in Christ Jesus has set me free from the [oppressive] rule [*tou nomou*] of Sin and Death" (Rom 8:2). We take Paul to mean this: the Spirit is present due to Christ's death and resurrection victory; thereby believers receive new life when they enter Christ's Kingdom of Light; the Spirit of life in them drives out, and takes the place of, Sin as the ruling power within them. The

---

[22] *Romans*, 213.

[23] We translate the verb *dedikaiotai*, which elsewhere often has the judicial sense "acquitted," as "freed," as do the NRSV and Barrett, *Romans*, 125.

result is that Sin cannot coercively re-enter the lives of believers, forcing its way back in to where it had previously ruled, so they are free from its oppressive power. Thus the Spirit conquers Sin, driving it out and building a fortress wall that Sin cannot break through.

## (4) The Army (Body) of Sin Defeated (Rom 6:6)

> We know that our old man was crucified with him so that [*hina*] the body of Sin [*to soma tes hamartias*] might be defeated [*katargethe*], and we might no longer be enslaved to Sin. For whoever has died is freed from Sin. (Rom 6:6–7)

The divine defeat of the Seleucid Empire, freeing Judea from its oppression, provides an apt symbol for Paul's story: "the body of Sin," a corporate entity also called "our old man," is the Seleucid Empire of the whole human race, and in Christ God defeated it.

We hypothesize that Paul had in mind the way a victorious army (or champion) defeats the enemy's "armed body" and drives it out of the homeland it had invaded. The divine champion's ultimate purpose is to follow up the victory and destroy the enemy army completely so it will never harm a single other person. In the short run, however, some people still remain under the old tyranny. The support for this corporate military interpretation is as follows:

"Our old man" (*ho palaios hemon anthropos*) is singular, and thus on its face refers to a single reality that belongs to many. Earlier when Paul referred to "one man" (*henos anthropou*) through whom Sin entered (Rom 5:12), he was referring to Adam. Therefore it is plausible that this "old man" in 6:6 is also a reference to Adam, but this time in his corporate role because he is "ours." Probably therefore Paul was thinking of the corporate life "in Adam," the united human race/family/body of Adam. This is the whole corporate life of humankind, inherited from Adam and now lived imprisoned under the slavery of Sin, which forces the prisoners to fight in its army.

As we have already suggested (section 2 above), "the old man...crucified with Christ" is another way Paul speaks of believers having died with Christ, being baptized into his death, i.e. sharing his death to Sin. However, this crucifixion of the old man happened "once for all," presumably because Christ took upon himself the whole body of Adam (becoming "the last

Adam," 1 Cor 15:45), and so his crucifixion was its crucifixion also.

When Paul uses a singular phrase, such as "the body of Sin," we should take the singularity seriously as referring to a single reality, unless that reading turns out to be impossible. By his phrase he presumably meant a single, corporate, reality. "Body" suggests a corporate human entity, parallel to the way Paul uses "body of Christ" to symbolize a corporate human reality (Rom 12:5). "Of Sin" suggests that this corporate reality is ruled by Sin, i.e. animated by, characterized by, Sin, parallel to the way that the body of Christ is ruled by Christ in the Spirit. In this same passage Paul speaks of humans as enslaved to Sin, so by his phrase "the body of Sin" he is suggesting that humankind as a whole is united in slavery, as the Judaeans were under the Seleucids. Further, since this body was "defeated," he was probably imagining it as an army. Thus Paul's "body of Sin" is humankind (before Christ's coming) seen as a unified, Sin-enthralled, army—the Army of the children of darkness. This is the inner, humanity-wide, tyranny within the cosmos-wide Kingdom of Darkness.[24]

The body of Sin is something that Paul pictures as defeated, rendered powerless, at least as far as believers are concerned, for in them the freedom from Sin has arrived. The verb *katargeo*, usually meaning "to defeat" or "to destroy," suggests a military image. Normally such defeats have an army as their object, and that is probably the case here in Paul's imagery. The enemy army is overpowered, rendered ineffective, stopped from exercising its tyranny.[25]

From Paul's other statements we can be sure that he did not think that the body of Sin was "destroyed," i.e. so thoroughly defeated that it can never again harm anyone. Rather, this defeat (like the defeat of the Seleucids in 164 BC) is effective at first only for a chosen group. Therefore when Paul speaks of the body of Sin (the tyranny of darkness chaining together the whole human

---

[24] Many commentators take the phrase "the body of Sin" to refer to the individual human physical body, e.g. Murray (*Romans*, 220), Leenhardt (*Romans*, 162) and Sanday and Headlam (*Romans*, 158–159). Many others give a corporate interpretation, e.g. Barrett (*Romans* 125), Ridderbos (*Paul*, 63) and Whiteley (*Theology*, 42). The prima facie corporate meaning is far more plausible as long as it makes good sense, which it does.

[25] See 1 Cor 2:6, 15:26 and 2 Thess 2:8 for Paul's other military uses of *katargeo*.

race) as "defeated" he means that has happened *as far as believers are concerned*. Within the Kingdom of Light the old tyranny of Sin is ended forever. As far as those inside the Fortress of Light are concerned, they no longer experience life inside the body of Sin. Those on the outside, however, still live in the darkness, still live in the slavery of Sin. Therefore the body of Sin still exists for a while, though its final doom has been foreshadowed. The Seleucid tyranny has been ended in Judea and Jerusalem, but it continues in the outer provinces. Thus the translation "defeated" catches that dual result, as the Seleucids were defeated and driven away from Jerusalem.

### Summary of Paul's Defeat of Sin Myth

We can present Paul's myth of Christ's victory over Sin and its army as a story that he hints at in various passages:

Christ entered the world of darkness as God's champion (Phil 2:6–7), bearing the divine light within him as his supreme weapon (2 Cor 6:14–15). Outwardly he wore the armor of light which is faithful obedience to God (Rom 13:12). He was a human like all other humans in that he had passions and desires, and so was vulnerable as they all are (Rom 8:3) underneath his armor of light. Because he was fully human, Sin, the demonic spirit enslaving everyone else in the Kingdom of Darkness (Rom 6:17), attacked him constantly. Using the law under which Christ was born (Gal 4:4) Sin attacked through his normal human passions (cf. Rom 7:5), tempting him to give in to his natural desires—for long life, security, comfort, pleasure.

Unlike all other humans before and since, he refused the temptation, fighting back instead of surrendering (2 Cor 5:21). By constantly warding off the fiery darts of Sin, letting them hit his armor of light (cf. Eph 6:16), Christ won his earthly battle against Sin. He was a soldier standing alone on the battlement of his personal fortress, with an army of thousands set to smash through the gates. From below, their general urged him to surrender, to open the gate, or else they would kill him. Standing firm, he refused to surrender, preferring a faithful death to a faithless life (Phil 2:8). So the Army of Darkness, animated by Sin, stormed the castle and killed him (1 Cor 2:6–8).

His death, however, was his final victory, for his greatest temptation had been to hang on to life. When he refused that temptation of Sin, and so was killed, the battle was finally over. He had won, for he had never given in. He had permanently escaped the Kingdom of Darkness, died to Sin (Rom 6:10), so Sin could no longer even tempt him.

That victory, however, was not his alone, for he was the last Adam, one who took upon himself the whole human race: his victory was the race's victory. By gaining the world's first permanent victory over Sin he defeated and drove back the Army of Darkness. Through his resurrection God created a Sin-free zone on earth, a beachhead of light pushing back the Kingdom of Darkness (Col 1:13). Into that new Kingdom of Light any human can enter by God's gift (Gal 1:4). The Adamic mass possessed by Sin has been split in two, with one group transformed into the Christic community energized by the Spirit. Now the Spirit takes the place of Sin as the spiritual animating power in the children of light (Rom 8:3; 1 Thess 5:5), who are spiritually safe within the Fortress of Light.

Outside the fortress, in the diminishing Kingdom of Darkness, the body of Sin is still alive, though retreating and fighting a rearguard battle. All the children of darkness are still chained together in the Sin-possessed body of Adam. In the end, however, that body of Sin will be annihilated when the last enemy Death is finally destroyed (1 Cor 15:26, 54–56).

Of course though believers have spiritually died with Christ and so entered the Kingdom of Light, they are still physically alive in the Kingdom of Darkness. Though Sin no longer oppresses them, it does tempt them, for they are free to open the door to Sin again if they choose. Thus the threat of Sin regaining its tyranny remains, so Paul emphasizes that it would be crazy to allow Sin back in (Rom 6:2). It would be as foolish to live in Sin now that we are freed, as it would be to go back and live in the darkness of an underground prison cell once we have been rescued and brought out into the freedom of the light.

## E. GOD (Partially) DEFEATED DEATH

Christ being raised from the dead will never die again; Death no longer has dominion over him. (Rom 6:9)

As we showed in the previous chapter, Paul pictured Death as a cosmic tyrant, a demonic spirit that follows wherever Sin goes, taking over as the ruling agent in all the newly conquered territory. Once inside the human castle, Death went its own way, spreading out to enslave every human being (Rom 5:12; 1 Cor 15:22). Then it spread to every biological creature, producing nature's bondage to decay (Rom 8:21). The result is that in this world, this Kingdom of Darkness, Death is King, reigning (Rom 5:14, 17) over all living creatures. Sin and Death are not independent outlaws, but the demonic agents of Satan, the Prince of Darkness, his spirits sent out to test, then punish (Rom 3:9; 1 Cor 5:5), and finally oppress humankind.

Christ's defeat of Sin included the partial defeat of Death, for Sin reigned in, with and through Death (Rom 5:21). In Paul's military gospel, Christ's death and resurrection was the way God created the new Kingdom of Light (in the midst of this Kingdom of Darkness), into which neither Sin nor Death can enter: just as Sin no longer can enslave believers, so also Death no longer has an eternal hold on them. However, as the children of light carry on their lives in the flesh as continuing participants in this present age, they remain subject to the power of temporal, physical Death, just as Christ himself was. Still, even when they die they remain in Christ, for the new realm of the dead in Christ is an extension of the Kingdom of Light into the world of the dead.

## (1) Victory Through Christ's Death

Death, in Paul's military symbolism, where it is one of the great enemies, oppressed all humankind from the beginning until the death and resurrection of Christ. In that event God conquered Death. Paul's myth of how God defeated Death seems thus to have the following steps:

(a) Christ was innocent, Sin-free, but as a son of Adam he was subject to death, like every other person in Adam (1 Cor 15:22). Because Death spread to all those in Adam, it reigned over Christ also, even though in him it did not come through the reign of Sin. Christ, as a man of the flesh, as a part of Adam's body, inherited mortality naturally, for "in Adam all die" (1 Cor 15:22). Paul sees voluntary identification with mortal humanity as the fullness of Christ's sacrifice, for he humbled himself even to the point of death on the cross (Phil 2:8). He *volunteered* to enter the battlefield where Death reigned supreme, in order to become one with all those in Adam (Phil 2:5–8).

(b) When the innocent Christ was killed it was an act of oppression, not an expression of God's just wrath against him. Death's assault on Christ was injustice, evil, an aggressive attack of the Evil One.

(c) Because Christ volunteered for death, taking upon himself the condition that was due punishment for all other humans, therefore God liberated him from the oppression and highly exalted him through the resurrection (Phil 2:9).

(d) In and through Christ's resurrection Death was completely and finally defeated *as far as Christ personally is concerned*, for he arose to eternal life, so Death can never rule over him again (Rom 6:9). This most interesting text reads: "We know that Christ being raised from the dead, will never die again; death no longer has dominion [*kurieuei*] over him" (Rom 6:9). While that "no longer" seems like mere common sense, it is not. In the world of mystery religions, whose dying and rising gods continually died and rose again, this finality needs to be stated. As Murray says in commenting on this text: "The resurrection from the dead is the guarantee that he vanquished the power of death and this victory over death is an irrevocable finality."[26]

(e) Further, by his resurrection and exaltation (Phil 2:9–11) Christ became the ruler of the new Kingdom of Light (Col 1:13), the fortified beachhead into which Death cannot enter, for light keeps out all darkness.

(f) Since Christ died for all humankind, it is possible for any human being to die and be buried with Christ by faith and baptism (Rom 6:3–4), thereby also rising with him to newness of life (Rom 6:4; Col 2:12). This union with Christ, which Paul elsewhere calls being crucified with Christ (Rom 6:6; Gal 2:20), is the most mysterious of the elements in the story. In military terms it suggests that Christ is the champion who has gone ahead and conquered the champion of the enemy, so now all his followers can then enjoy the benefits of his victory. As David beat Goliath and the Israelites enjoyed the fruits of his victory with him, so also Christ defeated Sin and Death and his followers join him in the victory.

(g) Thus any human beings who join Christ enter the Kingdom of Light and receive the benefit found there—the Spirit which gives freedom from Sin and from Death's eternal threat (Rom 8:3). DeBoer explains the benefit this way: "Insofar as a person is 'in Christ,' viz., in the realm of his Lordship and thus conformed to Christ's death to sin, he or she shares in Christ's victory over

---

[26] *Romans*, 223.

the power of sin and *therefore also over the power of death.*[27] We take him to mean that Death no longer is the ultimate threat for those in Christ's Kingdom of Light.

(h) When Sin was defeated, Death lost its "sting" (1 Cor 15:56). By that Paul probably meant its power to bring eternal death (Rom 6:23). Those who have been rescued from Sin's slavery have been given God's promise of eternal life through the Spirit (Rom 8:11).

(i) Eternal life is still only a promise, not a present reality, for those still on earth. The earthly members of the Kingdom of Light remain with one foot in the old Kingdom of Darkness, where they are subject to the physical power of Death (Rom 8:10; 2 Cor 4:10-11). Thus only at the End will Death be finally and completely defeated, when they are raised up in Christ (1 Cor 15:22, 26).[28]

## (2) Transformation of the Realm of the Dead?

We argued in the previous chapter that Paul probably adopted the traditional Hebraic picture: before Christ's victory over Death all human beings when they died descended into the realm of the dead, Sheol, the Underworld. There they were ruled by Death, which is one of the spirits of Satan, and were unable to escape from its slavery. Possibly, because some of his contemporaries did so, Paul may have pictured a division in the Underworld so that faithful Israelites and righteous Gentiles were separated from all evil-doers. However, it is unlikely that Paul believed in rewards and punishments beginning immediately after death, for he spoke of them beginning on the Day of Wrath

---

[27] *The Defeat of Death*, 185.

[28] Thus we disagree with Beker who sees "an inconsistency that cannot be ignored" (*Triumph*, 232) in Paul's picture of the defeat of death. He asks: "if sin, which is 'the sting of death' (1 Cor 15:56) has been removed, how can death still be 'the last enemy?'" (229) Our view is that Sin has only been removed from the believer's new armed camp inside the fortress, the Kingdom of Light; Sin, however, still reigns outside in the Kingdom of Darkness, into which believers must still venture in their daily lives and in their battle against the Darkness. Thus outside the fortress, where Sin rules, Death remains. It is the last enemy because believers are still subject to physical death as long as they are still in this age. However, they need not fear this enemy (Rom 8:38) because it can no longer usher them into eternal death.

(Rom 2:5), which is the End of the Age.

Though Paul never specifically refers to the effect of Christ's resurrection on the realm of the dead, we can make some plausible inferences from various hints that he offers. Our conclusion is that Paul did believe that Christ's resurrection had changed the realm of the dead: henceforth all those who are "dead in Christ," i.e. the dead members of Christ's body, are separated from the rest of the dead, protected from the threat of eternal Death. The best image from his time that suggests this kind of division is the traditional Greek and Roman division of Hades' realm into Tartarus, the place for evil people, and the Elysian Fields, where the good are rewarded. Paul did not adopt most of the details of that mythical picture, except that the division into two realms of the dead probably reflects his picture.

Paul's hints that the realm of the dead has been changed forever by Christ's resurrection are found in the following passages:

When he says that Christ being raised from the dead, Death no longer has any hold over him (Rom 6:9), it is clear that the omnipotent power of Death/Satan in the Underworld has been broken. For the first time, one of the dead, one of the slaves in Death's concentration camp, has been rescued. Therefore the hold of Death over the rest has been threatened. Those who are in Christ (though dead) share in this new freedom from the tyranny of Death, for they are no longer heading towards eternal death.

Secondly, Paul proclaims that even though believers die physically, no longer can Death separate them from the love of Christ (Rom 8:35–37). Thus the picture of believers inside the fortress Kingdom of Light probably informs Paul's picture of their condition after death: they remain in Christ's protection, even in the Underworld. Probably Paul when a Pharisee assumed the old Hebrew imagery of Death separating people from God, so Romans 8 suggests that he believed something new came with Christ's resurrection. Now dead believers are protected by the love of Christ in some way. Christ's kingly power still surrounds them, perhaps because the Kingdom of Light extends into the Underworld.

Thirdly, Paul says that at the Parousia "the dead in Christ" shall rise first (1 Thess 4:16). Certainly that phrase refers to dead believers, but it is likely that it means more than simply that identification. For Paul life in Christ probably always suggests the corporate, communal life in the body of Christ, for "we are one body in Christ" (Rom 12:5). This is an organic image that illuminates the same reality Paul points to in the military image of the fortress Kingdom of Light over which Christ rules. Therefore, "the dead in Christ" probably are those who have died who still remain members of the body of Christ, still remain inside his Kingdom of Light. Though they have died and descended to the realm of the dead, they are still united with Christ, are still integral members of Christ's body and kingdom and so protected by him. Thus Paul's picture seems to be that believers when they die remain in the realm in which Christ is Lord, where Christ's love is still operative and powerful. Thus we are probably not far from his image if we believe that the dead in Christ are still in the Kingdom of Light, though now in the Underworld portion of that kingdom.

Many scholars believe that Paul spoke elsewhere of this state of dead believers, in Philippians 1 and 2 Corinthians 5.[29] In the former Paul says "my desire is to depart and be with Christ for that is far better" than his present state as a prisoner fearing execution (Phil 1:23). The vagueness of "be with Christ" does not allow us to decide what his picture was here: he could have been imagining a conscious experience of communion in a paradisal setting; equally well he could have been imagining an unconscious protection (among the safe "dead in Christ") which provides an escape from the persecution of the present. Since this passage is vague, we must depend on what Paul says elsewhere and nowhere does he specifically speak of dead believers as already enjoying eternal life with Christ. Instead, they are "asleep," indeed "dead in Christ," so their hope is that they will be raised (from the Underworld) first when Christ returns (1 Thess 4:14-16).

A second passage that is (we believe mistakenly) used to uncover Paul's view of the present state of dead believers is 2 Cor 5:1-10. There Paul says, "if the earthly tent we live in is destroyed, we have a building from God, a house not made with hands, eternal in the heavens" (5:1). One traditional interpretation is that the tent symbolizes individual human physical bodies and that the building symbolizes individual spiritual bodies that believers receive immediately upon death. That interpretation is quite unlikely: such an image of a person (spirit)

---

[29] E.g. Shires argues that these passages show that "Paul was convinced of an immediate resurrection at death" (*Eschatology*, 90).

living in a tent (body) would be Platonic, not Hebraic, so Paul probably did not imagine the individual body as an external covering that could be removed. Secondly, this tent is communal, for "we" the Christian community have a single tent. Therefore it is more likely that the tent symbolizes something of the experience of believers entering into and so belonging to the Christian community. In this age the community is temporary and vulnerable (like the tabernacle, where God occasionally appeared). In eternity, however, the Christian community will become permanent, a temple (like the Jerusalem temple) where God is forever present.[30]

The chief evidence for our view that Paul saw dead believers as still unconscious in Sheol, not in conscious, joyous communion with Christ, is his consolation to the Thessalonians who were apparently concerned that their dead brothers and sisters had missed eternal life. If Paul had believed that dead believers immediately entered into eternal life, and so already were in conscious communion with Christ, then he would have said that. His consolation would have been just like those offered by millions of pastors beside Christians' graves. Instead Paul consoles by something far less (psychologically speaking), saying that the dead will rise first, before the living are united with Christ (1 Thess 4:15–17). That suggests that the dead are not yet in conscious communion with Christ.

Further, Paul's emphasis on the last day as the time when rewards and punishments arrive (Rom 2:5) makes it likely that he did not picture believers as already entering into the reward of conscious communion with Christ. Further, this apocalyptic image of the Last Day in Romans (one of his last letters) flies in the face of the theory that his views changed, that in the Thessalonian letters he saw the Last Day as decisive but in later letters saw the death of the individual as the decisive event. That last day emphasis stands out in 1 Corinthians 15 also, for he suggests that only at the end will the dead in Christ be raised (1 Cor 15:22) and Death finally defeated, as we will show in

---

[30] We have presented a detailed argument for this communal meaning of 2 Cor 5:1–10 in: "St. Paul's Collage of Metaphors in II Cor 5:1–10: Ornamental or Exploratory?" We also show that "away from the body and at home with the Lord" is probably meant existentially, meaning "no longer centered on this world (the body of Adam), but now making our home, our center of commitment, in Christ."

chapter VII below.

Our conclusion is that Paul pictured Christ's resurrection as a victory over Death in its role as the ruler of the Underworld. By God's power, the resurrection had a decisive effect, changing the realm of the dead. Prior to Christ's death and resurrection all the dead were gathered together in the Underworld under the tyranny of Death. By entering the Underworld, Christ, through God's power of resurrection, defeated Death, ending not only its threat over living believers but also its eternal hold on dead ones. By bringing the light of God into that gloomy realm Christ drove back the darkness. We can aptly take Paul as picturing the heavenly Kingdom of Light, which believers experience on earth, as beginning in the Underworld where it holds back the power of Death, Satan's spirit. Thus for Paul, dead believers, though in the Underworld, remain in Christ's Kingdom, remain members of his body, remain under the protection of Christ whose love still surrounds them.

## Conclusion

According to Paul's battle myth, God, through Christ's death and resurrection, defeated the angelic powers and Sin and Death and created the new Kingdom of Light, the fortress into which believers may enter and be spiritually secure.

Paul's image of the new Kingdom of Light spiritualizes the old prophesied picture of Jerusalem as God's City of Light set on a hill (Isa 2:2-4), impregnable to all the forces of evil because God is the wall of fire protecting her (Zech 2:5). That prophecy had been partially fulfilled in the Maccabees' victories. Paul knew well that story of the way that God through the Maccabees freed Jerusalem from the Seleucid oppressors. That enabled them to clean out all the idolatry, rebuild the fortifications, and light all the lamps again, so God was present within Jerusalem as the Lord. In Christ, Paul imagined, God had done the same kind of thing, but this time on a cosmic, eternal, battlefield: the angelic forces lying behind the oppressor nations had been defeated, driven out of the new, spiritual, Holy City, so all those inside were free from spiritual oppression; the idolatry of the demon Sin had been cleansed from the Fortress of Light, so the faithful people within were no longer forced to sin; Death too was defeated, for God's Spirit of Life was the inner reality within all the children of light who dwell within.

One interesting aspect of Paul's myth of the initial victory of God in Christ is that he never explicitly mentions any defeat of Satan. However, since the principalities, Sin and Death were all Satan's subordinates, we can be certain that Paul pictured God's victory in Christ as a victory over Satan too. Henceforth the Prince of Darkness is hemmed in by the advancing Kingdom of Light, over which he has no power.

Of course, as the Maccabees in their free kingdom centered on Jerusalem were forced still to deal with the Seleucids, so also the children of light have to come out into the darkness in order to carry on the business of this world. None of the forces of darkness can enter the Kingdom of Light, for Christ's light keeps them out. However, the children of light do not simply remain in their safe haven, for their task is to bring the light out into the darkness. So outside the fortress they carry their attack, and out there they are physically vulnerable to the counter-attacks of the darkness. Therefore their life in this age is an Ongoing War, a continual battle against the darkness, to which we now turn.

# VI. THE ONGOING WAR

# BETWEEN THE TWO KINGDOMS

> Though we live in this world, we do not fight [*strateuometha*]
> by worldly means, for the weapons of our warfare [*ta hopla
> tes strateias*] are not worldly, but divinely powerful to destroy
> [*kathairesin*] fortresses [*ochuromaton*]. (2 Cor 10:3–4)

## Introduction

By his initial victory in Christ, God for all time rescued believers
spiritually from "this world," "this evil age," the Kingdom of Darkness over
which "the god of this world" rules. God rescued them by creating in the midst
of the darkness the Kingdom of Light over which Christ rules (Col 1:13) and in
which believers find safety (Gal 1:4), as in a fortress. Perhaps Paul imagined
the new kingdom as the heavenly Jerusalem come invisibly to earth (Gal 4:26),
a spiritual kingdom which provides protection from all spiritual and eternal
evils. However, believers still live in the flesh, that is they live their physical
lives still under the oppression of the Kingdom of Darkness. Paul imagined them
as having their home base in the beachhead of light which God created in Christ,
but living their daily lives outside that safe haven, as stars shining in, and so
overcoming, the darkness (Phil 2:15). Of course the forces of darkness are not

pleased with these enemies who continually destroy their darkness, so a battle
ensues. Arnold aptly summarizes this situation after Christ's initial victory:

> The church continues to live in this 'mopping up' period.
> Final victory is assured, but it is still a dangerous time, and
> there are many battles to be fought. Satan and his powers
> continue to attack the church, hold unbelieving humanity in
> bondage and promote every kind of evil throughout the world.
> Believers will continue to suffer the painful effects of the
> large-scale evil spurred on by the powers of darkness...But the
> powers can no longer take us captive, separate us from God
> and keep us in sin.[1]

Like the Maccabees, who created a beachhead of Free Judah around
Jerusalem and then fought to expand it to include the whole nation, so also the
children of light must advance from their fortress and fight continually until the
complete victory is won. Thus we will begin by briefly considering **The
Maccabean Model**, supposing that for Paul their story was well-known, the
most immediate source of imagery of an ongoing war against the forces of evil.

## The Maccabean Model

As the heavenly Jerusalem come invisibly to earth (Gal 4:26), the new
Kingdom of Light resembles the Maccabees' kingdom after their initial victory,
when Jerusalem was retaken and cleansed and Free Judah arose in the midst of
the Seleucid darkness. Then, to expand their free territory, they had to go out
and attack fortresses, conquering them and occupying them once they had driven
the forces of darkness away. That may well be the most useful background for
our understanding Paul's similar image of the children of light attacking and
conquering the fortresses of the enemy.

The story of the Maccabees' successful revolt against the Seleucid
empire emphasized God as the source of the army's power. Just before the first
decisive battle, the author of 1 Maccabees has Judas pray to God, the "Savior
of Israel, who crushed the mighty warrior by the hand of your servant David,"
and ask God to "hem in this army" and "strike them down" (1 Macc 4:30–33).

---

[1] Arnold, *Powers of Darkness*, 123.

This, of course was standard Hebrew theology, so it is not surprising that Paul adopted the same imagery, saying that believers fight with the power of God (2 Cor 10:4), with divinely given weapons (2 Cor 6:6–7).

When the Maccabees won the battle which gave Jerusalem back to them, they went into the city, cleansed the Temple, rebuilt the altar, renewed the sacrifices and re-lit the lights (1 Macc 4:34–50). Then, in order to make the city invulnerable to Seleucid attack, they rebuilt its defenses. This provides an apt model for our picturing Paul's Kingdom of Light (Col 1:13) in the midst of the darkness, for it provided similar protection from the forces of evil, so believers gathered in it (Gal 1:4).

In particular we find significant background in the stories of the Maccabees for understanding Paul's imagery of fortresses. First of all the author pictured the enemy Seleucids building their citadel in the middle of Jerusalem when they first conquered it: "Then they fortified the city of David with a great strong wall and strong towers, and it became their citadel…an ambush against the sanctuary, an evil adversary of Israel at all times" (1:33, 35). It is quite conceivable that this passage lies in the background when Paul writes of believers attacking the fortresses of the enemy (2 Cor 10:3–6).

How one attacks such fortresses is pictured numerous times in the Books of the Maccabees. For example Judas attacked the sons of Baean: "They were shut up by him in their towers; and he encamped against them, vowed their complete destruction, and burned with fire their towers and all who were in them" (1 Macc 5:5). Thus fire was one of the chief weapons used in siege warfare (see Eph 6:16 on the flaming arrows used in such fighting), but other weapons were common too. For example, Simon's attack on Gazara (142 BC) is described this way: "He made a siege engine, brought it up to the city, and battered and captured one tower. The men in the siege engine leaped out into the city, and a great tumult arose in the city" (1 Macc 13:43–44). Here we have an account that provides very useful background for Paul's imagery of believers conquering fortresses (2 Cor 10:3–6) and making them into part of the Kingdom of Light.

Since the Books of the Maccabees do not describe the siege engines used to batter down the walls of fortresses we need to look to later sources for a description of them. Paul presumably knew the Romans' equipment, so the following description of a Roman siege tower which broke down Jerusalem's walls in the AD 66–73 war perhaps hints at part of what Paul was imagining when he spoke of conquering fortresses:

> These mobile towers, the front and sides of which were protected by iron plates, contained three compartments. The bottom one was filled with men who pushed the tower forward along the leveled ground. The first floor [Americans call this the second] contained arrow-throwing catapults and fire appliances. The second [third] and top floors reached above the walls. In these were placed the slingers and archers. Their duty was to immobilize the defenders and prevent them from interfering with the working of the battering ram. This was a heavy, iron-tipped baulk of timber. Suspended from the sides of the tower, it swung backwards and forwards, pounding the wall.[2]

That is the equipment used in Paul's day to destroy fortresses, so it is likely that Paul had that kind of image in mind when he pictured himself and his fellow soldiers in action (2 Cor 10:3–6).

Our thesis in this section is that the similarities between Paul's battle myth and the history of the Maccabees' ongoing war from 164 to 142 BC are great enough to make plausible the view that Paul used the latter as his model. Both speak of God giving a great initial victory, through which God's own kingdom, which is marked by light, is set up centered in Jerusalem. Both depict the forces of darkness as still very threatening, so the war must go on and on. Both show God's people venturing forth from their safe fortress to carry the battle to the enemy, for there will be no peace until the darkness is burned completely away. Both speak of conquering fortresses into which the army of darkness has retreated. Both look forward to the day when God's victory will be complete and the whole nation will be free from oppression. Thus as we describe Paul's story of the ongoing war we will use this Maccabean background

---

[2] Furneaux, *The Roman Siege of Jerusalem*, 168–169. See Josephus, *The Jewish War*, 300–301 for the ancient, somewhat briefer, description of the same towers, which he says were 75 feet high.

wherever it can help provide useful details.[3]

Our task here is to show how Paul describes the ongoing war. We will begin with **A. The Army**, believers as Christ's soldiers (Phil 2:25), fighting side by side (Phil 1:27). As soldiers they must **B. Attack**, just as Christ attacked the forces of darkness. Similarly his army must over-run its fortresses (2 Cor 10:3-6), using weapons of righteousness (2 Cor 6:7). Of course they have **C. Armor for Defense**, the full armor of light (Rom 13:12). Even so protected Paul knew there was **D. Cost to the Soldiers**, great suffering for the sake of victory. However, Paul was confident that though they are struck down they will not be destroyed (2 Cor 4:9), just as he suffered great physical harm (2 Cor 11:23-27) but still continued to attack fortresses successfully. Indeed he saw their present life as **E. Christ's Triumphal March**. Marching behind him they proclaim his victory and bring the aroma of death to all those who refuse to bow to his rule (2 Cor 2:14-17).

## A. THE ARMY

In the Army of Light Christ is the commander and all believers are soldiers. Whether they are evangelists like Paul or housewives creating Christian havens in their homes (Phil 4:3), they are soldiers of light fighting side by side (Phil 1:27-30), for they bear the light into battle against the darkness.

### (1) Commander and Soldiers

In the ongoing war that Paul and his fellow believers fight every day, Christ is the commander-in-chief (1 Cor 15:25; Col 1:13) while believers are Paul's fellow soldiers (Phil 2:25), sometimes fellow prisoners of war (Rom

---

[3] The basic picture of Paul's ongoing war is well summarized by Pfitzner when he writes: "The internal conflict of the believer against sin (Rom 6:12-14) is part of the great cosmic struggle against Satan and the powers of darkness (Eph 6:12). In this conflict the 'sons of light' (I Thess 5:4-8 and Rom 13:11-14) are joined with the powers of the old aeon in the last great eschatological struggle until God 'has put all his enemies under his (i.e. Christ's) feet' (I Cor 15:25). It is the *ekklesia*, God's military summons in the world, which is at war, not merely the individual believer." (*Paul and the Agon Motif*, 163).

16:7, Col 4:10; Philem 23) under Christ.

Paul's view of Christ as the commander-in-chief in this ongoing war comes out specifically in 1 Cor 15:25 where he says, "He (Christ) must reign until he (God) has put all his enemies under his (Christ's) feet." Though this could be taken to refer to a millennial reign, one that begins after the parousia mentioned two verses earlier, there is no ground for believing that Paul believed in such a millennial interlude. Thus the alternative reading—that Christ is now reigning, and now subjecting more and more of the powers to his authority—is preferable. As Whiteley says, 1 Cor 15:25 is military imagery describing the present: "Christ is like a general whose command lasts only during the period of the military emergency. As soon as a victory is won he must hand over to the civil ruler. Here is no doctrine of the millennial kingdom."[4]

Since Christ is the commander then Paul and other believers are soldiers. He specifically uses that image when he says that he and others are "fellow soldiers," *sustratiotes* (Phil 2:25; Philem 2). That makes it clear that he sees himself as part of an army, not a lone fighter going out against the darkness. In another passage he likens himself to a soldier since both have a right to be paid for their services: "Who serves in the military forces at his own expense?" (1 Cor 9:7).

Among the many points that Paul probably saw as significant in his soldier symbolism we include not only comradeship and the right to support, which he mentions but some of the following: soldiers only fight vigorously, risking their lives, when they desire the victory of their side; soldiers must obey their commanders or the battle will be lost; soldiers must stand together with their comrades, or each will be picked off by the enemy; soldiers will suffer, not just the fatigue of battle but sometimes the great pain of wounds, and some even death; even if they die in battle, glory is theirs for giving all for their

---

[4] *The Theology of St. Paul*, 270. Hill also concludes this after a detailed investigation of the alternatives: "It appears inescapable, therefore, that Paul understands the kingdom of Christ in I Cor. 15:24–28 to be Christ's present, cosmic lordship which he exercises from heaven...This intermediate kingdom is for Paul the period of Christ's dominion over but yet amidst the inimical forces" (Hill, "Paul's Understanding of Christ's Kingdom in I Corinthians 15:20–28," 317). See also Barrett (*First Corinthians*, 358) and Ridderbos (*Paul*, 559).

community.

When soldiers are captured, then they become prisoners of war. Thus the military symbol of the Christian life as a war against the Army of Darkness probably lies behind Paul's reference to himself and others as "fellow prisoners of war," *sunaichmalotoi* (Rom 16:7; Col 4:10; Philem 23). Though the word could simply refer literally to imprisonment, a good case can be made that Paul was thinking militarily here. Pfitzer argues that other words would have served better for referring simply to imprisonment, e.g. *sundesmios* or *sundesmotes*. Paul chose otherwise, so,

> The use of this specific word is no doubt meant to recall the familiar military metaphor. They who have taken an active part in all his struggles for the Gospel as his "fellow soldiers" have also faithfully stood at his side through persecution, trial, and imprisonment as "fellow captives."[5]

When prisoners see themselves as prisoners-of-war their attitude is very different than it is when they are individuals imprisoned for their own misdeeds. Clearly Paul saw himself and his fellow prisoners as only temporarily under the power of the enemy, for he believed that in the end Christ would conquer all the powers, and thus would free all the prisoners. Thus for Paul being in prison was not a defeat, but simply a part of the suffering that is required of a faithful soldier, suffering that he rejoices in (Rom 5:3; Col 1:24). In fact, for Paul imprisonment was no great drawback, for he continued his battle even there, since his main weapon was his preaching and other prisoners were a captive audience.

## (2) Fighting Side by Side (Phil 1:27–30)

> I will know that you are standing firm [*stekete*] in one spirit, with one mind fighting side by side [*sunathlountes*, struggling, competing, together] for the faith of the gospel, in no way intimidated by the enemies [*antikeimenon*]. For them this is a sign of their destruction [*apoleias*] but for you of your victory [*soterias*, salvation]. And this is God's doing. For he has

---

[5] *Paul and the Agon Motif*, 161.

> graciously granted you the privelege of not only believing in Christ but also of suffering [*paschein*] for him; so you are having the same battle [*agon*, struggle] that you saw I had and now hear that I still have. (Phil 1:27–30)

In this passage Paul seems to evoke the comradeship of warfare, not only the unity in fighting but also the willingness to suffer wounds in battle, as the picture he hopes the Philippians will adhere to. This is not a description of what they have already done, but is how Paul hopes to be able to picture them, for this is what he says he wishes "to hear about you." He hopes they will be faithful soldiers, fighting and suffering for Christ, for that is the example he has given them.

The primary clue to this as military imagery comes in the designation of the opponents as *antikeimenon*, which normally means an enemy, a person actively opposed to you, seeking to defeat you in your mission. It is used of the Man of Lawlessness in 2 Thess 2:4 who is called *ho antikeimenos*, the ultimate, final, enemy of God's people. This destructive figure is clearly not just a person who disagrees with them, but is pictured as a real enemy, i.e. one who seeks to destroy them. Similarly Paul uses it in 1 Cor 16:9 to speak of those who opposed his work in Ephesus, saying "there are many enemies [*antikeimenoi*]." The implication of "enemies" is that these opponents will fight, will bring suffering, perhaps even death, and so must be fought back against.

In addition, the use of *apoleias* (destruction) as the end waiting for those enemies further supports the view that Paul is imagining them not just as opponents to be avoided or silenced but as enemies who must be destroyed. Opponents, those who stand in opposition by their words, can be silenced. Enemies, those who fight with their swords and spears, must often be destroyed. Thus, for example, the Man of Lawlessness is called "the son of destruction [*apoleias*]" (2 Thess 2:3). Presumably he causes great destruction, and so in the end he must be destroyed (*katargesei*) in the coming of Christ (2 Thess 2:8). Thus by speaking of the destruction of these enemies in Phil 1:27–30 Paul suggests that the struggle they are in is really warfare.[6]

---

[6] The particular destruction Paul was thinking of was probably eschatological, for *apoleia* was often used to refer to the final destiny of the wicked (Rom 9:22; Mt 7:13; Rev 17:8, 11; Heb 10:39; 2 Pet 3:7). Since Paul

In the third place the verb *sunathleo*, which Paul uses here to describe the activity of believers, was used for warfare. Its general sense is "to contend or struggle together" against an opponent, especially in sports or warfare. Thus it can represent the infantry fighting together in their battle against their enemy. In this case Paul elaborates the infantry image by saying he hopes they will "stand firm [*stekete*] in one spirit."[7] By this imagery—standing firm together, fighting side by side—he conjures up a defensive line. Though under attack, these soldiers stand locked together, refusing to retreat, united in their defense of their homeland. At other times the verb can be used in an offensive sense, as in the other use of this verb in Philippians. There it can aptly be translated "these women...have fought by my side [*sunethlesan*] in the work of the gospel" (Phil 4:3),[8] referring presumably to those who helped in the preaching of the gospel by standing up against its enemies.

Perhaps the element in the Phil 1:27 military image that was most important for Paul was the absolute necessity for unity, for he speaks of it both as having one spirit and being of one mind. He evoked the image of a defensive line of soldiers standing firm, all side by side, in contrast to the alternative where some soldiers break ranks, heading towards the rear. When that happens the soldiers left in the front line become vulnerable, liable to attack from the side, or from two attackers at once. These remaining soldiers are then strongly tempted to retreat also, which would allow a rout and possibly the destruction of the whole army. Therefore Paul strongly urged the Philippians to stand together, to fight together, for in unity there was strength. The central theme of the Christ hymn in the next paragraph of Philippians emphasizes this unity, for Paul says "be of one mind" so each will "look to the interests of others" (Phil 2:2, 4). That is precisely how an army must act: only when all the soldiers stand firmly together in face of the enemy, concerned about the others and not first about themselves, can they be strong enough to endure the attack.

The fourth word in this passage with a military reference is *agon*. Paul

---

here speaks of the believers' unity in battle as the "sign" (*endeixis*) of the enemy's destruction, he was probably thinking of a foreshadowing, rather than of a present event.

[7] Grayston points particularly to this verb "standing firm" as one taken from "the soldier's life" (*Philippians and Thessalonians*, 26).

[8] So translated by Arndt and Gingrich, 791.

says "you are having the same *agona* [struggle, battle] that you saw I had..."
(Phil 1:30). Later in the Pastorals this term was used in the famous imperative
"fight [*agonizou*] the good fight [*agona*]" (1 Tim 6:12), so it is clearly a word
that can refer to warfare. In this present passage in Philippians, the connection
with war is also clear, not just because of the previous words used, but because
physical suffering is the evidence that points to a battle. Paul describes this
battle as their "suffering for him (Christ)" which we know from other passages
was one of the central reasons he used warfare imagery: it made clear that the
suffering was an essential element in the Christian life. When believers picture
themselves as soldiers in battle, they will expect to suffer wounds, and will
expect that some of their number will be killed. Thus the battle imagery
provides a clear rationale for Christian suffering—it is a normal by-product, one
that contributes to the battle against the Kingdom of Darkness which Christ will
eventually win through them.

## B. ATTACK

Paul's image of believers translated into Christ's kingdom (Col 1:13;
Gal 1:4) and there kept safe from the forces of evil (Rom 8:37–39) could
mislead readers into believing that Paul wanted them to remain hidden in their
safe fortress. His own example shows that this is not the case, for he
understands the believers' task as advancing into the darkness in order to drive
it back, as the Maccabees drove the Seleucids further and further away from
Jerusalem. His most detailed picture of the soldiers of light provides just that
kind of attacking imagery, for in 2 Corinthians Paul pictures them destroying the
enemy fortresses.[9]

---

[9] Paul's many warfare images in 2 Corinthians may be due to the
Corinthians' special knowledge about fortifications, as Malherbe notes: "His use
of military imagery in writing to Corinth was particularly apt. The location of
the city on the isthmus lent it great strategic importance. It was known for its
extensive fortifications, particularly those of Acrocorinth, from which, according
to Strabo, one could look down on the isthmus. Formidable in appearance and
in fact it could withstand a direct onslaught but was not immune to stealth"
("Antisthenes and Odysseus, and Paul at War," 173).

## (1) Destroying Fortresses (2 Cor 10:3–6)

> Though we live in this world [*en sarki*], we do not wage war
> [*strateuometha*] in a worldly manner [*kata sarka*], for the
> weapons [*hopla*] of our warfare [*strateias*] are not worldly
> [*sarkika*], but divinely powerful [*dunata to Theo*] to destroy
> [*kathairesin*] fortresses [*ochuromaton*]. We destroy arguments
> and every rampart [*hupsoma*] raised up against the knowledge
> of God, and we take every thought captive [*aichmalotizontes*]
> to Christ. When your obedience is complete, we are ready to
> courtmartial [*ekdikesai*] all insubordination [*parakoen*]. (2 Cor
> 10:3–6)

Here we find Paul's fullest use of military symbolism to describe the
believers' way of life while physically still in this world, the age of darkness.
He sees himself and his comrades as armed by God to attack and destroy
fortresses, breaking through the high walls with irresistible battering rams. Once
inside the walls, Christ's soldiers take captives, specifically taking thoughts
captive, and thus presumably bringing the defeated soldiers over to the side of
the light. Then, when the victory is complete, the general will turn his attention
to any who have sabotaged the campaign by disobedience. They will be
courtmartialed, and then presumably drummed out of the corps.

Paul begins this description by speaking of the weapons of their warfare
as not worldly, not of the flesh. By this he presumably means that they are not
physical, not literal weapons by which people can be killed. Thus he intends to
make clear at the beginning that he is not advocating literal warfare, using
physical force to repel or conquer the Army of Darkness. Still he wants to
emphasize that he sees himself in a war (by using both *strateuometha* and
*strateias* in his first sentence) so this image is a significant one for his self-
understanding. As Pfitzner suggests, "*The image of the strateia pictures the life
and work of the Apostle in its totality.*"[10] It is not surprising that Paul saw his
life this way, for he found himself continually in conflict with opponents, not
only outsiders persecuting all Christians, but even more insiders who preached
a different gospel.

Secondly Paul speaks of his weapons as not worldly, not of the flesh,

---

[10] *Paul*, 60.

but as divinely powerful. As he mentioned earlier in speaking of the weapons of righteousness (2 Cor 6:7), God is the one who supplies the power for his soldiers, for they in themselves are weak, empty vessels, mere flesh in comparison to his Spirit. The soldiers themselves are God's weapons in this war (Rom 6:13), while within their own experience they find that God's Spirit and love and truth are the powerful means of overcoming the darkness (2 Cor 6:6–7). The necessity for such spiritual weapons is due to the nature of the enemy—hidden, spiritual forces of darkness, i.e. Satan, the angelic powers, Sin and Death. As Hughes suggests:

> The satanic forces against which the soldiers of Christ's army contend are not forces of flesh and blood; therefore to attempt to withstand them with weapons of the flesh would be nothing short of folly. ...Only spiritual weapons are divinely powerful for the overthrow of the fortresses of evil.[11]

The target for these supernatural weapons is a fortress (*ochuroma*), with a rampart (*hupsoma*) raised up as its high protective wall in front. Though *ochuroma* is not found elsewhere in the NT, it "was widely used...for military fortifications" in other Greek literature.[12] One example often cited as possibly a source of Paul's imagery is Prov 21:2, which in the LXX version says, "The wise man attacks strong [*ochuras*] cities and destroys the strongholds [*ochuroma*] in which the ungodly trusted." Another prime example of this word used for fortressses is in 1 Maccabees (e.g. 5:65; 8:10), which we suggested above may very well provide a model for Paul's symbolism here. The Maccabees (as well as the Romans) are described there as attacking and breaking into fortresses, using battering rams to knock holes through the walls. In Paul's imagery here he apparently speaks of the high, thick walls with protected walkways on their top (and perhaps towers at the corners) as "ramparts raised up." This phrase refers to "the high bulwarks from which the defenders of a city may oppose a besieging army." Thus Paul's symbolism evokes "the tactics of siege warfare as practiced in the Greco-Roman world."[13]

---

[11] *Second Corinthians*, 350.
[12] Malherbe, "Antisthenes," 144.
[13] Furnish, *Second Corinthians*, 458.

Among the interesting suggestions raised by this symbol of the Army of Light besieging and breaking into a fortress of darkness are these: (i) The Army of Light attacks, for just as Christ advanced boldly into the darkness and drove it back, so also his soldiers actively seek out the enemy and force the battle; (ii) in fortresses the defense has all the advantages, so this direct attack on a strongpoint means the Army of Light does not seek easy victories, but strikes at the strongest fortification the enemy has; (iii) of course that is the intelligent way to conduct a campaign, for once this fort is taken, then all the territory over which it ruled is taken too; (iv) the Army of Light has power vastly superior to its enemies', for only with such power is it possible to batter down the walls behind which the enemy army hides; (v) since the major force in the attack is the battering ram, perhaps Paul imagines that his attack has some qualities of a battering ram, e.g. an invulnerable point, endurance, insistence, never giving up; (vi) perhaps Paul imagined himself with his word of the Gospel breaking down defenses by refusing to give in. Thus by bringing up their siege towers and battering rams believers knock down the walls of the fortresses, destroying them as centers of power. Once the walls are broken down, the Army of Light advances inside.

Inside any conquered fortress the victorious army takes captives. This stage of the campaign may be easy or bloody, depending on how vigorously the defenders fight on. Almost certainly the defenders' cause is hopeless, for they depended on the strength of their fortress to make up for their weakness in numbers of soldiers, so when their "champion" is broken down, they are done for. Of course in the ancient world the attackers sometimes killed everyone in the fort, but Paul has no interest in hurting people, indeed he is not even interested in capturing people. He says that they take captive every "thought" or "mind" (*noema*) of the enemy soldiers (2 Cor 10:5).[14] Presumably when the thoughts are taken captive the soldiers themselves are freed to join the Army of Light. Paul only conquers when he frees people to join Christ's army, for his

---

[14] Malherbe suggests that Paul knew Seneca's views and "describes his opponents' fortifications in terms strongly reminiscent of the Stoic sage....The self-sufficient, self-confident Stoic, secure in the fortification of his own reason, represents a type antithetical to Paul's own self-understanding and provides him with the description of his opponents. Like Seneca, they feel secure in their elevated citadel" ("Antisthenes," 166, 171).

task is extending the Kingdom of Light by bringing more and more former enemies into it.[15] That is essentially what Judas Maccabeus did when he captured Gazara, for he treated the captives inside with mercy, letting them go free. Instead of destroying the fortress city he cleansed it, removing all idols, and made it into a faithful city again (1 Macc 13:43–48). Similarly, instead of making the enemy soldiers prisoners, Paul and the other gospel soldiers free them from the prison of their sinful, idolatrous, thoughts. That is the victory of the light, when the darkness in their minds is overcome by light. The result then is that the fortress and all the territory over which it ruled comes to be integrated into Christ's Kingdom of Light.

Then at the end of the battle the commanders turn to deal with any of their own soldiers who were insubordinate, disobedient (*parakoen*), or failed to obey orders during the fighting; those traitors are courtmartialed (*ekdikesai*, 2 Cor 10:6). Presumably they are banished from the army back into the darkness, perhaps to bring them to see the folly of their ways and so repent and be saved (see 1 Cor 5:5). Neither *parakoe* nor *ekdikeo* is a technical military term, for they are simply standard terms to express disobedience and judging. In this context, however, they clearly suggest disobedience and judging after a military victory. In fact one other phrase does come directly from the military realm, as Malherbe points out: "Paul's claim to be prepared to punish is also stated in a phrase (*en hetoimo echontes*) used of military preparedness," e.g. in Polybius.[16]

Thus we can be confident that in this last assertion Paul was still thinking in military terms: during the battle some members of the attacking army failed to do their duty, refused to obey orders, perhaps even sabotaged the attack. The most common form such insubordination takes is for fearful soldiers to refuse to attack strong positions, afraid for their own safety. Sometimes, of course, active treason and sabotage by disguised enemies is the problem. While the battle is going on that behavior may have to be ignored. However, once the battle is over the insubordinate will be dealt with, in order to prevent others

---

[15] Furnish suggests that Paul's idea here is that "The gospel conquers unbelief" (*Second Corinthians*, 463).

[16] Malherbe, "Antisthenes," 145. See also Furnish, *Second Corinthians*, 459.

doing the same later. Presumably the punishment meted out to the insubordinate is that they are banished from the army.

## Summary

When the soldiers in the Army of Light come upon a fortress of darkness in their path, they take up the divinely powerful weapons God has given them and break down the walls. By that means they overcome the defenses people put up to keep themselves from hearing the gospel. So when the soldiers enter the fortress they take captive the thoughts of the defenders, bringing them over to allegiance to a new commander. Their old commander, Satan/Sin, is deposed, so the soldiers are freed from its tyranny. Then all those who were insubordinate in the battle are courtmartialed and driven into the darkness beyond Christ's kingdom, once again made slaves of Sin.

As each fortress of the enemy's · army is destroyed the territory surrounding it becomes part of the Kingdom of Light. Thus with each victory Satan's power is diminished, the Army of Darkness continually squeezed into a smaller area. Therefore as Paul takes the gospel further and further, bringing the light to destroy the fortresses of darkness, the angelic rulers of this present age are being destroyed (1 Cor 2:6). That ongoing victory is happening because Christ, in Paul and other believers, is continuing his war against the Powers (1 Cor 15:25), the war he began at the cross (Col 2:15), and will end with his victory in the Last Battle when he returns in glory (1 Cor 15:24).[17]

---

[17] One other passage in 2 Corinthians in which Paul may have been thinking in military terms is 10:12–18, in which he says that he will stay within the territorial limits (*kanonos*) that God has assigned to him. Hall argues that this is battle imagery "because Paul speaks here of *territory*. To press the military metaphor, we can say that where Paul has founded churches, there the new age, the sphere of God's power, has established a beachhead, from which the battle can be carried further. This might be regarded as over-interpretation or a highly figurative way to speak, were it not for 11:8. There Paul speaks explicitly about the founding of the Corinthian church made possible by military support from another 'beachhead.'" (*Battle Imagery in Paul's Letters*, 76–77). Though Hall has correctly understood Paul's imagery in general, this probably is over-interpretation of this particular passage, for 2 Cor 11:8 does not specifically mention another "beachhead" but other "churches." Paul could have been thinking in military terms here, since he has just finished doing so in verses 3–6.

## (2) Weapons of Righteousness (2 Cor 6:7)

> As servants of God we have commended ourselves in every
> way: through great endurance, in afflictions...calamities,
> beatings, imprisonments, riots...by purity, knowledge,
> patience, kindness, the Holy Spirit, genuine love, truthful
> speech, and the power of God; with weapons [*hoplon*] of
> righteousness for the right hand and the left. (2 Cor 6:4–7)

In battle the weapon of the right hand is usually the sword and that of
the left is the shield, so it is likely that in this passage Paul intended to evoke
the image of himself and others with those two weapons.[18] The sword is
usually seen as a weapon of attack, for by it the soldier can disarm, maim or kill
an enemy. Thus Paul probably imagined himself and other believers as able to
conquer their enemies using the sword that God supplied them. As we saw in
his picture of believers attacking fortresses, Paul imagined himself and the rest
of Christ's army as heading into the darkness, knocking down the defensive
walls of the enemy, and then capturing their thoughts. In Ephesians the
believer's sword is specifically called "the sword of the Spirit, which is the
word of God" (Eph 6:17), which fits very well with Paul's view of how he
attacks: by preaching the gospel of the light and thereby conquering the
darkness.[19]

Calling these weapons "of righteousness" provides several suggestions.
First of all it implies that God supplies them, because Paul's view was that
righteousness comes from God. As Barrett states: "the Gospel is a manifestation
of the righteousness of God (Rom. 1:16f), so that when Paul acts as a preacher
of the Gospel he is like a soldier whose weapons are righteousness."[20] Paul's
view was that he had no righteousness of his own, but only that which comes
through faith in Christ (Phil 3:9), so these weapons are divine weapons. This fits

---

However, he uses no specifically military symbolism in 12–18, so we cannot
know if that was what he was thinking.

[18] Furnish, 346. Hughes suggests that Paul is thinking that believers are
prepared to meet attacks from any side (*Second Corinthians*, 231).

[19] While the sword is largely for attack, the shield is largely for defense, so
we will speak of it in the next section on Armor for Defense.

[20] *Second Corinthians*, 188.

well with Paul's view that in the battle against evil his own human powers get in the way, so only when he is weak and empty can he really be powerful by the work of God's Spirit within him. As he said later, "when I am weak, then I am strong" (2 Cor 12:10).[21] Thus in the spiritual battle against the forces of evil in the world, Paul relies on the spiritual powers given him by God, through the Spirit.

Secondly, "weapons of righteousness" implies that the battle is one between forces of righteousness and forces of evil, which is the basic picture Paul often presents. This division into two warring sides comes out clearly in the other passage in which Paul uses this phrase, in Rom 6:13. He urges his readers, "present your members to God as weapons of righteousness," in contrast to their previous life in the Army of Darkness when they had presented their members "to Sin as weapons of wickedness" (Rom 6:13). Here Sin is the immediate commander in the Army of Darkness.[22] That army stands in direct opposition to the Army of Light of which God is the ultimate ruler. In Rom 6:13 "members" stands for the whole of their bodies, and thus for the whole of their selves. The believers themselves were God's weapons, those through whom God spreads righteousness in the world by attacking the darkness.[23] The crucial point in this Romans passage is that people have only one choice—whether they will allow themselves to continue as weapons in the hands of the rulers of the Army of Darkness, or will give themselves to Christ and so be his weapons in the Army of Light. Apparently neutrality is impossible.

Thirdly, "weapons of righteousness" may be taken as a genitive of result. Thus it may imply that the outcome of the battle is to be the spreading of God's righteousness, i.e. God's salvation, God's light, God's rule over that

---

[21] Furnish sees this as a central point of the military imagery: "Paul is fond of military imagery...perhaps because it enables him to emphasize that the resources for battle against the forces of the world come from God" (346).

[22] Leenhardt says "*Hamartia* is pictured as a reigning prince, who has subjects and armed troops at his disposal for...the consolidation of his reign of *iniquity*" (*Romans*, 165).

[23] Roberts emphasizes the military imagery here by saying that in Rom 6:13 Paul presents "the marching orders of a militant faith...a trumpet call to active combat in the cause of righteousness against evil" (*Romans*, 164–165).

which previously was covered by the darkness. Since the weapons are divine, they are unbeatable, for no creature, not even the god of this world, is able to withstand the attack of the divine sword.

## C. ARMOR FOR DEFENSE

In several passages Paul uses the symbol of armor to speak of the ways that God protects believers from the attacks of the forces of darkness. Perhaps the most evocative of them is the image of believers covered with "the armor of light" (Rom 13:12), for that fits artfully with the picture of them as members of Christ's Kingdom of Light. Particular pieces of armor he mentions include "the breastplate of faith and love" and "a helmet" which is the hope of salvation (1 Thess 5:8), as well as the implied sword and shield (weapons for the right hand and left) of 2 Cor 6:7. The fullest picture comes in Ephesians 6, which, if it was not written by Paul, was written by a Paulinist who develops this imagery that Paul had already used, showing aptly how the basic image can be expanded.

### (1) The Armor of Light (Rom 13:12)

> The night is far gone, the day is near. Let us then put aside the works of darkness and put on [*endusometha*] the armor [*ta hopla*, weapons, arms] of light. Let us live honorably as in the day, not in reveling and drunkenness...Instead put on [*endusasthe*] the Lord Jesus Christ, and make no provision for the flesh, to gratify its desires. (Rom 13:12–14)

Since believers are members of Christ's Kingdom of Light (Col 1:13), it was highly appropriate for them to picture themselves as covered with an armor of light. In fact, in this passage, since believers are called to "put on the Lord Jesus Christ," Paul implies that Christ is the light, the armor they will put on. Thus when believers enter Christ's kingdom they become like him, carriers of light, for he is the darkness-defeating power at work within them.[24]

One intriguing element in this passage is the imagery of night and day. Quite naturally the night is connected with the age of darkness, for night's darkness is the traditional cover used by forces of evil to hide their destructive ways (Isa 29:15; Psa 91:6; Prov 4:19). When Paul says the night is far gone and the day is at hand (Rom 13:12), he suggests that the sun is sending its light over the horizon, beginning to light up the dark world.[25] Presumably, Paul was thinking of the full arrival of the sun as "the day of the Lord," which was to come swiftly (1 Thess 5:2). Presumably he was picturing Christ's ministry as the light that comes before dawn, the sun's rays that have begun to drive away the darkness on earth. Thus all those who awake, arise, and assemble outside will be in the light, and so be covered with the armor of light. By this imagery Paul suggests how inevitable the victory of God in Christ is: just as certain as the rising of the sun to banish all the darkness, once we see its predawn light around us.

In the present, before the sun arises, Christ is the light that believers wear, which suggests that they have his power over the forces of evil. As we showed above, Paul saw Christ as having driven Satan's Army of Darkness into its fighting retreat. Thus the armor of light protects believers from the attack of Sin, enabling them to be free from its coercion as long as they have put on Christ. Further, the Powers can no longer enslave them, and Satan can no longer blind them, though temptations from those quarters still arise constantly.

---

[24] Since he uses *ta hopla*, which can mean weapons or arms, the translation armor is suggested by the verb, for the armament that soldiers "put on" is usually that which protects them. Their attacking weapons, the sword and spear, are "carried" rather than put on. Still, Paul may have been thinking of the total armament of a soldier, including a sword or spear. Since the "works of darkness" are removed it is plausible that Paul was imagining "works of light" as put on in their place, e.g. spreading the gospel by loving behavior towards others. Such works that conquer the darkness are appropriately understood as the sword of the faith. Barrett states: "'armour' includes offensive weapons" (*Romans*, 253).

[25] Nygren comments: "The Christian lives on the frontier between the two aeons, and his entire existence is marked by that fact. He is still in the old aeon, but the new sheds its light on his life and that life is a moving forward toward the new day" (*Romans*, 435–436).

Most of all, the light they wear means that Death is no longer an eternal threat, that its sting has been drawn.

Normally armor is designed to protect the wearer from the attacks of others, so that is the first implication of Paul's image here. In addition, however, the armor/weapons of light probably should be imagined as playing an attacking role, for when light goes into the darkness the darkness is driven back. Perhaps the image Paul had in mind was this: believers are covered with the light which comes from Christ, so they are protected from the arrows of darkness and so are able to stride forward with impunity into the battle.

As in his other picture of the believers' weapons, in 2 Corinthians 6, Paul here points to their lives of righteousness as the visible element of the light which they wear. Presumably Paul pictured their honorable lives as providing an attack on the decadence around them, but it also provided protection from the forces of evil. He probably saw the believers in their sober lives as fighting side-by-side, united in the Spirit, helping each other reject the easy slide down into the indulgence in which they had lived before their conversions.

By calling this new life "armor" Paul intended to convince these new believers that they had divine protection, that they could successfully break away from the lives of vice that they had previously lived. But by calling it armor "of light" Paul proclaimed that they were given the opportunity to be Christ's light in the world. Clothed with him, they would shine forth as an example of the eternal life that was about to break in when the sun soon rose above the horizon. Then all the darkness would be destroyed forever.

### (2) Breastplate and Helmet (1 Thess 5:8)

> You are all children of light and children of the day; we are
> not of the night or of darkness....Since we belong to the day,
> let us be sober, and put on the breastplate of faith and love,
> and for a helmet the hope of salvation. (1 Thess 5:5, 8)

Here, as in Rom 13:12, Paul connects the armor of believers with the light which comes to them from Christ, further supporting our contention that the Kingdom of Light and its corollary children of light are military images. Once again he is picturing them as awake before dawn, basking in the light that comes from the sun which is still down over the horizon, so they are "touched by the first light of the day."[26] Here, unlike in Rom 13:12, he specifies two particular pieces of the armor, both of them defensive, which the children of light wear in their battle against the forces of darkness. Quite conceivably Paul was here alluding to the one OT passage which speaks of God as covered with armor, Isa 59:17, where the prophet pictures God this way: "He put on righteousness like a breastplate, and a helmet of salvation on his head." The specific combination of breastplate and helmet strongly suggests that Paul was alluding to this passage. In Isaiah the meaning apparently was that the prophet, "was certain of the justice of God's cause (the meaning of righteousness in this context) and his final victory (which is how *salvation* should be translated in Thessalonians also)."[27] The difference between Isaiah's image and Paul's is that the former pictures God with this armor and the latter pictures believers. The connection between the two suggests that Paul thought that God's own armor, God's own power, God's own protection, were given to believers when they received the light which Christ is.

Roman breastplates, which Paul presumably had in mind in his image of the breastplate of faith and love (1 Thess 5:8), were typically made of iron (Rev 9:9) in overlapping strips. They covered the whole of the chest and the back to protect the soldier from spear and sword thrusts to the vital organs.[28] Thus when Paul spoke of the breastplate of faith and love he suggested that these two inner qualities provided a similar kind of protection from the attacks of the forces of darkness. Faith does it because faith is the means by which believers enter the Kingdom of Light, become members of Christ's army, those who are protected by the divine power. Love has a similar function because it brings believers to stand together, fighting side by side, considering the needs of their comrades first rather than worrying about their own lives. Thus if all the members of the community are covered with faith and love, the community will be united in Christ's triumphal procession.

The helmet which is "the hope of (eternal) salvation" is a parallel image, for it is the means by which the head of the soldier is protected. The

---

[26] Williams, *1 and 2 Thessalonians*, 88.

[27] Grayston, *Philippians and Thessalonians*, 88–89.

[28] See the pictures and description in Webster, *The Roman Imperial Army of the First and Second Centuries A.D.*, 124–125.

purpose of a helmet was to ward off sword blows, and the pounding of falling projectiles, to protect the vital organ of the brain from fatal attacks. When the Romans faced especially heavy barbarian swords they had to get rid of their bronze helmets and issued "helmets made of iron with a polished surface to cause the swords to be deflected."[29] Of course wearing these helmets was absolutely essential in battle, for without them the soldier was highly vulnerable.

In a similar way Paul presumably imagined the hope of salvation as a way for Christians to ward off the blows of the enemy. Most likely those blows were physical afflictions which could lead them to compromise their faith, to give in and renounce Christ. If their view was that this life is the only one we have, that there is no hope for eternal life, then they were vulnerable to the attacks of those with superior physical or political power. But if they had a strong hope of salvation, a conviction that if they endured to the end they would gain the eternal kingdom, then they could deflect the blows of their enemies' swords, as we will show in (5) below.

One intriguing aspect of Paul's exhortation here is that he says "let us be vigilant, putting on [*endusamenoi*]" the armor. Of course the verb is a perfectly natural one when used with armor, but the implication of the aorist seems to be that his readers have not previously put it on. As Best remarks, "we might have expected that Christians would be already armed with faith, love and hope."[30] Since the two pieces of armor here are purely defensive, and the armed one is called to be vigilant, perhaps Paul is thinking of a sentry,[31] who puts on his armor before taking up his post where he must exercise vigilance in order not to be overtaken by enemies. Then the armor of faith and love is a special protection for special duty, not the same as the faith and love which are common to all believers. This sentry stands guard during the night: by faith he can see the dawn coming and can see any enemies who approach; by love he is concerned for his comrades and will be vigilant to warn them; by hope of salvation he is confident that the day is at hand, so the forces of darkness will shortly be defeated. Thus Paul may here have in mind a special role in the community while it is at rest, not the common role of soldiers in the army

---

[29] Webster, *Roman Imperial Army*, 23.
[30] Best, *Thessalonians*, 214–215.
[31] Best, 215.

fighting the ongoing battle. Ezekiel's watchman who sees the enemy coming and
blows the trumpet in warning (33:1-6) may be a model. If this is the case then
Paul is here calling on the Thessalonians to wake up fully, to recognize their
enemies, to warn each other when those forces of darkness approach, and to live
in confidence that the victory of God in Christ is near.

## (3) The Whole Armor of God (Eph 6:11)

> Put on the whole armor [*ten panoplian*] of God, that you may
> be able to stand against the wiles of the devil...encircling your
> waist with the truth, and putting on the breastplate of
> righteousness...the shoes of the gospel of peace...above all
> taking the shield of faith with which you can extinguish all the
> flaming arrows of the Evil One...and take the helmet of
> salvation ...and the sword of the Spirit. (Eph 6:11, 14-17)

In this famous passage, Paul (or a Paulinist who knew his penchant for
armor imagery) elaborates on the pieces of armor as spiritual qualities. As we
have already shown, Paul spoke elsewhere of armor in general (Rom 13:12), the
breastplate and helmet (1 Thess 5:8), and alluded to the shield and sword when
he spoke of weapons for the right hand and left (2 Cor 6:7). Thus the only new
symbols in the picture, ones found only here, are the belt and shoes.[32]

The most interesting point in the picture in Ephesians 6 is the direct
reference to the battle against the Army of Darkness, when believers take "the
shield [*ton thureon*] of faith with which you can extinguish all the flaming
arrows of the Evil One [*tou ponerou*]" (16). Flaming arrows were shot into
walled cities not only to kill any humans they hit but also to burn up homes and
food and everything people need for their lives. Thus when the Enemy shoots
flaming arrows, he is not seeking just to kill, but to destroy everything. Facing
that barrage, defenders raise their shields, deflect the arrows, then put out the
fires so they do no harm. Thus in this passage Paul probably pictured believers

---

[32] Perhaps one source of this passage is Wis 5:16-22, which Paul may have
read. It speaks of God *shield*ing his people with his arm, using zeal as his
*armor*, putting on a *breastplate* of righteousness, wearing a *helmet* of justice,
taking holiness as a *shield*, wrath as his *sword*, shooting lightning from his *bow*
and hailstones from his *catapult*.

as inside the Kingdom of Light, defending themselves from attack. Though they are inside the impregnable walls of the divinely-created kingdom, still there are attacks from beyond, and believers must be ready for them.

By the Enemy's "flaming arrows" Paul probably symbolizes all the threats that the Army of Darkness makes against believers: Satan tempting them to take the easy path; Sin inviting them to seek pleasure by indulging their passions; the powers offering them freedom from persecution; Death promising to stay away a while longer if they join the Army of Darkness. These arrows are flaming because if they are only deflected, then allowed to remain nearby, they can start a fire that will destroy the community. Therefore they must be extinguished, destroyed.

The first step in protection, however, is the shield, which plays a role quite like the breastplate that we described earlier. Barth comments:

> *Thyreus* is derived from *thyra* ("door") and describes the large, door-shaped or vaulted "shield," in contrast to the small, round, convex shield...The Roman legionary's *scutum*, to which Paul alludes, had an iron frame and sometimes a metal boss at the center of the front. This shield served well even against incendiary missiles when its several layers of leather were soaked in water before the battle.[33]

Such large shields then became a mobile roof over the soldier, a way to guard against the attacks that came through the air. Unlike the breastplate which was fixed to the body, the shield was flexible, movable, a way to deal with flying dangers.

Paul's metaphorical use of the shield is probably based on the many OT passages in which God was depicted as the shield of Israel (e.g. Gen 15:1; 2 Sam 22:3; Ps 3:3; 18:35; 28:7 etc.; Prov 30:5). This imagery was often connected with God as the Rock or Fortress, with the shield offering an alternative image that suggested the intimacy of God's protection of the individual. Perhaps the most famous of these pictures is in David's psalm, given in 2 Sam 22:2-3, in which he thanks the Lord for keeping him safe: "The Lord is my high rock, my fortress and my champion...the one in whom I take refuge,

---

[33] M. Barth, *Ephesians*, 771-772.

my shield and...my stronghold...who saves me from violence."[34] The value of seeing the OT connection is this: when Paul uses the shield image he may well have been connecting it with the fortress image, which is the "shield of the community," and so provides the overall safety of the believer. Just as the fortress of light keeps them from ultimate evil, so also when they fight in the world of darkness the shield of Christ is over them to provide the same protection.

In sum then, we discover that Paul pictures himself and the rest of Christ's soldiers as protected from evil by God's armor of light. Inside the Kingdom of Light they are united to Christ, have put on Christ, and so are shielded by the light which Christ is. Further, Paul pictures them as fully armored, with helmet, breastplate, shield and sword, so that when they go into battle with the Army of Darkness they can carry the light with them and not be eternally harmed. Of course they are often temporally harmed, wounded, even killed, but that is quite natural, wholly expected, for it is the cost that all soldiers must be prepared to pay.

### D. COST TO THE SOLDIERS

As we have noted several times already, one of the chief attractions of the military imagery for Paul was that it made sense of the innocent suffering of believers: soldiers expect to suffer in order to win the battle against evil. By contrast, the theology of Job's friends left no room for the innocent suffering that Christ, Paul and many other believers endured. The Maccabean experience, and the apocalyptic imagery which flowed from it, however, emphasized the battle that has to be fought in the present. This gives a prominent place to the innocent, inevitable and praiseworthy suffering of God's soldiers.

In his own experience Paul knew of two kinds of suffering that the soldiers of Christ had to bear as the cost for winning the war: **(1) Physical Oppression** that comes from persecution by the Rulers of this Present Age and their subordinates, the children of darkness; **(2) Spiritual Suffering** that comes through constant temptation from the spiritual forces of darkness. We will

---

[34] See above **II. The Lord as a Man of War**, B. (1) "Israel's Shield and Fortress."

consider how Paul describes both these costs that the soldier for Christ must pay.

## (1) Physical Oppression

Paul was no stranger to physical suffering in his battle against the darkness, for he was many times beaten almost to death, both by Jews and Romans (2 Cor 11:23-25). These battle blows and their resulting wounds became for him a normal part of his warfaring life, something he had to recover from in order to go on with the battle.

While Paul does not explicitly say this, there can be little doubt that he pictured most of the physical suffering of believers as due to the oppression by the human rulers of this present age and their subordinates among the children of darkness. When Paul received the Jewish punishments of 39 lashes or stoning, or the Roman punishment of a beating with rods (2 Cor 11:24-25), the source of this oppression in each case was some ruler of this present age. He acted through one or more of the children of darkness who administered these undeserved, life-threatening punishments. Thus Paul was constantly aware of the battle against the rulers and their subordinates, since he bore in his body the marks of their warfare.

One passage that offers insight into his attitude towards this physical oppression is in 2 Corinthians:

> We are afflicted in every way but not crushed; perplexed but not driven to despair; persecuted but not forsaken; struck down [*kataballomenoi*] but not destroyed [*apollumenoi*]; always carrying in the body the death of Jesus...always being given up to death for Jesus' sake, so that the life of Jesus may be made visible in our mortal flesh. (2 Cor 4:8-11)

The clue to the military imagery here is the picture of a person struck down, implying a fight in which the opponent had superior force, or got in a lucky blow. Of course that image could evoke boxing, or a street fight, but the contrasting word makes a battle more likely: *apollumi* suggests death, for a person "destroyed" is normally a person killed. In other passages Paul uses this verb to describe the killing of Israelites by snakes and the angel of death (1 Cor

10:9-10) so it is likely that Paul means such physical killing here too.[35] The picture this passage evokes is thus one of a soldier in battle who has fallen at the hand of an enemy soldier, but is not knocked forever out of the battle. He may be lying on the ground unable to fight at the moment, but he knows that his condition is temporary.

The parallel Paul seems to suggest between believers' suffering and Christ's makes it likely that Paul sees suffering battle blows is a necessary step on the way to victory. First of all, by saying he is "carrying in the body the death of Jesus" he implies that his battle blows, his wounds, his suffering, are the continuation, or imitation, of Christ's. Christ fought the great fight against the powers and was struck down, but that was the necessary step on the way to victory in the resurrection. Therefore, Paul apparently saw himself as imitating his commander's fall in battle. Further, this fall was necessary for Paul also, for he says that he and others are given up to death for Jesus' sake, "so that [*hina*] the life of Jesus may be made visible in our mortal flesh" (11). Only through the battle wounds will the victory come.

The soldiers' temporary defeat, when struck down, makes it clear that the ultimate victory is due to their commander. In themselves, in their physical flesh, they are too weak to conquer the enemy; thus when victory comes anyway, in the pushing back of the darkness, it is clear that it is God's power at work, the victorious life of Christ working in and through them. Thus Paul rejoices in his weakness (2 Cor 12:9-10), for then his rescue from death, which had always happened in the many instances of persecution (2 Cor 11), makes clear that God is the power at work. As Hughes comments on "struck down but not destroyed": "Hostile forces press in upon him from all sides and threaten to crush and immobilize him, but a way out of the desperate straits in which he finds himself is always provided; contrary to all human probability, God brings him safely through."[36] That safe extrication from destruction in the battle is thus God making visible in him the life of Christ (2 Cor 4:10-11), the power

---

[35] His other uses of the verb refer to the already working eschatological destruction of unbelievers, e.g. Rom 2:12; 14:15; 1 Cor 1:18; 8:11; 15:18; 2 Cor 2:15. Since no readers would think that Paul was a candidate for such eschatological destruction it is not likely that Paul had it in mind here. So temporal destruction must have been his meaning.

[36] Hughes, *Second Corinthians*, 138.

of the light which conquers the darkness (6).

Elsewhere Paul speaks of the Christian soldier's suffering as a gracious gift from God, in the military imagery passage from Philippians 1 that we discussed above. He says God "has graciously granted you the privilege not only of believing in Christ but of suffering for him as well—you are having the same struggle [*agona*] that you saw I had" (Phil 1:29–30). Far from being incidental, or evidence of the superiority of the darkness, suffering seems to be an essential mark of membership in the Army of Light, a part of the privilege of belonging.

## (2) Spiritual Suffering: Temptation to Desert

Our thesis here is simple: believers suffering from the sword blows of the soldiers of darkness find themselves tempted to give up the fight. They are tempted to desert the Army of Light and hide again in the darkness, in order to escape this suffering. This temptation is the latest in a series that the forces of darkness have pressed on God's people throughout their history. The ultimate threat came when the Seleucid king commanded them to adopt the Greek religion and abandon their own, enforcing it with this threat: "Whoever does not obey the command of the king will die" (1 Macc 1:50). Paul the soldier experienced the same kind of temptation, so he warned his readers to be ready for it, and to reject it.

The clearest passage in which Paul speaks of this particular temptation is in 1 Thessalonians where he refers to the tempter. Paul recalls the persecution the Thessalonians had suffered (2:14) and tells them that he was eager to come to them to support them but could not. So he sent Timothy,

> to establish you in your faith and to exhort you, that no one be moved by these afflictions. You yourselves know that this is to be our lot. For when we were with you, we told you beforehand that we were to suffer affliction; just as it has come to pass, and as you know. For this reason, when I could bear it no longer, I sent that I might know your faith, for fear that somehow the tempter had tempted you and that our labor would be in vain. (1 Thess 3:3–5)

"Moved by these afflictions" suggests that the physical persecution, their suffering in the ongoing war, could lead the believers to have to choose between staying alive and staying faithful. They are like soldiers under devastating attack who have to choose between continuing to fight and surrendering. Their natural desire to live might tempt them to abandon their faith, which would then entail that Paul's "labor would (have been) in vain." In that case a soldier of the light would become again a soldier of the darkness. As part of his fore-arming them, Paul had told them that they were to expect "to suffer afflictions" because he understood the Christian life as warfare, and soldiers know that they will have to suffer. Referring to "the tempter" as the source of this temptation is very likely a reference to Satan, the ruler of the Kingdom of Darkness. Therefore Paul probably saw the persecutors as Satan's agents, and the whole process was then Satanic temptation, the attempt to lead people to choose continued physical life over eternal life.

Though Paul does not use explicit military language here, there are five clear hints that the ongoing war is in the back of his mind: first, the imagery of the suffering that believers know they must endure at the hands of the forces of darkness makes it likely that he was picturing them as caught in the midst of the ongoing war between the two sides. Secondly, Paul pictured the persecutors as agents of the darkness, for he speaks of them as agents of Satan, those who killed Jesus and the prophets, drove Paul and others out (of synagogues?), displease God and stand in the way of the preaching to the Gentiles that would save them by spreading the light (2:15–16). Thirdly, when he says that "God's wrath has come upon them at last" (16) he probably was imagining the Army of Light breaking in and driving back their darkness. Fourth, when he says that he could not get to Thessalonia because "Satan hindered us" (18), he was imagining himself in an ongoing struggle, a war, with the forces of darkness standing in his way. He perhaps saw himself and his entourage as a relief column sent to break through to a beseiged fortress, but prevented from getting there by the enemy army surrounding it. Fifth and finally, his hope that the believers will "stand fast in the Lord" (3:8) suggests a defensive line in battle, with the defenders suffering considerable losses but refusing to bow to the enemy, refusing to surrender or to turn and flee in order to save their lives.[37]

Thus Paul imagined Satan as a spy sneaking inside the walls of Christ's

---

[37] The verb Paul uses here for "standing firm" (*stekete*) is the same one he used in Phil 1:27 to describe the believers fighting side by side, as we showed above in A.2.

advancing Fortress of Light. The Enemy appears as an "angel of light" (2 Cor 11:14), i.e. disguised as a friend, an ally, a guide. This spy offers an easy way out of the difficulty: Why not surrender, and so save yourself from being badly hurt or even killed in this battle? If the soldier gives in, then this secret agent will lead his victim outside the fortress into slavery to Sin again.

Paul's imagery of the Prince of Darkness tempting believers to abandon the Fortress of Light is symbolized secondly by the picture of them bowing again to the slavery of the demon Sin. Giving up the fight entails giving in to Sin, that is, allowing oneself to become again "a weapon" in the hands of the Army of Darkness.

Of course in Paul's warfare imagery Sin cannot coerce believers, but it can still tempt them, for it is Satan's presence. Paul makes it clear that by joining in Christ's victory believers have been freed from the slavery of Sin, so that no longer are they coerced into sinning by this demon that formerly possessed them: "Having been set free from Sin, you have become servants of righteousness" (Rom 6:19). Yet they still are vulnerable, for they are free and so can turn back to the old slavery if they succumb to temptation: "do not let Sin exercise dominion in your mortal bodies, to make you obey your passions [*epithumiais*]. No longer present your members to Sin as weapons [*hopla*] of wickedness" (Rom 6:12-13). As Beker asserts, this situation can aptly be described as a paradox: "Sin has become an *impossible possibility*—impossible, because of the victory of Christ over sin, which is mediated to us through the Spirit, and possible because Christian life remains threatened and liable to...attack or temptation."[38] Paul seems to picture believers as protected from Sin's direct attack because they are members of Christ's Kingdom of Light and so covered with the armor of light. But if they remove the armor and allow Sin in to tempt them into following their passions, then they can be enslaved once more. The citadel of the human inner person is invulnerable to Sin's direct attack, but vulnerable to subversion and sabotage if the armor is opened and one of the disguised agents of the enemy is allowed in.

Presumably the weak point in the armor of the soldier is found in his natural passions, i.e. inner urges and desires which are good servants but bad masters (Rom 6:12; 7:5; Gal 5:16, 1 Cor 7:5). Paul seems to imagine Satan

---

[38] *Triumph*, 217.

working as a voice, or perhaps even an urge, within believers' passions, when he describes the tempting they have to face. In 1 Cor 7:5 he suggests that good inner impulses may provide the means by which Satan can work. Speaking to Christian wives and husbands, concerning their sexual relationship, he says: "Do not refuse one another except perhaps by agreement for a season, that you may devote yourselves to prayer; but then come together again, lest Satan tempt you *through lack of self-control.*" The abstinence practiced here was presumably a means to fight the battle against evil, reminiscent of the abstinence forced upon soldiers by their having to leave home when they go to war. While that abstinence is a good thing, Paul also saw it as eventually opening a door to the enemy. Apparently Paul was thinking of prolonged abstinence as providing an increasingly strong sexual desire, which, if it was not satisfied, could tempt the person to do something improper.

Here the bodily impulse and desire, when they have become strengthened well beyond their usual power, stand in conflict with the spiritual decision to abstain in order to give full attention to the war against evil. When the desire becomes as strong as the decision, then the temptation is constant to give way to the desire. Paul apparently pictures Satan as emphasizing the desire, perhaps urging the person to believe that giving in is not really a bad thing. We should imagine here the enemy agent Sin at work within as a spy or saboteur which finds its way in through the chink in the armor provided by natural passions. Still it must depend on the believer bowing to it before it can come to rule again. Thus for Paul Sin remains a great threat in the battle, not as a physically attacking army, but as an inner saboteur that must be imagined, then recognized and rejected.

Paul's third way of picturing the temptation to desert that all believer-soldiers constantly face is by pointing to the ongoing siren call of the law, which is one weapon used by the angelic powers to try to re-gain control over their freed slaves. From outside the advancing Fortress of Light these powers call out, like the Assyrian messenger. Speaking for his emperor outside the walls of the beseiged Jerusalem in Hezekiah's days, the messenger said: "You are relying now on Egypt, that broken reed of a staff" but that reed will "pierce the hand of any man who leans upon it" (2 Kgs 18:21). Likewise the powers and the law call out to believers saying that their reliance simply on faith is foolish, that they need to obey the law also (Gal 3–4). Of course, the effect of returning to the law was that they would immediately re-enter the darkness, coming under the slavery of the powers and Sin again (Rom 7:5; Gal 3:10–12; 4:8–11; 5:2–4).

Here again, as with Satan and Sin, temptation of free soldiers, not coercion of slaves, is the problem. The temptation apparently works by offering believers a supposedly greater security (a false security of course), urging them to conform to the law in order to earn God's approval. In fact, in Paul's military myth, such an attempt entails giving up the freedom of Christ's Fortress of Light and returning to the slavery of the Kingdom of Darkness (Gal 5:2).

Paul spoke most clearly about this temptation from the law and the powers when he warned the Galatians against returning to the slavery under the elemental spirits of the universe (another name for the angelic principalities and powers) that they had previously experienced (Gal 3:23; 4:3). By their bowing to the demands of religious laws governing rituals, they were "turning back again to the weak and beggarly elemental spirits," which would enslave them again (Gal 4:9–10). Paul was adamant that adopting religious laws as a way to find more security was in fact giving up Christ (Gal 3:10), giving up the security of the fortress which is the Kingdom of Light. Indeed, bowing to the law again is one of the ways by which Sin can enter and take control of the inner person again (Rom 7:8, 5). Thus bowing to the law was opening the gate to the Enemy's disguised saboteur, thus allowing the Enemy to come in and rule again.

## Conclusion

Paul clearly pictured the enemy attack as both open (physical) and insidious (psychological/spiritual), so the costs paid by the soldiers are both external and internal. The external, physical, persecution brought on by the human rulers of this present age and the rest of the children of darkness is simply the more obvious battle that believers must endure. That is the frontal assault on the soldiers advancing with the Fortress of Light, the open warfare in which the children of light suffer physical wounds and even early death. By means of that threat of death the Prince of Darkness also attacks insidiously: it tempts the soldiers to give up the fight, to desert, to come back over to the Army of Darkness in order to escape the pain and suffering that is their lot as soldiers of Christ.

## E. CHRIST'S TRIUMPHAL MARCH

In warfare, as in all other human struggles, hope for success is an essential ingredient if the soldier is to fight diligently. As long as the soldier believes that his side will win in the end, then he will be able to fight to the death, knowing that his death will not be in vain if it contributes to the victory. Such confidence in God's eventual victory was central to Paul's battle myth, as we will elaborate in the next chapter. He firmly believed that in the end God through Christ would triumph over all the forces of darkness, defeating all the enemies, even Death and Satan. As an expression of that confidence Paul imagines himself and other believers already marching in God's triumphal procession.

He writes of the triumph in these words:

Thanks be to God, who in Christ always [*pantote*] leads us in triumphal procession [*thriambeuonti*], and through us spreads in every place the fragrance that comes from knowing him. For we are the aroma of Christ to God...among those who are perishing...a fragrance from death to death. (2 Cor 2:14–16)

This army advances in a triumphal procession because the decisive victory has already been won (Col 2:15). The beachhead has been created which allows the overwhelming forces of the light to begin streaming into the land of those oppressed by the darkness. Now the Fortress of Light, in the persons of the soldiers in their armor of light, advances directly into the darkness and overcomes it. As the army marches, its soldiers are a poison gas that foretells death (and perhaps even brings it, see 2 Cor 3:6) to their enemies.

Barclay sets Paul's implied scene well when he writes:

In his mind is the picture of a Roman *Triumph* and of Christ as a universal conqueror. The highest honour which could be given to a victorious Roman general was a Triumph. To attain it he must satisfy certain conditions. He must have been the actual commander-in-chief in the field. The campaign must have been completely finished, the region pacified and the victorious troops brought home. Five thousand of the enemy at least must have fallen in one engagement. A positive extension of territory must have been gained, and not merely a disaster retrieved or an attack repelled. And the victory must have been won over a foreign foe and not in a civil war.[39]

At the head of the parade were the Roman civil officials, followed by the spoils of victory and pictures or models of the conquered land and ships. Then came the defeated princes and generals, as if driven along by the victorious general in his chariot. "...finally came the army wearing all their decorations and shouting *Io triumphe!* their cry of triumph."[40]

Probably Paul's image here is of Christ as the triumphant general. Though the subject of the verb to triumph is God, it is God "in Christ," i.e. presumably invisibly present in the visible Christ, who is the victor. Thus Paul's picture suggests that Christ was the commander in the field, against a foreign foe (the Army of Darkness), and the victory has been won already. Here Paul was thinking of Christ's victory over the powers and Sin and Death, which came in his death and resurrection. Further, Paul may well have been alluding to an extension of territory by conquest which would aptly symbolize the creation of the new Kingdom of Light.

The dispute concerning Paul's picture is whether Paul and other believers are in this procession as victorious soldiers or as captives displayed by God their conqueror. Furnish discusses an array of interpretations and concludes that a parallel with Seneca provides the clue to Paul. Seneca used the image of a Roman triumphal march to describe his own humiliation as a captive under his benefactor. Furnish then makes the leap to Paul, saying:

> It is not impossible that Paul uses the Greek verb *thriambeuein* for a similar reason...Thus the verb would not just mean "to display"...but would carry the additional connotation "as humiliated" (cf. 1 Cor 4:9b, "we have become a spectacle"); that is, *as if we were prisoners in a triumphal procession.*[41]

Furnish is right that this view is not impossible, but it is unlikely, for Paul never spoke of himself as humiliated by God, but always as blessed by God. The

---

[39] Barclay, *Corinthians*, 183.

[40] Barclay, *Corinthians*, 184.

[41] *II Corinthians*, 175.

reference to apostles as a spectacle (*theatron*) comes in a context in which Paul speaks of apostles as examples of those who reflect the behavior of Christ, e.g. "when persecuted, we endure" (1 Cor 4:12). Thus the spectacle is that they are "set on the stage in a theatre" because they are the examples that God wants the world to know and believers to follow.

Most important of all, Paul did not elsewhere imagine himself as defeated by Christ but as Christ's soldier in the defeat of others (especially in 2 Cor 10:3–6). Therefore, since a Roman triumph included both victorious soldiers and defeated enemies we have a choice as to which of them Paul identified himself with. He and other believers bring a fragrance that is life to believers and death to enemies, so that strongly implies that Paul and his colleagues are victorious soldiers in the parade, one which is a continuing battle, not just a celebration of previous victories. Barrett supports this interpretation, saying:

> In this verse he is describing himself and his colleagues as collaborating with God, and not as exposed by him to disgrace. Notwithstanding the lack of supporting lexical evidence it is right to follow L.S., Allo, and Kummel in taking Paul to represent himself as one of the victorious general's soldiers sharing in the glory of his triumph.[42]

Our interpretation of this passage is thus in line with the Paul-as-soldier-of-Christ imagery that we are elaborating in this chapter. Paul pictures himself and other believers as soldiers marching in God's victory parade through the world, into the darkness of this present age. As they go they bring the light, the victorious light, God's power to overcome the darkness. In this passage he specifies that power as their knowledge of God which comes through Christ, and symbolizes it as a fragrance, an aroma, a gas which arises from them and has varying effects: to those who welcome God, it is a fragrance of life; but to those who oppose God, who are his enemies, it is poison.[43] That is precisely how an

---

[42] Barrett, *Second Corinthians*, 98.

[43] Barclay and others suggest that this aroma refers to the smell coming from priests in the parade swinging incense censers. To the victors then the incense could remind them of their victory, while the prisoners took it as a foretelling of their coming execution (*Corinthians*, 184).

advancing army would affect the inhabitants of the region into which they march: all those who welcome the army, rejoicing in the freedom from the powers that it brings, will receive life. But those who object to the army's advance, who see it as the threat of death, and thus fight against it, will be right—it is death for them.

## Conclusion

By his initial victory in Christ, God created the advancing beachhead of the Kingdom of Light over which Christ rules and in which believers find safety as in a fortress. As the heavenly Jerusalem come invisibly to earth this new kingdom resembles the Maccabees' initial kingdom, when Jerusalem was retaken, cleansed and its lights relit, so Free Judah arose in the midst of the Seleucid darkness.

Paul's picture of the victorious Army of Light begins with Christ as the commander, and all believers as fellow-soldiers fighting side-by-side against the Army of Darkness. When they attack the enemy fortresses they use weapons of righteousness, driving back the enemy soldiers and finally defeating them. Central to the military imagery of an ongoing war is Paul's picture of believers as covered with the armor of light, which is Christ's own power that covers them and keeps them from any spiritual or eternal harm.

Even though Christ's soldiers are fully protected from spiritual and eternal harm, they remain vulnerable physically, socially and economically, for they still live their daily lives in this age of darkness. They must go out and attack the darkness in order to keep up the string of victories that began with the suffering victory of the cross. Paul knows from experience that Christ's soldiers must suffer, bearing the cost of this ongoing war. The forces of darkness can cause them pain, at times maim them, or even kill them. While they are alive the physical persecution they inevitably suffer in their role as soldiers provides one central opening to temptation. By threatening to maim or even kill Christ's soldiers, the forces of darkness seek to get them to desert, to choose freedom from persecution now and give up their eternal life in the Army of Light. In order to keep them from deserting, Paul offers the picture of present triumphs and hope of eventual complete victory in the Last Battle, to which we now turn.

# VII. THE LAST BATTLE


The Lord himself, with a cry of command, with the
archangel's call and with the sound of God's trumpet, will
descend from heaven, and the dead in Christ will rise first. (1
Thess 4:16)

Then comes the End, when (Christ) hands over the kingdom
to God the Father, after he has destroyed every ruler and
every authority and power...The last enemy to be destroyed is
Death. (1 Cor 15:24, 26)

The God of peace will soon crush Satan under your feet.
(Rom 16:20)


**Introduction**

In Paul's complete cosmic war myth, the original invasion of evil in the
fall (Gen 2-3; Rom 5:12-21) is reversed by the destruction of all evil in the
Last Battle, an image he received from the Jewish tradition. Here the story of
human history, the conflict of good and evil, will end, for God will finally
destroy all evil forces and so bring about the perfectly good and peaceful world
that had been his intention from the beginning. The cosmic battle imagery makes
it clear that evil will not give up easily, and cannot be overcome simply by
human beings. Rather evil is basically supernatural, and only the power of God
in Christ will finally conquer it. However, as believers are Christ's soldiers in
the ongoing war, so they will take part in the war until the final defeat of all the

forces of evil.

Our goal in this chapter, as in the previous chapters, is to describe this military version of the End, the symbolic expression, not to try to discern the reality it symbolized. In order to discover Paul's full myth we will explore his various hints and elaborate them. Those hints come mainly in 1 Corinthians 15 and 1 Thessalonians 4–5, with further details coming from 2 Thessalonians 2. Even if the latter is from a Paulinist, not Paul, it probably reflects the Pauline tradition and so is an appropriate source for developing a fuller picture. We postulate that Paul had in his imagination a much fuller story of the Last Battle that he could have told if he had found it necessary. Thus our task is to look at those tips of the mountains standing above the clouds, and try to discern what lies beneath, hidden from our eyes. Our main source for discerning that undercloud detail is the traditional Hebraic Last Battle Myth, as we painted it in chapter II above. We will use the details of that traditional picture, especially from Daniel 7 and 11, Ezekiel 38–39 and Zechariah 14, to fill in the canvas on which Paul simply painted a few highpoints.

In outline, the story we will tell in this chapter has these main elements: **A. The Increasing Oppression of the Darkness**, for the ongoing war continues and probably grows in intensity until the End. **B. The Final Conqueror Arrives**, when the parousia of Christ takes place with the sounding of the last trumpet. **C. Final, Complete, Victory: The End of Evil**, when the returned Christ shall defeat the last of the angelic principalities, bring an end to the oppressive reign of Death, and crush Satan.

## A. THE INCREASE OF EVIL

In Paul's story the present is the time of the ongoing war which we described in detail in the previous chapter. Though believers are spiritually protected in Christ's Fortress of Light, they venture out to attack the darkness and thereby join in the battle that Christ began. When he says that "the mystery of lawlessness is already at work" (2 Thess 2:7) that presumably refers to the power of Sin doing the work of Satan through the oppression of the angelic powers and their subordinates, the children of darkness.

Paul's most direct expression of this ongoing war is his statement in 1 Corinthians 15 that Christ is now reigning and is now carrying on the war against the rulers, authorities and powers (24–25). As we argued earlier, this is not a reference to a millennial rule after the parousia, but to the ongoing battle in the present, as the age to come presses forward, like a beachhead moving outward, and gradually conquers the present age of darkness.

One obscure element in the story is Paul's reference to "the restrainer" in 2 Thess 2:6–7 who will eventually be removed, thus allowing the forces of evil to mount to their greatest oppression. No agreed interpretation of this force or person has arisen, so it remains a mysterious element in Paul's myth. Perhaps the War Scroll provides a hint, for it says that the beginning of the last battle comes on the day that God has appointed (1QM i), which suggests that the will of God, the timing of God, is the restraint.[1]

In Paul's tradition, especially in the prophets' writings, the Last Battle begins with a final, physical, attack on Jerusalem by the forces of darkness. Our concern here is to determine what Paul, with his new understanding of God's victory in Christ, may have imagined as the triggering event of the end. Did he simply adopt the OT picture and also imagine a physical attack on Jerusalem? Or did he transpose that physical attack into a spiritual one on the Fortress of Light?

### (1) The Tradition

In the Hebrew tradition, the final rebellion against God and his Kingdom of Light was prophesied to take place when God calls the forces of darkness together to attack God's people (usually in Jerusalem). According to the prophets, God says:

> In the latter days I will bring you against my land, so that the nations may know me, when through you, O Gog, I display my holiness before their eyes. (Ezek 38:16)
> I will gather all the nations against Jerusalem to battle. (Zech 14:2)

Further, the Qumran visionaries looked forward to the day "appointed from

---

[1] See Vos, *Pauline Eschatology* (132), Whiteley (237–240), Ridderbos (521–526), Best, *Thessalonians* (295–301) and Marshall, *Thessalonians* (193–200) for discussions of the various options here.

ancient times for the battle of destruction of the sons of darkness" (1QM i). Thus the apocalyptic visionaries foresaw the powers of evil gathering like a pack of greedy hyenas in Judah, surrounding Jerusalem, at a time determined by God. Then the persecution done by the forces of darkness will reach unprecedented heights. In the tradition, this explosion of evil was foreseen, e.g. when Daniel said that Michael would arise in "a time of trouble, such as never has been since there was a nation" (Dan 12:1).

## (2) Paul's Spiritual Viewpoint

Paul as a Christian held a different view of God's people than did his Jewish ancestors among the prophets and his contemporaries among the people of Qumran. Those Jewish believers understood God's protection as a physical power at work in the land of Palestine. They understood God's people as the people of Judah, of that particular land, so the attack on them naturally took place as a physical attack on Judah, especially on Jerusalem.

Paul, however, did not believe that God's new people in Christ were located physically in any particular land. Instead they were located spiritually in the Fortress Kingdom of Christ, an invisible place. Thus attacks on that kingdom would have to be different from the prophets' imagined attacks on Jerusalem. Thus Paul probably did not simply adopt the prophetic picture of a physical attack on Jerusalem as the precipitating event of the End.

Paul never explicitly spoke of a final attack of the forces of darkness against the light, so it is possible that he did not think such an event would take place. The passages which speak of the End offer only sparse information.

1 Cor 15:24–25 suggests that the battle against the principalities is ongoing, that Christ is now defeating them and will keep that victory streak up until they are all defeated. The triggering event of the End thus seems to be here the defeat of the last angelic power.

2 Thessalonians 2 has more details, speaking of the *apostasia* and the coming of the Man of Lawlessness. Neither of these is a clearly military event. The term *apostasia* has a primary political sense, "rebellion," and a secondary religious sense, "apostasy" which means the renunciation of prior belief. Marshall argues that the rebellion is a general increase of godlessness in the world, rather than apostasy among believers, because the apocalyptic writings refer to such a general increase of wickedness and opposition to God as the end

draws near.[2]

The Man of Lawlessness, who seems to be a version of the Antichrist spoken of later in the Johannine letters, is not a clearly military figure, so his coming does not necessarily entail a physical attack. The central characteristics of this figure are these: (i) he claims divine status, for he "opposes and exalts himself against every so-called god and object of worship, so that he takes his seat in the temple of God, where he proclaims himself to be God" (2 Thess 2:4); (ii) he works by propaganda rather than force for he uses Satan's signs, lying, wonders and deception (9-10). As Ridderbos observes, he "bears much more the character of a false prophet who leads men astray not so much with outward force as with lying wonders, and whose character is defined above all by his godlessness and immorality carried to an extreme;"[3] (iii) he is apparently the personification of all evil, for when Christ defeats him it seems that all evil is defeated. No other battle is mentioned and so none seems necessary (2 Thess 2:8)

That claim to divine status and self-enthroning in Jerusalem seem to be allusions to Dan 11:36 which speaks of a king (Antiochus IV, who called himself "Epiphanes") who considers himself higher than any god. Further, Dan 11:31 speaks of an abomination set up in the temple, which could be the source of the image of the Man of Lawlessness enthroned in the temple. Thus it is plausible that in 2 Thessalonians 2 we find an updated version of Daniel's endtime imagery. Then the reference in 2 Thess 2:9–10 to the use of propaganda is reminiscent of Antiochus' attempt to turn the Jews into Hellenists. Finally, the possibility that the Man of Lawlessness is a personification of all evil is reminiscent of the Fourth Beast in Daniel 7, for that beast (with Antiochus as its little horn) too seemed to be the final symbol of all evil.

If Daniel's visions are the chief background for understanding 2 Thessalonians 2 that implies that the kind of attack that comes at the End is primarily a religious one rather than a strictly military one. Antiochus tried to destroy Judaism by getting Jews to convert to his Hellenism, so he acted by tempting them to give up their tradition in order to save their lives. That seems to be quite similar to Paul's picture of himself and others as they endure the

---

[2] *Thessalonians*, 189.
[3] *Paul*, 513.

ongoing war: they too are tempted to give up their faith in order to escape the persecution that is the way the darkness seeks to blot out the light. Thus the ongoing persecution of believers is the battle that takes place up till the very end, and Paul probably thought this would increase for the Daniel story included this end-time prophecy: "There shall be a time of anguish, such as has never occurred since nations first came into existence. But at that time your people shall be delivered" (Dan 12:2). That same image of the messianic woes is repeated in the Synoptic Apocalypse, showing that it had indeed been taken over by the early Christians (Matt 24:8–24).

Given the apocalyptic nature of 2 Thessalonians 2, and the background of the sea monster imagery in Ezek 38:4 and Dan 7:2–3, Bousset suggested that Paul's rebel, this false Messiah, is a literary descendant of the sea serpent used as a symbol by the prophets:

> As may still be seen in Revelation, there existed in the popular Jewish belief the foreboding of another revolt of the old marine monster with whom God had warred at the creation, but who in the last days was again to rise and contend in heaven-storming battle with God...To me the Antichrist legend seems a simple incarnation of that old Dragon myth, which has in the first instance nothing to do with particular political powers and occurrences. For the Dragon is substituted the man armed with miraculous power who makes himself God's equal—a man who in the eyes of the Jews could be no other than the false Messiah.[4]

Our conclusion thus is that Paul transformed the traditional picture of a final physical attack on Jerusalem into the culmination of the ongoing spiritual attack on believers. Quite possibly, in order to keep faith with his tradition, he pictured this as an attack on the spiritual Jerusalem, the new Fortress of Light. Having been squeezed back into a small space, the united armies of the Enemy attack the Fortress of Light, whereupon God's people will suffer their greatest persecution ever (Dan 12:1). God allows that suffering of the chosen people because that will be the means by which they are refined, purified, cleansed (Dan 11:35; 12:10). It is also the means by which God will finally defeat the

---

[4] Bousset, *The Antichrist Legend*, 144.

forces of evil, for they are gathered in one place and so are conquerable. In Paul's picture that gathering of all the enemies in one place seems to be presented in the personification of all evil known as the Man of Lawlessness, who is conquered by Christ.

## B. THE FINAL CONQUEROR ARRIVES

> For the Lord himself, with a cry of command, with the archangel's call and with the sound of God's trumpet, will descend from heaven. (1 Thess 4:16)

At the heart of Paul's last battle story, the main image he wished his readers to take away in their memories, is this: the supernatural Christ descends with an overwhelmingly powerful angelic army behind him to conquer the Army of Darkness finally and forever. This is the Pauline version of the OT Day of Yahweh, a day of God's intervention that had been part of Hebrew myth since Amos' day. Of course, since Paul had a different picture of God's People than did the prophets, Paul's picture of the final victory differed from theirs also.

### (1) The Day of the Lord Arrives

Paul used the phrase "the day of the Lord (or of Christ)" often to refer to the day when Christ comes in glory (1 Thess 5:2; 2 Thess 2:2; 2 Cor 1:14; 1 Cor 1:8; 5:5; Phil 1:6, 10; 2:16). That same day he spoke of as "the day of wrath" (Rom 2:5) which is "the day when...God, through Jesus Christ, will judge the secret thoughts of all people" (Rom 2:16).

Amos was perhaps the first prophet to use the phrase, when he warned his hearers that the Day of Yahweh would be a day of darkness not light, for God would punish all evil-doers, Israel included (Am 5:18). Isaiah spoke constantly of the day of the Lord (calling it often just "that day"), seeing it as a day of judgment (2:12-13; 2:20-21; 3:18-24; 5:30; 7:18, 24-25; 10:3) and a day of salvation for a remnant (10:20-27).

While the day of the Lord as used by Amos and Isaiah was a time in history in which God would come to punish the evil and rescue the oppressed, it later became an eschatological threat and hope. Perhaps one of the earliest expressions of it is in Isaiah 13, from the time of the exile, in which the day of the Lord is a day of cosmic judgment:

(4) Listen, an uproar of kingdoms, of nations gathering together. The Lord of Hosts is mustering an army for battle. (5) They come from a distant land, *from the end of the heavens*, the Lord and the weapons of his indignation, *to destroy the whole earth*. (6) Wail for the day of the Lord is near, it will come like destruction from the Almighty...(9) See the day of the Lord comes, cruel, with wrath and fierce anger, to make the earth a desolation, and to destroy its sinners from it. (10) For *the stars of the heavens and their constellations will not give their light*...(11) I will punish the world for its evil and the wicked for their iniquity.

Later Joel foresaw "the great and terrible day of the Lord" when "the sun shall be turned to darkness and the moon to blood" (Joel 2:31). Zephaniah saw the day of the Lord as imminent, for he said "the day of the Lord is near" (1:14), "a day of trumpet blast and battle cry against the fortified cities" (1:16). Though that suggests earthly warfare, that is not the whole of this prophet's vision for he also says that "on the day of the Lord's wrath...the whole earth shall be consumed; for a full and terrible end he will make of all the inhabitants of the earth" (1:18).

Paul's use of the traditional phrase "the Day of the Lord" suggests that he had these passages in mind. He too foresaw a day of judgment which would be a cosmic invasion since the descent of the conqueror was so central to his picture. However, since for Paul God's people were spiritually safe in the Kingdom of Christ, and the enemies were mainly spiritual forces, the invasion had to be somewhat different from the traditional picture of earthly armies clashing physically. Instead the attack of the darkness on earth takes the form of attacks on believers all over the world, and the propaganda proclaiming a false messiah in Jerusalem.

## (2) The Last Trumpet Sounds

Traditionally the visionaries had foreseen evil reaching its heights just before the End comes, so it is plausible that Paul held a similar picture. When the persecution and attempted seduction of believers reaches its height, then Christ will descend from heaven to rescue them. First comes his cry of command, then the archangel's shout mobilizing the Heavenly Army of Light, and finally the trumpet will sound to call the army to battle (1 Thess 4:16, see

Isa 27:13).[5]

Like a voice crying in the wilderness, when hope has almost disappeared, so the sound of God's messenger will announce the coming of the Lord at the head of his relieving army: It is the Commander-in-Chief of the heavenly army crying "Attack!" as he leads his legions of light into the battle.[6]

Along with the commander's cry comes the archangel's call. Here Paul probably imagines the handing on of Christ's command by Michael, the military leader of the Hosts of Light. Though the NT writers rarely referred to the archangels (Jude 9 is the only other reference, to "Michael the archangel") the tradition clearly pictured the chief angel Michael as the commander in the battle on earth. In fact Dan 12:1 describes the End as the time when "Michael shall arise, the great Prince who has charge of your people." The Scrolls go even further in saying that the defeat of Satan will result in "eternal succour to the company of His redeemed by the might of the princely Angel of the Kingdom of Michael" (1QM xvii). In Paul's myth, of course, Christ is the one who has the kingdom. If it were not for this Thessalonian reference to the archangel's call we would have taken Paul to have put Christ completely in the place of Michael as the commander of the forces of light on earth. As it is, this brief phrase suggests that Paul is simply making an allusion to the traditional picture given in Daniel, because that is the story that his readers know. By having the archangel Michael at Christ's side, Paul emphasizes that Christ has been given the role of the Lord of all creatures, "the head of all rule and authority" (Col 2:10). When the king cries "Attack!", the general at his side gives the specific order, "All troops, forward at attack speed!"

---

[5] Some interpreters identify the cry and the call with the sounding of the trumpet, all as ways to describe a single event. Marshall says, "this is quite possible since Rev. 1:10; 4:1 contains the idea of a voice which sounds like a trumpet" (*Thessalonians*, 129). While that is possible, when we take the scene as a military one the order of events makes good sense as Paul wrote it and as we will expound it.

[6] The phrase *en keleusmati* has the sense "with a signal," or "with a cry of command." Bruce says "This military noun occurs once in LXX: Prov 30:27, 'the locust marches at one word of command.'" It is also used by Thucydides (Hist. 2.92) "of the cheer with which the Athenian fighters encouraged one another at the battle of Naupactus" (*Thessalonians*, 100).

Following the king's cry and the general's call comes "the sound of the trumpet of God" (1 Thess 5:16), which is the way the command reaches the troops in an army. In the Hebrew tradition the trumpet also announced the coming of the king, first at the Sinai covenant-making (Exod 19:16), next when the Lord comes to bring the exiles home (Isa 27:13), and finally at the Last Battle (Joel 2:1; Zech 9:14). Perhaps the best background for this aspect of Paul's battle picture comes from Zeph 1:14–16: "The great day of the Lord is near...A day of wrath is that day, a day of distress and anguish...a day of trumpet blast and battle cry against fortified cities and against the lofty battlements." When the trumpet sounds, it sends the heavenly host into the battle against the forces of darkness which have surrounded the children of light, seeking to tempt them to fall away.[7]

## (3) The Heavenly Host Descends

At that blast of the trumpet, the chief warriors Paul imagines as called into battle are the angelic ones, those who are the subordinates of the archangel. Paul refers to them in another phrase in 2 Thess 1:7 when he says: "The Lord Jesus is revealed from heaven with his mighty angels, in flaming fire." That flaming fire expresses the divine awesomeness and power (Exod 19:18; 24:17; Dan 7:9–10). Presumably both the descending commander and the angelic army are armed with the flaming fire for they represent and symbolize God's power of light that will destroy the darkness. Like David descending from the hill-top to do battle with Goliath, Christ will have behind him the whole army of God, the host of heaven, ready to destroy the enemy army once the single combat is over.

Such an accompanying angelic host was common in the tradition, e.g. in the last battle picture of Zechariah which says "the Lord your God will come, and all the holy ones with him" (14:5, see also 1QM i). A more detailed picture of the angelic army comes from 2 Maccabees in which the armed help of the

---

[7] This trumpet call is the last sound before the End according to 1 Cor 15:52 where Paul writes: "We will not all die, but we will all be changed, in a moment, in the twinkling of an eye, at the last trumpet. For the trumpet will sound, and the dead will be raised imperishable, and we will be changed." Here, the resurrection comes at the last trumpet because the Enemy defeated in the last battle is Death (26).

angelic army is described, first of all in a vision:

> For almost forty days there appeared over all the city goldenclad cavalry charging through the air, in companies fully armed with lances and drawn swords—troops of cavalry drawn up, attacks and counterattacks made on this side and on that, brandishing of shields, massing of spears, hurling of missiles, the flash of golden trappings and armor of all kinds. (2 Macc 5:2-3)

Later, in a battle, another epiphany occurs which helps the Jews win, for the angelic soldiers "showered arrows and thunderbolts on the enemy, so...they were thrown into disorder and cut to pieces" (2 Macc 10:29-30). These visions could well have provided inspiration for apocalyptic visionaries imagining the Last Battle.

Paul presumably included his brief references to the angelic army at Christ's side because it was a traditional part of the picture that he had learned long before, not because it was a central element in his own imagining. Indeed he plays down the angelic role in order to play up Christ's role, for Christ wins the battle instead of Michael and the other angels. Still the angelic army probably had symbolic value for Paul: first it elevates Christ the commander, making him appear to be far greater than a single champion, by showing the supernatural army he has at his command; in addition, it suggests that the battle on earth is also supernatural, emphasizing that the enemies are not simply human, but the angelic princes of the nations united under the Prince of Darkness.

### (4) The Fiery Champion Descends

> The Lord himself will descend from heaven. (1 Thess 4:16)
> The Lord Jesus is revealed from heaven, with his mighty angels, in flaming fire. (2 Thess 1:7)

When believers engulfed in the last flames of the ongoing war suppose that defeat is imminent, when everything seems dark, then like a thief in the night Christ will burst into glorious view, revealed from heaven with his mighty angels in blazing fire. As God appeared in fire on Mt. Sinai, announced by the sound of a trumpet (Exod 19:16–20), so Christ will appear at the last day. The sun will appear at midnight, and night will no longer hold sway. Then will be fulfilled the promises such as this one:

> Arise Jerusalem, rise clothed in light;
> Your light has come
>  and the Glory of the Lord shines over you.
> For, though darkness covers the earth
>  and dark night the nations,
> The Lord shall shine upon you
>  and over you shall his glory appear. (Isa 60:1–2)

In that descent of the light, the promise will be fulfilled that the Lord will go forth and fight against the nations as when he fights on a day of battle (Zech 14:3).

Of course Paul did not believe that before the last battle Christ had been absent, separated from his people on earth. All through the time since the Age to Come broke the universal hold of the Present Age, Christ has been present within his people, the Lord of the Castle where they find their home. But he has been invisible, not only to believers but also to the Rulers of the Present Age, fighting them mainly through the faithfulness and love of the children of light. In that ongoing war Christ continued to subdue the powers (1 Cor 15:25), spreading the walls of the Fortress of Light further and further into the domain of the god of this age.

The picture of Christ visibly descending at the head of an angelic army is thus a dramatic change, one we can perhaps think of as the change from a guerilla war by underground resistance fighters into an all-out confrontation against the darkness. Previously the guerillas had to venture out into the darkness and seek to conquer fortresses with stealth. Now the whole heavenly army attacks, so the slow fortress-by-fortress war is over. Now the overwhelming power of the heavenly army appears, with the Lord the champion of his people (e.g. Ezek 38:19–22; Zech 14:3–4; Isa 26:21; 27:1; 1QM xii).

Paul describes this event as "the Lord Jesus revealed from heaven with his mighty angels *in flaming fire*" (2 Thess 1:7). This blazing fire which surrounds Christ is a symbol from the tradition. God often was imagined as appearing in fire, especially in the beginning at Mt. Sinai (Exod 3:2–6; 19:18), but at later times also (Ps 18:8; Ezek 1:13, 27; Hab 3:4). The fire symbolizes mystery, power, the possibility of purification, but most of all the threat of destruction. Thus the most likely immediate background for Paul's picture is the divine judgment tradition, e.g. in the vision of Isa 66:15: "Behold the Lord will come in fire, and his chariots like the stormwind...to render...his rebuke with flames of fire." Even more striking is the Danielic picture of the Judge and Conqueror at the End: "His throne was fiery flames, its wheels were burning fire. A stream of fire issued forth from before him" (Dan 7:9–10). Thus when Paul depicts the returning Christ in flaming fire, he probably was using this traditional symbol of God's mystery, awesomeness and conquering power as a way to say that Christ is the Power of God at the end.

## C. FINAL, COMPLETE, VICTORY: THE END OF EVIL

When the heavenly champion, the King of the Kingdom of Light, arrives on earth, the darkness cannot endure his presence. The Man of Lawlessness is burned to a cinder, the angelic powers are all dethroned, Sin is disintegrated, Death is finally defeated, and Satan is crushed under the feet of the soldiers of the King of Light. All these are probably complementary symbolic expressions of Paul's main hope: at the end, God in Christ will destroy all evil forever.

### (1) The Tyrant Annihilated

> Then the Lawless One will be revealed, and the Lord Jesus
> will slay [*anelei*] him with the breath [*pneumati*] of his mouth,
> and destroy [*katargesei*] him by the epiphany [*epiphaneia*] of
> his coming [*parousia*]. (2 Thess 2:8)

As the rising of the sun drives away the darkness, so the simple epiphany of Christ clothed in heavenly fire (which perhaps is the Glory of God) will defeat the Lawless One, whom Paul seems to have meant as the personification of all the forces of darkness. Christ's epiphany is the arrival in power of the true king, the one whose simple presence so terrorizes the rebels that they break ranks, turn to flee and so are easily destroyed.[8]

How the arrival of that heavenly warrior will defeat the enemy, by the breath of his mouth, we can picture from the tradition which spoke of it vividly in the Coming of the Divine Savior (God): "The Lord thundered in the heavens...uttered his voice, hailstones and coals of fire...and the foundations of the world were laid bare, at your rebuke, O Lord, at the blast of the breath of your nostrils" (Ps 18:12–15).

In that day Gog and his army will be the great sea monster bringing the chaos of the sea against God's people (Ezek 38:4), but it will not succeed. For the Lord with his great sword will conquer Leviathan the fleeing serpent, destroying that dragon of the sea (Isa 27:1). In single combat the divine hero will face the tyrant, striking his weapons from his hands and so killing him and his armies on the mountains of Israel (Ezek 39:3). When that monster is slain by the Champion of Israel, then its body will be burned with the fire that streams out from the throne of God (Dan 7:11).

Paul's picture of Christ conquering the great enemy by his breath is foreshadowed also in Isa 30:27–28 where God's approaching wrath is pictured this way:

> His tongue is like a devouring fire; his breath is like an overflowing stream that reaches up to the neck, to sift the nations with the sieve of destruction...The Lord will cause his majestic voice to be heard and the descending blow of his arm to be seen, in furious anger and a flame of fire...The Assyrians will be terror-stricken at the voice of the Lord, when he smites with his rod...a burning place has long been prepared...the breath of the Lord, like a stream of brimstone, kindles it.

---

[8] The image of an *epiphaneia* "has a Hellenistic background in the visitations of deities to save and help men, and is applied in a similar way to the visitations of kings and emperors to cities" (Best, *Thessalonians*, 303). Paul's picture of a conquering "epiphany" echoes the story in 2 Macc 3:24 when a foreign general came to plunder the temple treasury. Then "the Sovereign of Spirits and of all authority caused so great an epiphany that all who had been so bold as to come were astounded by the power of God, and became faint with terror."

Here the prophet combines God's word of judgment/destruction with the image of the warrior using his rod to destroy. Perhaps Paul had a similar combination in mind.

Then will be fulfilled the promise that the Lord roars from Zion and utters his voice from Jerusalem and the heavens and the earth shake, but his own people take refuge in him (Joel 3:16). Then too will come true Isaiah's prophesy of the coming king of Judah, who "will strike the earth with the rod *of his mouth*, and with *the breath* of his lips he *will slay* the wicked" (Isa 11:4). That victory comes when he "judges the poor with righteousness," i.e. speaking forth saving judgments.[9]

When Christ descends from heaven he will come as the heavenly hero long foreseen by Israel's prophets and called by them "the Lord." Since the tradition offers these pictures, Paul may well have imagined something like this: Christ will stand on Mt. Zion and face the Armies of Darkness, with the angelic Army of Light behind him and perhaps the underworld powers of nature joining in the battle. By his fiery breath (his Spirit, his Word) he will burn up the Man of Lawlessness, which, like Daniel's Fourth Beast probably symbolizes, embodies, personifies, the whole Evil Empire (since he is the only enemy Christ has to defeat in this vision). By his word of judgment he will condemn them all and destroy the darkness by declaring the advent of universal light. In Paul's imagination this was probably a spiritual battle, not a physical one as it seems to be in the OT. Simply Christ's coming and the power of his Spirit are enough to defeat and destroy all evil forever.

One intriguing question that Paul leaves open is what role the human children of light will play in this last great battle. Paul never clearly describes them taking part in it. In addition, most of the traditional pictures have God alone, or with the angels, winning the battle, leaving no place for a human army. The one exception is the War Scroll, which pictures the Army of Light as including human warriors as well as angelic ones: "Valiant [warriors] of the angelic host are among our numbered men, and the Hero of war is with our congregation; the host of His spirits is with our foot-soldiers and horsemen"

---

[9] The italicized words are the ones Paul quotes in 2 Thess 2:8, probably from memory, combining them in his picture of Christ "slaying" the Lawless One "with the breath of his mouth."

(1QM xii).

The clues to Paul's picture of the believers' role at the End are two-fold: Paul pictured believers taking part in the (spiritual) ongoing war, so it would be natural for them to continue that fighting until the very end; Paul pictures God finally crushing Satan "under your (believers') feet" (Rom 16:20), which we will argue below suggests that believers are in Christ when Christ defeats the powers of darkness. Thus we conclude that Paul followed the Qumran model, seeing believers as taking part (spiritually) in the final battle, as they had in the ongoing war that led up to that battle.

## (2) The Angelic Powers Overthrown

> Christ must continue to reign until he has put all his enemies under his feet...defeating [*katargese*, destroying?] every rule and every authority and power. (1 Cor 15:25, 24)

In this passage, rule, authority and power refer to the angelic princes of the nations, the rulers of this present age whom we described in chapter IV. There we argued, following Caird and others, that Paul saw them as the angelic sons of God whom God had appointed as agents of divine justice over each of the nations. However, they had become corrupt in allowing themselves to be worshipped as gods, and had used their nations for their own benefit instead of the peoples'. Therefore God had condemned them, proclaiming that in the end they will be punished (Isa 24:21), indeed destroyed (Ps 82:7). As we showed in chapter V, Paul believed that in the death and resurrection of Christ the angelic powers had been initially defeated (Col 2:15; 1 Cor 2:6-8), their spiritual hold over believers ended (Gal 4:3, 8-9).

Though defeated and driven back, the angelic powers continue as powers in the world: they are still God's agents of justice in the nations (Rom 13:1-6); and they still are Satan's agents of oppression over all those who are in the Kingdom of Darkness, including believers as far as their physical lives are concerned. As far as their spiritual lives are concerned, however, believers are within Christ's Kingdom of Light, which is advancing forward into the darkness. As it advances in the ongoing war (see ch. VI above), its ruler Christ gradually subdues the angelic powers, for they are *ton katargoumenon*, i.e. the ones who are "passing away," or "being destroyed" (1 Cor 2:6). In the End, the powers will all be finally and forever defeated, dethroned (and perhaps destroyed) by the victory of Christ.

As we argued in chapter V, Paul probably believed that Christ's reign began at his resurrection, and thus that the battle against the principalities is a central element in the ongoing war which is now taking place. Vos plausibly argued that in Paul's story Christ began to reign at his resurrection when the powers were first subdued (Col 2:15), for Christ from then on reigned over them (Rom 8:38–39).[10]

Thus Paul probably believed that the end to the rule of the powers would happen immediately upon the return of Christ. Probably he imagined Christ defeating them in, with and by his destruction of the Man of Lawlessness, who is probably the embodiment or personification of all the evil forces (as the Fourth Beast was the symbolic embodiment of all the evil in Daniel's vision). This moment of Christ's epiphany, his presence on earth, then is the moment when he will finally defeat "every rule and every authority and power" (1 Cor 15:24). All the rebellious angelic rulers of every rank, and all the evil human rulers and soldiers, will be defeated forever, as had been foreseen in the Hebraic tradition.

Among the traditional roots of this defeat-of-the-angels myth are various passages in the Old Testament. Perhaps the oldest is Psalm 82 in which God denounces the gods of the nations, for injustice and declares that they all "shall die like mortals" (Ps 82:7). An Isaiah passage also foresees this defeat: "On that day the Lord will punish the host of heaven in heaven, and on the earth the kings of the earth" (Isa 24:21). The first clear expression of the battle with angelic rulers is found in Daniel 10 in which Michael the archangel joins with the unnamed chief angel in battles against the Prince of Persia and then the Prince of Greece (10:13, 20–21). Though the text does not specifically report their victory, it implies it in the proclamation of resurrection at the end (12:1).

The first full account of the final defeat (in the form of punishment) of the angelic rulers is in *1 En* 90:24–25:

---

[10] Vos, *Eschatology*, 245. For a similar view see Davies, *Paul and Rabbinic Judaism*, 292–297, Shires, *The Eschatology of Paul*, 68–72, and Hill, "Paul's Understanding of Christ's Kingdom in I Corinthians 15:20–28," 297–320.

> The judgment was held first over the stars [the sons of God of
> the Genesis 6 story], and they were judged and found guilty,
> and went to the place of condemnation, and they were cast
> into an abyss, full of fire and flame, and full of pillars of fire.
> And those seventy [angelic] shepherds were judged and found
> guilty, and they were cast in that fiery abyss.

Finally, the one Jewish work that specifically depicts the angelic forces of
darkness defeated in battle is the War Scroll. After a see-saw battle, the end of
the war arrives when God intervenes: "with the seventh lot, the mighty hand of
God shall bring down [the army of Satan, and all] the angels of his kingdom,
and all the members [of his company]" (1QM i). Thus we can see that Paul's
picture of the final defeat of the angelic powers is a traditional one.

### Destroyed or Reconciled?

When Paul said in Col 1:20 that in Christ God had reconciled all things
to himself, including things in heaven, that may suggest that he foresaw the
reconciliation of some at least of the angelic enemies. If he did expect that then
we could translate 1 Cor 15:24 differently to include that possibility. In that
verse Paul uses *katargeo* of the end of the powers' sway, a verb which is used
in the NT in the senses to make ineffective, to abolish, and to destroy. If some
of the powers are reconciled then we could say Paul meant the sense make
ineffective (as opponents) here. That may be what Paul suggests in Philippians
2 also, when he says every knee in all creation will bow to Christ as Lord
(10–11). Since the powers were originally God's agents, they can (theoretically)
repent and be reconciled to their Maker.

Berkhof suggests that the Powers will in fact return to the fold, saying
that "the Powers have their role also in the age to come."[11] In order to make
that interpretation fit Paul, Berkhof translates *katargeo* in 1 Cor 2:8 and
15:24–25 as "dethrone," so the powers are defeated but not destroyed by the
returning Christ. That same imagery is suggested by Caird who sees Paul as
offering both the image of Christ conquering the powers and the image of God
reconciling them to himself:

---

[11] Berkhof, *Christ and the Powers*, 42.

> The hope that the powers will be reconciled to God is thrown out without any elaboration, so that we are left to conjecture what such a hope involves. I think we may assume, however, that Paul developed his hope of cosmic reconciliation not as a substitute for his earlier belief in the defeat of the powers but as its complement, and that the powers could be reconciled to God only when they had been deprived of their evil potentiality and made subject to Christ.[12]

Though Col 1:20 is the only semi-direct expression of the idea of the reconciliation of angelic enemies, it does have weight since there is also only one passage (1 Cor 15:24) that speaks directly of the defeat of those powers, and it can be understood as allowing for reconciliation following the defeat.

To summarize: though he only speaks of the defeat of the angels briefly, Paul certainly believed that the evil angelic powers were finally defeated by Christ, their oppression and slavery finally ended by the return of the true king. Christ's parousia, the coming of the eternal light into the temporal darkness, will completely defeat the angelic forces of darkness by a single breath of his mouth. Possibly some of them may repent and become reconciled to their Maker. The rest, presumably, will suffer eternal death.[13]

## (3) Death Defeated

> Christ must reign until he has put all his enemies under his feet. The last enemy to be destroyed is Death. (1 Cor 15:25–26)
>
> The Lord himself will descend from heaven with a cry of command...and the dead in Christ will rise first; then we who are alive, who are left, shall be caught up together with them in the clouds to meet the Lord in the air. (1 Thess 4:16–17)

With the defeat of Satan's army comes the defeat of Satan's most feared

---

[12] *Principalities*, 83.

[13] Matt 25:41 refers to "the eternal fire prepared for the devil and his angels" which shows that in the first century at least some Christians saw fallen angels as destined for eternal punishment. Perhaps Paul thought that also, even though he never said so.

agent, Death, the last enemy (1 Cor 15:26). Since this is the last enemy, Paul probably pictured Satan's final defeat (Rom 16:20) as accompanying, happening in and with, the defeat of Death. Probably for Paul the defeat of the Man of Lawlessness, the dethroning of the powers, the end of Death's reign and the crushing of Satan underfoot are all complementary expressions of the end of all evil. When any of them is mentioned Paul probably thought it included the others, so he did not need to mention them.[14]

Our first question is how Paul pictured Death when he called it "the last enemy." As we argued in chapter IV above, Paul probably imagined Death as the Destroyer, the angel of destruction mentioned in 1 Cor 10:10 and various OT passages (Exod 12:23; Num 16:41–49). Paul probably understood this Destroyer along the lines of Revelation's Abaddon/Apollyon, the angelic ruler of Sheol (Rev 9:11). Since we also described Satan as the angel of death (ch. III above), we suggest that Paul saw Death the last enemy and Satan as two names for the same reality. Paul probably thought of Death as the last facade of Satan, the final expression of that angelic power. Perhaps, if he used the underworld imagery we find in Revelation, Paul pictured the Angel of Death ruling in Hades, hidden from the light of the sun. Probably he pictured Death ruling over all who have died, like a shepherd in control of his flock (Ps 49:14), or a warden ruling his prison as a tyrant (Rom 5:14, 17). This fits well with the picture that DeBoer presents when he says:

> In 1 Corinthians 15 death is an inimical power that has usurped God's place, standing in opposition to the divine purpose and desire; it is the power that encompasses the other powers and marks the human world as the realm of separation

---

[14] Of course we could create a consecutive plot and attribute it to Paul. We could say that first comes the defeat of the powers (since it is going on already); then perhaps comes the parousia and the destruction of the Man of Lawlessness; perhaps this would be the point when Satan is next crushed underfoot; finally could come the end of Death, with the resurrection of all believers. Our view is that Paul could have had a plot like that, but the absence of any suggestion of such consecutive events, and his way of mentioning just one and implying the end of all evil, suggests that the four pictures are four different symbolic expressions of the defeat of evil.

from God and thus from life.[15]

The other passage suggesting the defeat of Death is 1 Thessalonians 4. There the one and only event mentioned following the parousia is the resurrection or transformation of believers. Thus in that vision, when the Victor returns, his power invades the hidden, underworld empire, the Kingdom of Death, Satan's final stronghold. There (as we reconstructed Paul's probable picture in chapter IV) all the dead are found, though they are divided into various realms, so the dead in Christ are protected from any further harm. Still they are victims under the oppression of Death, asleep rather than enjoying blessedness, so Christ's final victory is the means of their final rescue. That is the reason for Paul's emphasis on the defeat of Death: only by that event are dead believers freed from its hold.

Paul probably pictured the defeat of Death as the same event as the resurrection of the dead, their rescue from Sheol/Hades, which happens immediately upon Christ's return to earth: "the Lord...will descend from heaven, and the dead in Christ will rise first" (1 Thess 4:17); the resurrection will happen to "each in his own order: Christ the first fruits, then at his coming those who belong to Christ" (1 Cor 15:23). Thus the last battle, and the defeat of death the last enemy, are pictured by Paul as happening immediately upon the return of Christ to earth, victory by "the epiphany of his parousia" (2 Thess 2:8).

One disputed issue is whether Paul pictured all the dead rising or just the faithful dead. On the one hand, Paul's military symbolism, if he meant death is "destroyed," suggests that death will be totally overcome, that all who have suffered death will be brought to life. Further, some early Christians did believe in the resurrection of all the dead (Rev 20:12-13; Acts 24:15), so Paul probably knew that belief, though he did not specifically mention it.[16] On the other hand,

---

[15] *The Defeat of Death*, 138.

[16] W. D. Davies presents the views of Schweitzer and other 19th century scholars who asserted that Paul conformed to the apocalyptic schemes of his contemporaries, which included a short messianic age and a resurrection of all the dead at the end of that age. Davies shows that there is no direct evidence for this in Paul, and that his eschatology is more directly influenced by his faith in Christ than those scholars allowed (*Paul and Rabbinic Judaism*, 292–297).

his tradition included the picture of a partial resurrection (e.g. Daniel 12 and 1 Enoch 22), so it is plausible that Paul believed in that too. Then he would have imagined death as "defeated" rather than "destroyed."

The evidence is in favor of the view that Paul believed only in the resurrection of the good, for he wrote: "But each [will be raised] in his own order: Christ the first fruits, then at his coming those who belong to Christ [*hoi tou Christou*]" (1 Cor 15:23). Similarly in 1 Thess 4:17 the ones who will be raised at the Parousia are "the dead in Christ" which presumably distinguishes dead Christians from everyone else. Further, when Paul says that "in Christ shall all be made alive" (1 Cor 15:22) that fits these other sayings best if it is interpreted "all who are in Christ shall be made alive." Thus Paul's specific statements seem to refer only to the resurrection of believers (though in Rom 2:7 he may imply that other doers of good will be included also).

If Paul pictured only the resurrection of the good, then the defeat of Death means that Christ defeats Death enough to rescue believers (perhaps all the good) from its oppression, for they are the only ones who are victims. He probably pictured Death as only an oppressor of the good, those who deserve life and so are innocent victims torn down by Death. All others are Death's prisoners as the result of God's judgment on sinners, so Christ leaves them in the hands of Death. Those who deserve eternal death (Rom 2:6–8; 2 Thess 1:9; 2:10) will presumably receive it immediately upon their natural deaths. Only those who are doers of good will be raised into their spiritual bodies.[17]

In fact, not just those who have already died will be freed from Death's slavery at the End, but those believers who are left alive at the Parousia will be also:

> We will not all die, but we will all be changed, in a moment,
> in the twinkling of an eye, at the last trumpet. For the trumpet
> will sound, and the dead will be raised imperishable, and we

---

[17] This view is supported by Vos (*Pauline Eschatology*, 216–217), Shires (*Eschatology*, 84–85) and Witherington (*End of the World*, 187). Whiteley (*Paul*, 272) is agnostic on this question, saying Paul has not told us, and Ridderbos is ambivalent, saying that Paul's teaching on judgment for all may presuppose a universal resurrection, even though Paul specifically only argues for believers' resurrection (*Paul*, 554–555).

[who are left alive at the Parousia] will be changed. For...this
mortal nature must put on immortality. (1 Cor 15:52–53)

This transformation of the living is a defeat and banishing of the destructive
power of Death within them, a rescue from the slavery of that cosmic power.
The transformation is also a re-creation, for they are given a new spiritual body
in which eternal life reigns where Death reigned before (1 Cor 15:44, 49).
Henceforth Death will no longer be an oppressor, an enemy, but will be solely
God's obedient servant, holding in eternal death those who refuse God's offer
of eternal life (Rom 2:6–8; 2 Thess 2:10).

Paul's picture thus seems to be that all those who by faith come into
Christ thereby receive immediately his eternal life along with his Spirit and his
righteousness. Thus when the end comes, when Christ returns, he will raise all
those who are asleep in Christ, the dead who are members of him (and perhaps
other doers of good described in Rom 2:7). At the end, then, when Christ
swallows up the enemy Death by his life, he will free all members of his Army
of Light from Death's hold forever.[18]

## (4) Satan Conquered, Crushed Underfoot

I would have you wise as to what is good, and guileless as to
what is evil; then the God of peace will soon crush Satan
under your feet. (Rom 16:20)

This is the only passage in Paul's writings in which he speaks of the
end of Satan, but it cannot be the only one which implies it. In each of his other
passages depicting the End he implies the end of all evil, which includes Satan.
Thus the destruction of the Man of Lawlessness (2 Thessalonians 2) implies the
destruction of Satan (whose power was incarnated in that figure). Further, the
dethroning of all the principalities (1 Corinthians 15) implies the dethroning of
their ruler, and the rescue of all believers from Death (1 Thessalonians 4)
implies that Satan (the Destroyer) has been deprived of the power of death. Thus

---

[18] Though Paul does not mention it specifically, the final victory must
include the final defeat of Sin along with that of Death. Since Sin rules through
Death (Rom 5:21), when Death is defeated that entails that Sin's rule is ended.

Rom 16:20 is another perspective on the End, another element in the complete picture that Paul probably held in his imagination as his cosmic war myth.

The issues we need to consider here are these: (a) Is this really an eschatological reference, for some scholars see it as a temporal one? (b) What are the important traditional passages that offer insight into this crushing of a supernatural enemy underfoot? (c) What is the best translation of the verb *suntribo*, to break, shatter, crush or conquer? (d) How are the believers (particularly their feet) involved in this supernatural victory?

## (a) Temporal or Eschatological?

Some interpreters take this as an elliptical reference to a temporal event, the expulsion of false teachers from the Roman congregation.[19] However, most take it eschatologically. For example, Barrett says "Paul is looking forward to the final defeat of the prince of evil, and believes that this defeat will take place soon (cf. xiii. 11)."[20] The chief evidence that Paul had the Eschaton on his mind in the last part of Romans is found in Rom 13:11–12: "you know what time it is, how it is now the moment for you to wake from sleep. For salvation is nearer…now than when we became believers; the night is far gone, the day is near." Probably that is a reference to the nearness of the Day of the Lord, the Parousia, when Christ will return to end the reign of the powers of evil on earth. Thus the crushing of Satan is probably also a symbol Paul offers as an expression of the hope for the final conquest of all evil.

## (b) Background to Crushing Enemies Underfoot

Many OT and later Jewish passages provide useful background to Paul's image here, for they speak of enemies ending up underfoot, which is probably a standard image for conquest.

Psalm 110 says that God will seat the king (later taken to refer to the Messiah) at his right hand "until I make your enemies your footstool," by shattering the heads of kings (1, 5). Since Paul directly refers to this passage (1 Cor 15:24) it was certainly one of his sources.

Another relevant image is the promise in Ps 91:9–13 given to those who "have made the Lord your refuge," just as believers had taken refuge in Christ's Kingdom of Light. The psalmist promises that God will "command his

---

[19] E.g. Sanday and Headlam, *Romans*, 431.
[20] *Romans*, 285.

angels...to guard you in all your ways...You will tread on the lion and the adder, the young lion and the serpent [*tannin*] you will trample under foot." The *tannin* mentioned here probably refers first of all to a snake, parallel to the adder, but it soon took on symbolic importance. In some Hebrew poetry, the *tannin* alludes to the sea serpents which are the cosmic enemies God alone conquers, e.g. when in Ps 74:12–17 the Lord crushes the sea serpent's heads.

Other interesting prophetic myths using the imagery of trampling enemies underfoot include Isa 63:3 which depicts God the Warrior trampling his enemies under his feet. Even more interesting is Isa 26:5–6 in which the lowly will trample the lofty, powerful people, quite like Paul sees lowly believers trampling the lofty Satan. This will happen (according to Isa 24:21) on the day when the Lord punishes the host of heaven and the kings of earth. On that same day the Lord will kill Leviathan, the dragon (*tannin*) in the sea (27:1). Thus the lowly trampling the lofty is an element in the divine conquest of the angelic powers and the earthly monsters.

Important intertestamental passages provide interesting background also. In 1 Macc 3:19–22, Judas says that God "will crush" (*suntribo*) the overpowering enemy, in the presence of his people. *The Testament of Levi* 18:12 says that the Messianic High Priest will "bind Beliar [Satan]" and give power to God's children "to tread upon evil spirits." *The Assumption of Moses* declares that when God's Kingdom appears "Satan shall be no more" (1), for God will appear on earth to punish all the Gentiles and destroy all idols (7), which presumably are the images of the angelic rulers. Even more striking is the parallel from the Dead Sea Scrolls, for the myth in the War Scroll can be summarized in these words: "The mighty deeds of God shall crush the Enemy...The wrath of God is kindled against Satan and against the men of his company, leaving no remnant" (1QM i, iv).

Finally, in the synoptic tradition of Jesus' teaching we find two significant images. Mk 3:27 has Jesus speak of his ministry as one of binding the strong man and plundering his goods, clearly referring to a conquest of Satan and his demons. Then in Luke 10 Jesus says he saw "Satan fall from heaven" (18), with the result that Jesus gave his disciples "authority to tread on snakes and scorpions and over all the power of the enemy" (19). Here too we see the dual emphasis, Satan defeated, God's people treading on his kingdom.[21]

This array of traditional passages, many of which Paul probably knew, provides us with substantial suggestions on the symbol that Paul was imagining in Rom 16:20. It is thus plausible that when Paul speaks of God crushing Satan beneath believers' feet, he was alluding to these passages and taking them to mean that believers will somehow be God's agents or weapons in this eschatological trampling of the dragon of evil.

### (c) To Break, Shatter, Crush or Conquer?

The verb Paul uses is *suntribo*, with further description of the action as "under your feet." Elsewhere in the NT the verb means: (i) to break (a bone, Jn 19:36), (ii) to shatter (jars, Rev 2:27), (iii) to harm, beat (a person, Lk 9:39). (iv) Outside the NT it can be used of enemies and then it has the sense conquer, annihilate or crush, e.g. in 1 Macc 3:22 where God crushes, conquers, destroys, the pagan enemies in the presence of the Jews.

With Satan as the object, the senses break and shatter, which apply to brittle physical objects, do not fit. The third sense of "harm" is possible, but is not likely because Paul makes no suggestion that this is a merely temporary defeat for Satan.

Thus we are left with the senses "annihilate/conquer" or "crush." "To crush Satan" makes good sense IF the means by which God deals with Satan is by using the feet of believers. However, "to annihilate," or "to conquer (finally and completely)" makes good sense if God does the conquering and believers simply enjoy the result—standing victorious over the dead body of the Enemy. Thus we shall have to leave this translation choice open until we discuss the

---

[21] Many Christian interpreters down through the ages have suggested that in Rom 16:20 Paul was alluding to Gen 3:15. E.g. Leenhardt says "the allusion to Gen. 3:15 is obvious" (*Romans*, 386). However, it is not obvious to every reader, and is indeed a more distant possibility than most of the others we have mentioned. The main differences between the two passages are these: In the Eden story the snake is the representative of all snakes, of earthly, creaturely enemies of humankind, not of a supernatural enemy. Further, Gen 3:15 refers to a mutual attack of snake on human and human on snake, whereas Rom 16:20 refers simply to the destruction of Satan. Thirdly Gen 3:15 speaks of a long-running battle, each bruising the other, not of a single decisive conquest. Thus if Gen 3:15 lies behind Paul's statement, it lies distantly behind, mediated by some of the destruction-of-the-dragon images in other parts of the OT.

relationship between God and believers in this mythical symbolism.

**(d) Who Does the Crushing?**

When Paul says "*God* will crush Satan under *your* feet," it raises an important question: what is the connection between the actor God (the subject of the sentence) and the believers' feet under which Satan will end up? At least three possibilities spring to mind: (i) Believers acting under God's power actually do the crushing. (ii) God (in Christ presumably) is the supernatural power which conquers Satan, and then afterwards leads the people of God (who were spectators to the battle) to stand on or over the dead enemy. (iii) God in Christ conquers Satan, but believers are in Christ, members of his body during the battle, so they too stand in victory over the conquered enemy.

(i) On first reading, taking the words at face meaning, the passage suggests cooperation: God supplies the power and believers supply the feet. Upon further consideration, however, that picture is unlikely. The great disparity between the weakness of the Roman believers and the awesome power of the Prince of Darkness makes it unlikely that they could conquer Satan, even with God's power. As we have seen in his other passages the conquest of the forces of evil is Christ's victory (e.g. 1 Cor 15:24).

(ii) Therefore we turn to an alternative picture, that God (in Christ) conquers Satan, and when the job is done believers are given a stance of victory over his dead body, for Paul pictured believers as victorious at the end (e.g. 1 Cor 6:3 where they will judge angels). That imagery is traditional, for in the earlier tradition two passages which we mentioned above do provide this order: God conquers, then God's people rule afterwards. The most important is the detailed conquest picture in Daniel 7: first of all the Fourth Monster is destroyed by fire coming from the throne of God (so God apparently is the conqueror); then God gives dominion to the Son of Man, i.e. the people of God (13–14, 18). A second passage providing this image is *T. Levi* 18:12, according to which the Messianic High Priest will first bind Beliar, and then God's children will tread on his evil spirits. Neither of these passages has precisely Paul's image, but they do suggest that the tradition included the picture of a divine conquest of Satan followed by believers standing victorious over evil forces.

The difficulty with this second theory is that it does not give enough prominence to the believers' feet as the medium through which Satan is crushed: if they just stand victorious over the dead dragon when it has been already defeated, then the statement "crush Satan under your feet" seems a bit misleading. Further, as we argued above, Paul probably pictured believers continuing their attacks on fortresses, their ongoing war against the forces of darkness, until the final conquest is complete. So believers do probably play a role in the final conquest.

(iii) Therefore we propose a third alternative as a compromise between the first two, one suggested by the fact that in 1 Cor 15:23 God puts all the enemies under *Christ's* feet. That is the image that comes from the often-quoted Ps 110:1, "The Lord [God] says to my Lord [the King, later the Messiah], 'Sit at my right hand, until I [God] make your enemies your footstool.'" Perhaps Paul thought that God would crush Satan through Christ's coming, and that believers would be in Christ when that happened.

Suppose when writing Rom 16:20 Paul was thinking of the Ps 110:1 prophesy; then "under your [the Roman Christians'] feet" could have been closely associated in his mind with "under Christ's feet." The connection could be that Paul was thinking of those believers as identified with (or incorporated in) Christ because he had just previously stated: "So we, who are many, are one body in Christ [*hen soma esmen en Christo*]" (Rom 14:4). Perhaps Paul was imagining the Roman congregation as part of the whole Christian community, and all of it as the body of Christ. Thus when he said "under your feet" he might have pictured a single figure (Christ, with all believers in him) standing victorious over the dead dragon. This then would be quite like Daniel's single "one like a Son of Man" who embodies or represents all the people of God in their dominion over evil (7:13–14, 27). This third interpretation seems to be the one with the fewest difficulties. Our conclusion then is that *God does the conquering, but does it through the returned Christ, who embodies in himself all believers*. In the end, then, the returned Christ, somehow including all believers in himself, will burn up the dragon Satan and crush its ashes under their feet.

If that interpretation is the most plausible one, then it answers the question we discussed above on how to translate *suntribo*. The best translation is "to crush" because that fits the picture precisely, whereas "to annihilate" is more vague and therefore less helpful. Thus we can now gather together the different parts of the symbolic picture we have been elaborating, and provide this more detailed version of Paul's brief promise that "the God of Peace will soon crush Satan under your feet":

Very soon, the Day of the Lord will dawn and Christ will return to earth in triumph with the fiery angelic army. In and through them God will bring peace to the world by ending the career of the war-making Prince of Darkness. Satan in Paul's image is probably a monster with human features (a gigantic Man of Lawlessness), modelled on the Fourth Monster of Daniel 7 and other references to the sea-serpent Leviathan who symbolizes all evil. When the two meet, Christ (acting in God's name and with his peaceful power) will conquer and so destroy Satan, i.e. all the Kingdom of Darkness. The peaceful means of conquest will simply be Christ's appearing, for the eternal power of goodness, the glory of God in the face of Christ (2 Cor 4:6) will be a fiery flame destroying all evil with which it comes into contact (as in Dan 7:10–11). The light destroys darkness by arriving.

While the conquest will be God's doing through Christ, all believers, as members of Christ's body, will take part in that event too. Thus when in the end Christ stands victorious over the dead body of the monster Satan, believers will stand in him, so Satan will be "crushed under their feet."

## Conclusion

In Paul's cosmic war myth the culmination comes on the Day of the Lord, when God in Christ will fight the Last Battle which the Hebrew prophets had foretold for centuries. Before that day, the ongoing victories of the light push the Prince of Darkness and all his forces into a corner where the final battle is their last stand. The darkness is personified by a single superhuman Man of Lawlessness (modelled on Goliath, Gog and the horn on the head of Daniel's Fourth Beast) who represents all evil in himself. In that final battle believers will find themselves tempted more and suffering more than in all the ongoing war beforehand, so they know the end is near.

Once the final battle begins the Day of the Lord will arrive. The last trumpet will sound, the heavenly Army of Light will descend, and the Prince of Light will arrive in fire on earth to confront the Champion of Darkness. Christ's epiphany alone conquers that Man of Lawlessness, burning him up by Christ's fiery breath, and so ending the reign of darkness.

Probably Paul believed that this single conquest by Christ's fiery word/breath will end (i.e. symbolizes the end of) all evil on earth and in the heavens: human evil, angelic evil, Sin, Death and Satan. Paul gives no indication that he foresaw a long campaign in which each of these enemies had to be defeated in some order. Rather his picture seems to be that when the light descends the day dawns, and then all darkness and night disappear. As the defeat of the Fourth Beast in Daniel ends the oppression of the whole Seleucid Empire, so the conflagration in which the Man of Satan is burned up reaches all the way through the Kingdom of Darkness and annihilates it.

Thus in and with Christ's conquest of the Man of Lawlessness, the angelic principalities and powers will be conquered finally, perhaps with some of them returning to the side of the light through God's offer of reconciliation. Sin too will be annihilated, so it can no longer tempt believers. Death also will be defeated, its oppression of the dead in Christ ended by their resurrection to eternal life. That will leave Death as simply God's agent of just punishment, holding all those who are separated from God and so deserve eternal death. Included in this final victory Paul imagines is a monstrous figure of Satan crushed beneath the feet of Christ('s body), an event that presumably happens in and with the destruction of the Man of Lawlessness, Sin and the angelic powers. God in Christ will conquer Satan, but all believers are in Christ's body and so will stand with him when all the forces of darkness are ashes beneath his feet.

Once Christ's followers have all been rescued from the prison of Death, then they will follow him in triumph to the presence of God (see 1 Thess 4:17). At that time the King of Light, who has conquered all the powers of Darkness, will hand the Kingdom over to the Father, so that God will be all in all (1 Cor 15:24, 28). There believers will always be with the Lord, sitting on thrones beside him, as rulers over the creatures of earth (1 Cor 6:2-3). Around the table of the Lord they will eat and drink and rejoice together at the Great Feast, celebrating God's victory over Death (Isa 25:6-8) and the rest of the forces of the Evil One.

# VIII. THE REALITY BEHIND

# PAUL'S ANGELIC ARMIES SYMBOL

## Introduction

In the previous five chapters we have explored Paul's many brief uses of military symbolism. In particular we have elaborated them using traditional Hebrew and Jewish imagery, which was summarized in our chapter on "The Lord as a Man of War." The result is a relatively complete military version of the gospel, Paul's Cosmic War Myth.

## (1) Paul's Cosmic War Myth

In the beginning, when God created the heavens and the earth, he called forth angelic spirits as his servants, courtiers, messengers, and rulers of the nations of the earth. One angel, the satan, had three tasks: it was God's tester of humankind, the accuser before God of those who failed the test, and the destroyer of those whom God condemned. In addition, to each nation God gave an angel as its prince, the one designated to bring God's justice to it by introducing and promoting law, order, testing and punishment.

Unfortunately, fallen humankind often failed the tests, and eventually came to worship their national princes, thereby making them the false gods of the nations. When the angels accepted that worship, then they (whom Paul called principalities and powers, thrones and dominions, elemental spirits of the universe, rulers of this present age, lords and gods) became God's enemies. Even then, however, they still remained God's agents of justice in the nations, for they still promoted justice, law, order and punishment—but now as the means to enhance their power.

Over them all Satan eventually came to preside, for he too rebelled against God: when God showed himself as gracious, Satan the agent of justice revolted and came to rule over the Kingdom of Darkness, becoming the god of this present age. In this kingdom the chief power comes from the angelic rulers' God-given authority to teach and practice justice, law and order. However, they misuse this power. By seeking self-enhancement (as human tyrants do), the angelic rulers also produce injustice, oppression, the domination of the strong over the weak, and conflict between their nations. Their visible agents are the human rulers of this present age, who are the leaders of the political and religious realms. Under them are the human children of darkness, all those who follow their lead and so become the infantry in the Army of Darkness.

Further, Satan's invisible demonic agents in this present age of darkness are Sin and Death. Sin is the invisible, enslaving spirit that Satan has sent out to capture the fortress of every human heart, through the divine law which provides the opportunity for rebellion. Like the Roman Empire subjecting every newborn within its boundaries to its oppression, so also Sin conquers and enslaves all who are born into this world. Following on the heels of Sin is Death, the power that enters after Sin into every human life. Death is the local procurator and armed guard that enforces the law of the empire in each conquered province. Indeed Death is not even limited to the human realm, for it has advanced throughout the whole organic realm, bringing decay to everything that lives, so it rules over the living universe as a tyrant.

Into this Kingdom of Darkness God sent his Son, as his agent bringing light to conquer the darkness. In his ministry Christ brought God's light, proclaimed God's grace to the outcasts, and pronounced God's judgment on oppressors, thereby stirring up their enmity. He fought the agents of darkness spiritually, never giving in to them, driving out their forces (e.g. demons) wherever he came upon them. But by coming as a weak and lowly human being Christ was vulnerable to their political powers. Thus the forces of darkness, through their human rulers, arrested, condemned and executed him, not knowing that by this means they had sealed their own fate.

In Christ's death and resurrection God exposed, disarmed, conquered the angelic princes of the nations, creating through Christ the new Kingdom of Light. This is the beachhead of the new age, the eternal light that has dawned and formed a fortified haven for all those who join Christ's army. Now Satan, Sin, the angelic princes and all the forces of darkness cannot enter this invisible kingdom, so Christ's soldiers inside it are spiritually safe from them.

Though they have been translated into the safety of the fortified Kingdom of Light, Christ's soldiers must not stay hidden there, for God's purpose is to advance the beachhead, pushing the walls of the fortress ever outward. So the army leaves its safe haven and attacks the forces of darkness in their fortresses. Paul was one of those who joined the army and saw his comrades as fellow-soldiers, members of the Army of Light which was daily advancing into the darkness. He saw himself as covered with an armor of light, bearing the shield of faith and fighting with the sword of the Spirit. So armed he attacked the fortresses of darkness, breaking down their walls, conquering the soldiers inside and thus continually taking new ground for the Kingdom of Light. Of course in this warfare the soldiers of light constantly suffered, for soldiers know suffering is their lot. Some, like Paul, were captured and then Paul spoke of them as his fellow prisoners of war. Indeed some of them died in the battle, as Paul often thought he might, but their confidence in Christ's eventual victory made them bold and courageous in facing the worst the Enemy could do.

As Christ's Kingdom of Light advances further and further into the darkness, the disunited forces of darkness will become more and more desperate because their end will loom over them like a tidal wave about to break. Finally, when God gives the word, the whole Kingdom of Darkness, imagined as a single Man of Lawlessness—Goliath, Leviathan and Daniel's Fourth Beast all rolled into one—will attack the forces of light.

Once the darkness has attacked, Christ will descend at the head of the heavenly host, with the archangel Michael as the general at his side. The loyal angels of the heavenly host, will descend with him as the Army of Light, clothed in fire. That final battle will be over in a flash: a single word of command, a life-giving breath from Christ, will destroy the ancient monster who embodies all evil, death and destruction. Thus by Christ's one breath, one word

of conquest, all evil will be destroyed forever: Sin will be dissolved; Death will
be defeated, overwhelmed by life; the evil human rulers and their armies will
be disarmed forever; the princes of the nations will be stripped forever of all
their power over human beings; Satan, the last monster, will be crushed under
the feet of Christ and his army.

## (2) Our Interpretive Task

This then is one military version of the Christian myth, the story of
how God and the supernatural world have intervened militarily in the natural
world for the bane and benefit of humankind. Our basic theory is that this
detailed picture was one of the four major, complementary ways that Paul
imagined the story of Christ. Parallel to it are his three other symbolic
versions—judicial, personal and organic—which we briefly described in the
introductory chapter.

Our task now is to look through the window of this military symbolism
to try to discern the mysterious subject that lies behind it. What is the reality
symbolized? Since we do not have space to interpret the whole battle myth, we
will focus on just one element, the picture of angelic hierarchies. In this chapter
we will consider what Paul intended to refer to by using the symbolism of
angelic armies.[1]

The issue of what to make of the supernatural angelic characters of the
biblical story is an ancient one. In the Old Testament some writers, e.g.
Jeremiah, never mention angels, whereas others such as Zechariah give them
prominent places. Early on the one angel mentioned is the *malak Yahweh*, who
seems to be an alter-ego to Yahweh, not a separate spirit, as we will show
below. Later there seem to be millions upon millions of them in the pictures of
God on the heavenly throne (Dan 7:10). Thus differences over angels are an
ancient tradition.

The first theory we will discuss in detail is **A. LITERALISM**. Taking
the myth as literally as possible is the fundamentalist approach, the most
traditional Christian approach. Here the angelic hierarchies are taken as

---

[1] For a discussion of the theory on which this connection of symbol and
subject is based see Macky, *Metaphors*, ch. II "Defining Metaphor" (especially
49–55).

companies of real spiritual beings, i.e. separate, individual, personal, created, supernatural spirits who are active under God's rule. We will consider a fairly sophisticated version of this literalism when we take up Arnold's arguments in *Powers of Darkness*.

A second popular theory today is one we call **B. ALLEGORISM**, the view that angels symbolize earthly political/social structures. This is a late twentieth century approach that bears a significant resemblance to Daniel's. His myth of the destruction of the Fourth Monster (7:9-11) was a symbolic way to describe God's conquest of the Seleucid oppressor, a human religious, political and economic structure. A development of this type of approach is Wink's allegorical theory. He suggests that Paul's principalities and powers (neuter terms) do not stand for supernatural realities but instead represent symbolically the earthly structures of existence that undergird all social and cultural life. We call this the allegorical approach because it proposes that the supernatural angelic imagery stands symbolically for something earthly that can be otherwise named and described.

Finally, the theory we will advocate in this chapter stands between the literalist and allegorical approaches, and we call it **C. TRUE MYTH**. Our view is that Paul's picture of angelic armies, and especially their participation in a cosmic last battle, was understood by Paul symbolically, mythically. By the name true myth we mean that Paul understood his angelic warfare imagery was a valuable symbolic story that expresses some of the mystery of the divine power and authority at work in the world. By the word "myth" we thus mean a supernatural, fantastic, story known to be symbolic by its tellers. By the word "true" we mean that the tellers of this story believed that it was the best way to symbolize the supernatural reality which they could not know directly and so could not describe literally.

## A. LITERALISM AND ITS WEAKNESSES

"Literalism" when interpreting Paul's angelic imagery is the theory that Paul meant the imagery to refer to individual, personal, spirits which were created as real intermediaries between God and humankind. Evil angels are then the fallen version of these spirits, servants of Satan, who is taken to be the highest of all the created spirits who revolted against God's rule. Satan in this literalist theory is an individual, intelligent, fallen spirit who has organized all the other fallen spirits into a force (usually squabbling) under his command. After presenting this theory and the arguments used to support it, we will evaluate it in the light of Paul's theology, especially his view that God is present in Christ and the Spirit.

## (1) The Arguments for Literalism

The traditional, pre-Enlightenment, theory was that Paul meant his battle myth essentially literally, that an evil hierarchy of individual spirits fights against God's good hierarchy of individual spirits in age-long battle. Basically the literalist argument is this: the fact that Paul (like the rest of the NT) talks openly and easily about Satan, angels, demons, principalities and powers, and never says he means them symbolically, is clear evidence that he meant them literally, i.e. as descriptions of real spirits and real battles of various kinds.

Such advocacy of a literal interpretation of angels does not necessarily entail a simplistic view of symbolism, i.e. taking the physical symbolism literally. For example, C. S. Lewis, in his preface to *The Screwtape Letters*, makes this distinction clear:

> A belief in angels, whether good or evil, does not mean a belief in either as they are represented in art and literature...Creatures higher in the natural order than ourselves...must be represented symbolically if they are to be represented at all. These forms are not only symbolical but were always known to be symbolical by reflective people. (viii)

It is this type of sophisticated literalism that we are considering, not the naive literalism of those who take the Bible's physical pictures of the angels literally.

## (a) Many References

The main argument used by the advocates of literalism is that Paul and the rest of the biblical writers often referred to angels, demons and principalities without any overt statement that they meant them any way other than literally.

For example, Calvin adopted a sophisticated literalism which he defended with the argument that the many passages which speak of angels contradict the Sadducees' dream that the angels are not real spirits. Beside the many passages he had already quoted, he wrote:

> There are other passages which most clearly prove that they are real beings possessed of spiritual essence. Stephen and Paul say that the Law was enacted in the hands of angels. Our Saviour, moreover, says, that at the resurrection the elect will be like angels...However much such passages may be twisted, their meaning is plain...it is not qualities or inspirations without substance that he speaks of, but true spirits.[2]

This perhaps could be called the "plain meaning" argument, the view that writers should be taken literally unless they specifically give indications otherwise.

A modern advocate of literalism presents a related argument. Arnold, in *Powers of Darkness*, presents his view in a chapter entitled "Reality or Myth?" The most important point Arnold makes in support of literalism in Paul is this: "In contrast [to modern disbelief in spirits] the apostle Paul never showed any sign of doubt regarding the real existence of the principalities and powers. He saw them as angelic beings belonging to Satan's kingdom" (169). In this Paul reflected his culture, for, "there is no question that people living in the first century believed in evil spirits, including all of the New Testament writers, particularly Paul" (176). Here Arnold, like Calvin, apparently argues that we should always take authors literally unless they specifically tell us to do otherwise.

## (b) Distinct Categories

Further, Arnold argues for his theory when he takes up Wink's allegorical interpretation and offers objections to several parts of it. His major difference with Wink is this:

> It is erroneous to equate the powers with the structures. As I will argue, we ought to distinguish between the powers of darkness and the structures of our existence. The two categories are ontologically distinct. One is personal, the other nonpersonal; one possesses intelligence and the ability to will, the other does not. Truer to Paul's letters is to say that the powers exert their influence over the structures of our existence than to make the powers coextensive with the structures. (195)

---

[2] *Institutes* I.xiv.9.

Though this is mainly assertion of his viewpoint, Arnold does here seem to imply an argument for it: personal spirits (the image used in the battle myth) and social structures (the reality Wink says they represent) are ontologically different; therefore (presumably) Paul would not have symbolized one (the impersonal structures) by the other (personal spirits); rather he would more likely have meant that the personal spirits are the forces at work within the impersonal structures.

### (c) The Reality of Evil Spirits

Arnold's third objection to taking Paul's principalities and powers as the impersonal structures of earthly existence is that it does not leave room for the evil spirits which Arnold believes are really experienced by human beings. Thus he says Wink's approach,

> is reductionistic. It unreasonably restricts how we understand the work of the devil in Paul's day and in our day. Specifically *it overlooks the direct and immediate work of an evil spirit* in the life of an individual—either through overt demonization ("giving a place to the devil") or the devil's classic work of directly tempting people to sin. (196)

Apparently then, Arnold believes there is independent evidence for the existence and work of evil spirits, as real, independent, personal entities within people. Apparently he believes that this independent evidence is support for his whole theory that all the supernatural angelic figures were meant by Paul and the other NT writers as distinct, individual, personal, created spirits.

### (d) Satan and God

Finally, a common argument in favor of taking the angelic hierarchies of the battle myth literally is that if the interpreter is consistent she should interpret God the same way as she interprets the rest of the supernatural hierarchies. For example, Green argues specifically for the existence of the devil as personal spirit, saying: "What is totally inconsistent is to accept one point of the spiritual realm, God, and to reject the other. The existence of a devil is a necessary part of consistent theism."[3] If we take the angelic hierarchy as symbolic of something earthly, so this argument goes, then consistency demands

---

[3] Green, *I Believe in Satan's Downfall*, 31.

we take God as symbolic of something earthly. Of course the advocates of a symbolic interpretation of the angels do not usually wish to take God the same way (though Process theologians do something quite close to that). Therefore, the literalist concludes, if you are to be consistent you must take the hierarchies as literally as you take God. When speaking of Paul, the argument is thus that Paul certainly took literally the picture of God as real, personal, individual, and spiritual, so in consistency he must have taken Satan and the rest of the angels the same way.[4]

## (2) Criticism of Literalism

In our evaluation of literalism we are not proceeding in the common post-Enlightenment way of bringing in modern philosophical viewpoints and using them to discredit ancient views. Instead we are seeking to use ancient understandings in order to get as clear a picture as we can of what Paul meant by his angelic hierarchies.

### (a) Answers to the Arguments for Literalism

The primary argument for a literalist approach to Paul's supernatural hierarchies is that he spoke of them often and never said that he meant them anything other than literally. However, the fact that a story uses recognizable characters does not determine what those characters represent. It all depends on what kind of story it is. In particular, throughout the OT characters enter the story who seem not be real, distinct, individual, spirits. For example, Second Isaiah uses of the myth of Rahab the Sea Monster (Isa 51:9-11): the prophet

---

[4] One argument we have not included here is a modern one based on evolutionary theory, something that Paul could not have known. MacGregor theorizes that evolution cannot have ended with humankind, that it must have gone on and developed beings at a higher level, "extraterrestrial beings who...could have developed along another evolutionary line to a higher form than ours and be more rational, more benevolent, and so capable of helping humans in the way that angels in traditional religious lore are said to do...even if there were no mention of angels in the Bible and nothing about them in the long and complex tradition celebrated in literature, a sincere believer in God as the Creator of the universe would nowadays be compelled to make some sort of hypothesis about beings more advanced than we and therefore more attuned than most of us to the will and purposes of our creator" (MacGregor, *Angels: Ministers of Grace*, 198-199).

probably did not take the monster literally, even though he did not make any explicit point disclaiming a literal use. Similarly we can look at the Bright Shining One of Isaiah 14, the morning star that tried to reach the highest heaven but fell to earth: presumably the author did not take this fallen star myth literally, for he used it here as a symbolic means to suggest what had happened to the King of Babylon. Therefore, characters in biblical stories, especially supernatural ones, may be meant symbolically even when their authors do not explicitly say so.

For Arnold, apparently, the necessary evidence for Paul not taking the supernatural imagery literally would be something he overtly said, as modern writers at times explicitly state that they are writing symbolically. This argument from Paul's silence is unconvincing, however, for all the silence shows is that there was not the same argument afoot in his circles that there is in ours. As we have shown repeatedly in the previous chapters, Paul constantly talked in symbolic terms—though he hardly ever stated directly that he was doing so. Usually he left it to the reader to discern that the speech was symbolic: sometimes by using two contrasting symbols together (1 Cor 3:9), sometimes by using the simile form (1 Cor 3:10), sometimes by using a standard biblical symbol (1 Cor 3:11), sometimes by using a physical image to speak of a spiritual reality (1 Cor 3:16), but often by expecting readers to recognize that taking the image literally will conflict with something else in his teaching (1 Cor 3:15).

Unlike many modern writers who are trained in philosophy, and in the post-Enlightenment disdain for metaphor and symbol, Paul was an ancient writer steeped in the poetic and mythical forms of his two worlds (Hebraic and Hellenistic). He knew that he and his readers "see a dark image through a dim mirror" (1 Cor 13:12) when they seek to view the supernatural world. Thus he often spoke symbolically without calling direct attention to it, e.g. when he said "Do you not know that you are God's temple and that God's spirit dwells in you?" (1 Cor 3:16). Elsewhere he spoke symbolically without saying so when he personified Sin by saying it "entered into the world," and "ruled" and "paid wages" (Rom 5:12, 21; 6:23). As a final example we can consider Paul's image of Christ as "above...seated at the right hand of God" (Col 3:1), thus quite separated from the earth. Paul does not here say that he meant this spatial imagery symbolically. However, we can hardly doubt that he did so mean it since he elsewhere spoke so often of Christ as present in himself and in all believers (Col 1:27; 2:6; 3:11). Thus Paul assumed that readers would discern the presence of symbolism without being directly told so.

Secondly, if we are right in seeing Arnold as arguing that Paul would not use personal images to symbolize impersonal structures, then our answer is fairly simple: Why not? It is precisely in order to suggest what an impersonal reality is like that we use personal symbolism: Israel was symbolized as a wife (Hos 1–2); Rome was symbolized as a whore sitting on seven hills (Rev 17:3–6); the destructive chaos of Egypt the oppressor was symbolized as Rahab the sea monster (Isa 51:9–11). In Paul's writing perhaps one of the central examples of such personification is his speaking of Death as if it were a personlike being, for Death is the last enemy (1 Cor 15:26), a foe that needs to be defeated in battle, swallowed up in victory (1 Cor 15:54). Thus it is quite conceivable that Paul in other places (principalities, rulers of this present age) used personal images to symbolize impersonal realities.

Thirdly, when Arnold argues that the experience of evil spirits provides evidence for the literalist approach to the supernatural forces, he is probably arguing in a circle. The interpretation of an experience as "the presence of a real, individual, evil spirit" is dependent on the literalist theory. Only if a person holds that theory will she interpret the experience that way. Experience is always to a certain extent theory-dependent, so we will not be able to determine the reality of distinct, individual, spirits by pointing to experiences that have been interpreted that way.[5]

Finally, we must consider briefly the theory that consistency demands that when we interpret the angels (including Satan) as symbols of something other than distinct, individual, spirits, then we must do the same with God. That parallel is unconvincing. God is clearly a quite different kind of character in the Biblical story than are angels: from the first verse to the last God is the center of the story, whereas angels, including Satan, are peripheral. Eliminating God as a real personal spirit would change the whole story dramatically; eliminating

---

[5] See C. S. Lewis's argument in *Miracles* (ch.1) that "the question of whether miracles occur can never be answered simply by experience" because "what we learn from experience depends on the kind of philosophy we bring to experience."

angels as separate, personal spirits, would make very little change in the story. Consistency does not require us to treat central characters the same way we treat peripheral characters. In fact, as we will argue below, God's omnipresent reality and power is the chief evidence that Paul probably did not take the references to angels literally.

## (b) General Arguments against Literalism

The blindspot in Arnold's approach is the traditional one of Protestant orthodoxy: it fails to recognize that most of the biblical references to the supernatural world are symbolic, not literal. Bultmann (like many before him) is right in saying that the NT speaks of the other world (the supernatural realm) in terms of this world, that the (*ex fide*) purely spiritual world of supernature is constantly depicted in images (and in theology, in concepts) taken from the natural (physical, mental and spiritual) world. Thus the angelic courtiers, messengers and soldiers are essentially elements of the symbolic picture of God as Emperor lifted up far beyond the natural world.

The central argument we will offer in this section has these steps:

(i) almost all biblical God-talk is symbolic, including the spatial image of God as Most High, far above earth in Heaven his dwelling place;

(ii) the angelic hierarchy serving God was one aspect of the picture of God as transcendent;

(iii) taking the good angelic hierarchy literally conflicts with the other image of God as the immanent spirit, the one who speaks directly to humankind, indeed is within them at times;

(iv) therefore Paul probably took the good angelic hierarchy symbolically;

(v) this argument applies by implication to evil angels, for the biblical myth seems to be that evil angels are good angels turned bad.

## (i) Most Biblical God-talk is Symbolic

The basic theory of theological symbolism we assume here is one we have developed in detail elsewhere. In *The Centrality of Metaphors To Biblical Thought* we argued at length that almost everything the biblical writers said about the supernatural realm was said using symbols. We argued that Paul and the other biblical writers said only a few things literally about God: first of all they spoke literally in saying that God is "real" (not imaginary) and "active" (not purely passive), as in Paul's description, "the living [*zonti*, active] and true [*alethino*, real] God" (1 Thess 1:9). Further, the biblical writers spoke literally of God in a variety of negatives, saying that God is invisible, incorporeal, immortal, incorruptible, eternal (non-temporal), uncreated, not sinful, and unchanging. Finally we argued that some biblical writers, including Paul, probably used the general assertion "God saves" literally in speaking of the spiritual renewal that believers experienced. Our argument then was that everything else the biblical writers said about God they said using symbols.[6]

In their description of the supernatural realm, which they believed was distinct from (though not completely separated from) the realm of visible nature, the biblical writers took images from this world and used them as symbols to represent aspects of the mystery of the other world. The best example perhaps is the use of spatial imagery to represent the unseen world and its relationship to this world. Heaven, the realm in which God "dwells," is up, in the sky, for that which is high represents power, vision, separation from the ordinary. Therefore God is called the "Most High," pictured as sitting "high and lifted up" on a throne (Isa 6:1), and descending from heaven when visiting humankind (Gen 11:5; Exod 19:18). Paul too adopted this spatial imagery, telling the Colossians to "seek the things that are above, where Christ is seated at the right hand of God. Set your minds on the things that are above, not on things that are on earth" (Col 3:1–2).

While at times they pictured God as separated from earth, dwelling far above in heaven, the biblical writers knew that the spatial separation was not to be taken literally because God is everywhere. One famous expression of this divine omnipresence is when a psalmist imagined God as inescapable, crying out that there is nowhere we can hide from him, not in heaven, or in Sheol, or in "the farthest limits of the sea" (Ps 139:7–10).

This dual perspective—God as both far above and in the midst of the chosen people—is apparently the standard developed biblical view. Paul, like the other biblical writers, believed God was present (immanent), indeed at times at work within them, but also spoke of God as exalted far above them in heaven, because that image expresses the divine transcendence, otherness, majesty. Thus the biblical writers used spatial imagery—God as both present and as transcendent—as a way to express their belief in both God's "omnipresence" and

---

[6] *Metaphors*, chaps. VIII and IX.

God's "otherness." Neither spatial image should be taken literally, for then it will conflict with the other. Indeed distorted theologies continually arise when one or the other picture is taken literally: Deists took the transcendence literally and so rejected the immanence; Process Theologians seem to take the immanence literally and so reject the transcendence. Further, we are probably wrong if we take "God is omnipresent" literally (as Tillich probably did in saying God is literally "Being Itself"). God, as dimly discerned through the great variety of biblical pictures, is beyond spatial categories. Saying "God is present everywhere," and "God is transcendent, beyond everything created," are both attempts to speak of a non-spatial reality in spatial terms. Paul, we propose, knew that neither is to be taken literally, but both are to be taken seriously, for each is needed to correct the deficiencies of the other.

### (ii) Angels: Part of the Imagery of a Transcendent God

The biblical picture of a good angelic hierarchy is apparently an integral element in the symbolism of God as transcendent, separated from earth. In order to suggest a connection between the God far away in heaven and human beings on earth, the model of messengers from the emperor was used. Thus angelic messengers fly between God's dwelling-place in heaven and the human subjects on earth. Similarly, when the Hebrews pictured God as sitting high on a throne, the Emperor of All, an essential part of the picture was the entourage, the courtiers and the millions of cheering heavenly subjects or soldiers (Isaiah 6, Ezekiel 1 and Daniel 7).

In Daniel 7 God is pictured as human-like, with white hair and white clothes, sitting on a fiery throne on wheels, with a hundred million courtiers (angels presumably) surrounding the throne (9–10). Most mature readers (of which Paul was certainly one) recognize that Daniel probably believed God is a spirit, not a physical being: thus the readers take symbolically, not literally, the white hair, the white clothes, the throne and the fire which picture God as corporeal. All of this is based on the symbol of a human king, with fantastic touches (the fiery throne) to show it is not simply a human king.

Some readers, however, may fail to recognize that the millions of angelic courtiers surrounding the throne are just as much taken over from the earthly realm as are the throne, the fire and the white hair. Earthly emperors show their majesty and power by the number of their courtiers, the size of the crowds that come out to cheer for them, the greatness of their armies. Thus in

Daniel's picture the millions of angelic courtiers in God's crowd are a concrete and vivid symbolic expression of the belief that God is more majestic, awesome and powerful than any earthly emperor.[7]

The purpose of the symbolic application to God of a human emperor's council (1 Kgs 22:19), entourage and army was to express the greatness, majesty, awesomeness and power of God. Thus the angelic hierarchy under God contributed admirably to the imagery suggesting God's transcendence, God's exaltation beyond nature (including humankind), God's awesome power over nature. Of course it did nothing to express God's immanence, God's personal presence with and in the people. Paul, we propose, believed that God is both transcendent and immanent, so he probably understood the problem with taking the angelic hierarchy literally.[8]

### (iii) The Good Angelic Hierarchy Conflicts with God's Immanence

The issue then is how we are to interpret this imagery of a vast hierarchy of angels, based as it apparently was on the picture of God as the transcendent, high and lifted up, Emperor of the Universe. Does taking the angels literally as distinct, individual, real spirits, conflict with anything else in the biblical understanding of reality? If it does so conflict, then one or both of

---

[7] Westermann seems to adopt this viewpoint when he writes of the servants surrounding God's throne in OT visions, saying: "All this is intended to do nothing but declare the majesty of God. Behind such talk there is a thoroughly human, one might well say primitive, idea of lordship. For thousands of years humankind could not conceive of lordship in any other way than by picturing a lord sitting upon a throne, surrounded by servants who are there to execute his commands but at the same time are the living reflection of his absolute power" (*God's Angels Need No Wings*, 97–98). Thus Westermann suggests that the angels are part of the symbolism for lordship.

[8] Some interpreters so emphasize the transcendence, essentially taking it literally, that they miss the problem. For example MacGregor says: "Of course angels have an obvious role in monotheistic religions such as Judaism, Christianity, and Islam: they are needed as a means of communication from God to man...The...role of angels as messengers or ambassadors of the divine is one that seems virtually indispensable in a severely monotheistic religion. Angels serve as intermediaries between God and the prophets" (*Angels*, 26-28). He apparently ignores the imagery of God speaking directly to Adam and Eve, Cain, Noah, Abraham, Moses, Samuel, Job, Elijah and most of the writing prophets, all of which shows that angels are not indispensable intermediaries.

the two opponents in the struggle need to be taken symbolically to resolve the conflict.

To a certain extent the picture of individual angels ranked in a hierarchy connecting God with humankind does conflict with the biblical emphasis on God's immanence, the picture of God as present and active with and in people on earth.[9] Both pictures depict God's influence on earth, but with different images: the transcendent picture uses the image of angels as God's intermediaries; the immanent picture uses the image of God personally, spiritually, present and active everywhere at all times. Since these two pictures conflict, and Paul presumably recognized the conflict, he must have taken at least one (and probably both) symbolically.

If we take the intermediaries literally, then we take literally the picture of God as (at least sometimes, in some ways) absent, separated from the creation. God is then elsewhere, the way the Assyrian Emperor was always absent from most of his subjects and so communicated via messengers (*malachim, angeloi*), e.g. in the story in 2 Kgs 18:28–35. So, if for example Gabriel in Daniel's story is a real intermediary spirit, at times doing something that God cannot or will not do, then that implies that God is limited in one or more of three ways: either (i) God is absent, or (ii) God cannot communicate with humans adequately at times, or else (iii) at times God refuses to condescend to communicate with humans.

None of these three limitations is plausible as the view of Paul, nor of most of the biblical writers.

(i) The tradition which Paul seems to have inherited spoke of God as both transcendent and immanent, present and powerful everywhere, never absent in fact.

---

[9] Westermann makes this point in these words: "In theory there is no need for angels, because God is present everywhere. If God is present everywhere, then he does not need to send messengers" (*God's Angels*, 13). Westermann then goes on to assert that God does send messengers, but just what he means is not clear. It is likely that his view is that stories of angels really refer to the presence and power of God: "the stories in the Bible that speak of angels relate the experiences of men and women to whom God drew so very near in moments of great personal crisis or danger that they sensed...the helping hand of God" (7).

(ii) The general picture in the Bible is that God can, does and will speak to human beings anywhere at any time, for God is not limited in location or in communicating ability in any way (see Exodus 19, Jer 1:4–10, Isaiah 6 for vivid examples). Thus it is unlikely that Paul believed that God was ever unable to communicate directly with humans.

(iii) The third possibility is that God needs angels to communicate with humans when God refuses to communicate personally. This is an image suggested in Exod 33:2–3 when God says: "I will send an angel before you and I will drive out the Canaanites...but I will not go up among you, lest I consume you in the way, for you are a stiff-necked people." This suggests that God may at times refuse to "come near" his people, and so sends an angel "in his place." If God is the omnipresent spirit, however, that imagery should not be taken literally. Instead it suggests a difference between God's wrathful presence and beneficent presence. The angel symbolizes God's presence even though God is still "angry" with the people.

Our conclusion is that for Paul then, God's omnipresence, God's power to act immediately in earthly life, God's immanence in the world, probably stands in conflict with a literal interpretation of angelic intermediaries.[10] Because God is omnipresent, Gabriel the heavenly messenger (Dan 8:16; Lk 1:19) as a character in the story plays some other theological role than as a real intermediary, a spirit wholly distinct from God, doing a job God cannot or will not do. That raises the question of why Gabriel is created and used as a character in the story, and in general why some of the biblical writers (especially those following the apocalyptic tradition that Paul used in his military imagery) came to spread angels all over the tapestry of their story.

**(iv) "Angels" are Visualizations of God's Presence and Power**

Calvin (though a literalist on this question of the existence of real,

---

[10] The angelic messengers are quite different from human ones: the prophets, the earthly Jesus and evangelists are literally God's messengers, intermediaries, beings distinct from God, because they can do something God cannot do. They speak from within the human situation, as a human person, with a human voice, to people who know them as fellow sufferers, sharers of their weaknesses and dangers. Angel messengers in the story have none of those qualities. Being spirits as God is, they cannot do anything that goes beyond what God can do.

distinct, individual spirits) hinted at the problem of taking angels literally when he explained that they are God's accommodation to human weakness. God uses angels as agents, but "as a help to our weakness, that nothing may be wanting to elevate our hopes or strengthen our confidence." When humans find themselves in trouble, they might be "driven to despair, did not the Lord proclaim his gracious presence by some means in accordance with our feeble capacities...(so he) assures us that he has numberless attendants, to whom he has committed the charge of our safety."[11] Our weakness is thus that we have difficulty imagining God, the single One, as protecting all. By contrast, we can easily imagine an army of millions of angels spread everywhere throughout the creation, armed and ready to protect God's people and all others who are in need.

That kind of vision is precisely what Calvin points to in the case of Elisha's frightened servant as he and his master face the besieging Assyrian army: God provides a vision of a fiery angelic army which convinces the servant that God is more powerful than the enemy (2 Kgs 6:17).[12] Thus the contribution that angels make is to the symbolic expression of the power and presence of God. By envisioning angels, a physical army, we can imagine God as present and powerful. However, as we argued in the previous section, if that army is real, distinct from God, standing between us and God, then God is not present, but absent.

To avoid that plausible conclusion, Calvin makes a strong case for seeing angels as merely extensions of God: "angels...have been appointed for the very purpose of assuring us of his [God's] more immediate presence to help us." Thus it is essential that when we think of angels they should "conduct us directly to him—making us look to him, invoke and celebrate him as *our only defender*." In order for that to happen we must think of angels "*merely as [God's] hands moving to our assistance* as he directs."[13] Hands are extensions of the person, not separate persons. Thus the metaphor suggests that the angels are aspects of God, not separate spirits. Of course Calvin believes that angels are separate persons. But the fact that he uses this metaphor indicates that he

---

[11] *Institutes*, I.xiv, 11.

[12] *Institutes*, I.xiv, 11.

[13] *Institutes*, I.xiv, 12, italics added.

sees the problem with the traditional view of angels as personal spirits separate from God: if they are separate from God (unlike God's Spirit which is God in some way present), then their presence is a substitute for the presence of God.

Here Calvin provides the clue to why the biblical writers developed their angelology: to help overcome human imaginative weakness. But Calvin's conclusion, that God created real angels in order to overcome that weakness, is unconvincing. God does not need real angels, real spirits to act in God's stead, for the problem is not in the external world. Rather the problem is in humans' inner world, in their imaginations. Indeed real angels, intermediaries between God and the world, are quite unnecessary because God needs no intermediaries. What humans need, and God supplies, is the vision of angels, a vast army in the story, in order to appeal to our imaginations. Symbolic angels, formed into a vast hierarchy with millions of angelic soldiers, thus giving visual form to the invisible and largely unimaginable power of God, can successfully overcome human imaginative weakness. Then, if we recognize the angels as symbolizing aspects of God, we eliminate the problem of interposing intermediaries between the omnipresent God and creatures.[14]

### (v) The Angel of Yahweh as Model

The chief biblical hint of this understanding—that angels are one of the human ways of visualizing (and so imagining) the invisible God—comes in the early pictures of "the angel [*mal'ak*] of Yahweh" who seems to be Yahweh, or perhaps some aspect of Yahweh. J. B. Russell emphasized this when he wrote:

> In the early Old Testament literature, the *mal'ak* is the voice of God, the spirit of God, the God himself...The concept of the *mal'ak* was meant to represent the side of God that is turned towards humans, or the aspect of God that humans perceive, or the manifestation of God in his relationship with

---

[14] Karl Barth followed generally in Calvin's footsteps, taking a literalist view of angels in his commentary on most texts, but then so interpreting the angels' ontological status that the distinction between God and angels sometimes virtually disappeared. He essentially defined angels by their functioning as making God present, so they have no essential being other than that. "They do not exist and act independently or autonomously. They have no mind or will of their own" (*Church Dogmatics*, III.3, 480).

humans.[15]

For example, in Exodus 3, Moses sees "the angel of Yahweh" in the
burning bush (2), but when he draws near Yahweh sees him and speaks to him
(3). Likewise, though Yahweh is the one said to strike down the firstborn
Egyptians (Exod 12:12), the one who will pass over the Israelites, later the
author says Yahweh "will not allow *the destroyer* to enter your houses to strike
you down" (12:23). Similarly the presence of Yahweh in the cloud that leads the
Israelites (Exod 13:21; 14:24) is also described as "the angel of God" going
with the cloud (14:19) and as "the glory of Yahweh" appearing in the cloud
(16:10). Another way of describing this angel is that Yahweh says "my *name*
is in him" (23:20). Similarly the temple is the place where Yahweh's name is
present (Deut 12; 1 Kgs 9:3) and is also the place filled with "the glory of the
Lord" (1 Kgs 8:10). That the "name" and the "glory" are expressions of the
presence of the Lord is clear in the statement that the temple is the place that
"the Lord your God will choose...as *his habitation*, to put his name there" (Deut
12:5). Similarly, when the people eat their sacrifices in the temple, they eat "in
*the presence of the Lord* your God" (Deut 12:18).

In Exodus 3, as in Judges 6, the reason for the pseudonym (the angel
for Yahweh) was probably to make this suggestion: Yahweh is present (so they
have Yahweh speak); but Yahweh is not localized here, and not visible (so they
say it is the messenger who is seen). Similarly the dwelling of the name of
Yahweh in the temple (Deut 12:5) was a way to say Yahweh was present (Deut
12:18) and yet not localized, not limited to this place as other gods were thought
to be located in their temples. The specific reason for the Yahweh/angel of
Yahweh dichotomy in the wilderness wanderings story comes in this divine
statement: "I will send an angel before you, and I will drive out the
Canaanites...but I will not go up among you, or I would consume you on the

---

[15] *Prince*, 36. Westermann seems to adopt this viewpoint also when he
writes: "Everything the Bible says about the guardian angel can be said about
God himself. It is not necessary to speak about a guardian angel. It is always
God himself who acts through the guardian angel...It is the intention of the Bible
not to provide a special figure apart from and in addition to God but rather to
emphasize God's care for what is endangered...This care of God can best be
understood by talking about an angel" (*God's Angels*, 104–105).

way, for you are a stiff-necked people" (Exod 33:2–3).

In all these cases **the angel is the presence and power of God, but is not to be simply identified with God**. The distinction between the two clearly makes a contribution, for it suggests that God is somehow separated from this operation, even though the divine power and presence is also within it. Thus this angel of Yahweh image is a way to suggest that God is not simply present and active, but complexly present and active. God the invisible cannot be seen, but seeing the angel of God suggests that God can be known.[16]

If we start from the view that the "angel of Yahweh" was a way to speak in a more sophisticated manner of Yahweh's presence and power, then we can see why the tradition developed the angelic hierarchy: because it served as an imaginative way to express the awesomeness and otherness of God. When Isaiah 6 pictures God the King surrounded by the fantastic seraphim, that set of courtiers makes the King seem more exalted than simply describing him as sitting alone, or with human courtiers. Likewise, when Ezekiel has God on his throne-chariot upheld by the fantastic cherubim, the otherness and awesomeness of God are vividly expressed by the strange, powerful, awesome throne-bearers. Further, when Daniel sees God sitting on his fiery throne surrounded by millions of holy ones (Dan 7:10), their numbers suggest how much greater this King/Judge is than any seen on earth.

A later example of angels as expressions of divine power and presence is found in 2 Maccabees 3. There a magnificent angelic intervention to protect the temple (24–26) is described not only as "the sovereign power of God" (28) but also by the words "the Almighty Lord had appeared" (30). The author evidently saw the angelic intervention as the presence and power of God himself, for "he who has his dwelling in heaven watches over that place himself and brings it aid, and he strikes and destroys those who come to do it injury" (39).

---

[16] Barth apparently agreed with this general viewpoint for he wrote: "It is the mystery of God which is concretely revealed and set before the reader in these constantly recurring references to the angel of God...the angel of Yahweh can hardly be distinguished from Yahweh Himself but seems very clearly to be one with Him" (*CD*, III.3, 489). "The angel has the character and task of a perfect mirror of God, in which He whose face no man has seen is disclosed, and He, the High and Hidden and Eternal, is present" (490).

In a similar way Paul seems to use good angels as a concrete way to express the awesomeness of Christ when he returns to conquer the forces of evil. When Christ returns he comes with his mighty angels in flaming fire (2 Thess 1:7), and the archangel's call is one step in the battle starting (1 Thess 4:16). In both cases the effect of adding the angels, the vast heavenly host flying at Christ's back, is to make the supernatural power of Christ more imaginable. If readers simply pictured Christ returning, then it would be very easy to imagine him in human form and so still completely vulnerable to the procurator of a tiny Roman province. But when Paul suggests that the fiery heavenly host headed by the archangel Michael accompanies him, then readers have no doubts about the outcome. Thus for Paul angels probably symbolize divine power coming into the world to conquer evil.

Our conclusion then is this: Paul probably believed that the soldiers in Christ's heavenly army, i.e. the angelic intermediaries and the millions of angelic courtiers, are not to be taken literally. The internal evidence that leads us to take them symbolically is this fact: taking them literally would make God an absent monarch in need of intermediaries, as all human kings are for almost all of their subjects. Instead we should take the Pauline allusions to angels symbolically: the millions of courtiers, as well as the archangels, the princes of the nations, and the heavenly host are the symbolic expression of the mysterious and awesome power and presence of God. Thus when Paul pictured God in Christ as commanding a vast angelic army, he was expressing the greatness of God's power and its presence everywhere. The members of the angelic army are God's hands, not separate, individual, free, spirits.[17]

### (vi) The Argument Applies Indirectly to Evil Angels Too

In essence we have argued here that Paul probably did not take the good angelic hierarchy literally as a collection of individual, personal spirits, because to do so would conflict with his traditional belief that God is

---

[17] This viewpoint can be aptly summed up in the words of Westermann: "Are there really angels? No! There are no angels...angels have no existence, no being in a sense comparable to what we mean when we speak of human existence" (*God's Angels*, 18). However, Westermann then goes on to speak of angels as in some way like God, so his theory is not entirely clear. Probably his theory is that angels are the symbolic way to express the human experience of encountering God in revelation and protection.

omnipresent and almighty. The same argument does not apply directly to Satan, principalities and evil spirits, for to the extent that they are evil they do not express the activity of God and so should not be thought of simply as visualizations of divine activity in the world. In the next section we will discuss Paul's views of Satan and the evil spirits directly, but here we offer a brief argument to complete this objection to literalism in interpreting the angels: if good angels are not to be taken literally, then evil angels are not either, for they are (so it seems in the biblical picture) simply good angels turned bad.

Though the biblical writers never specifically declare that evil angels are good ones gone bad, that seems to be the implication of several stories. The "sons of God" in Psalm 82, who appear to be the angelic rulers of the nations, are denounced by God for their injustice, so the implication is that they were assigned to play a good role but have turned from that to evil. This imagery is probably based on the practice of emperors giving authority to vassal kings, or governors; sometimes those underlings do not truly serve the emperor but become corrupt and use their power for their own ends. Thus the evil sons of God/angels are probably modelled on evil governors.

Similarly the biblical Satan seems to be the divine agent of testing, accusing and punishing who somehow turned bad. At first, "the satan" in Job and Zechariah seems to be simply God's agent, and therefore essentially good. Later, however, in the NT, he is depicted as God's enemy, while still continuing as God's agent of testing, accusing and punishing. This character too is probably modelled on a human agent of justice who has become corrupt, using his powers to become an independent center of power. From these two examples, we can conclude that it is likely that the biblical writers in general, and Paul in particular, believed that in the beginning all God's creatures were good, so the picture of evil angels probably entails the plot element of good ones becoming evil.

We argued at length in chapter IV above that the principalities are God's agents of justice in the nations, the expressions of God's will for, standards of, and inspiration of justice. Though they have gone bad, using their power for corrupt purposes, still they remain God's agents, for they carry out the divine justice to a certain extent. As the good angels are essentially visual expressions of God's transcendence and awesomeness, and of divine power and presence in the world, so **evil angels are appropriately understood as visual**

**expressions of the corruption of the divine power of justice in the world**. We will argue for this view in detail below.

### (3) Paul Meant "Satan" Symbolically, as a Personification of Evil

So far we have argued that Paul probably did not understand the angelic hierarchies literally. Our discussion has concentrated on the good angelic hierarchy in particular, so now we must concentrate on Satan. We have already refuted the argument that if one takes God literally one must take Satan literally in order to be consistent. Now we expand the argument by showing that Paul provides adequate evidence that he probably thought of "Satan and the powers" as personifications of the evil that pervades creation.

### (a) Paul's Theology Does not need Satan (Rom 1–15)

One argument used by advocates of the theory of a real, individual, spirit Satan is that NT theology does not make sense without him. For example Green asks rhetorically of those who reject his view, "How can they make sense of the atonement if there is no devil?"[18] Similarly Russell says that the NT's "central message" is that, "Christ saves us...from the power of the Devil. If the power of the Devil is dismissed, then Christ's saving mission becomes meaningless."[19] Clearly the military version of the gospel has come to seem central to these writers, so they apparently take that version as a literal account.

Our response is that Paul knew better, for he gave his most complete summary of his gospel, in Romans 1–15, without ever mentioning Satan. Clearly Paul (at least when writing Romans) did not believe that the character Satan was essential to his gospel. Instead Paul was able to take the role Satan plays as the chief power of evil in his other writings and give it to Sin (and perhaps Death and Law).

As we argued above in chapter IV, "The Enemy Hierarchy," Paul probably saw the power Sin, which appears in Romans 6–8 and nowhere else in his writings, as the agent, or even the presence, of Satan. Paul does not call

---

[18] Green, *Satan's Downfall*, 31.

[19] Russell, *The Devil*, 229. It is not entirely clear how this fits with Russell's later observation that "The idea of the Devil ultimately does little to solve the problem of *why* there is evil in the cosmos...if God is responsible, why do we need the idea of the Devil?" (*Mephistopheles*, 390).

Sin that, but the similarities between the activity of Sin and the picture of Satan given elsewhere are too close to be coincidental. Apparently Paul believed that his whole understanding of the evil powers at work within people could be appropriately expressed by speaking of Sin and its agent Death while never mentioning Satan. Probably, Sin is not a person, not a distinct spirit, or else Paul would have chosen a different name for it. Instead it is a personification of human experience of enslavement to moral evil. Clearly Paul thought that this experience was more than simply something that came from inside the individual, for he spoke of Sin coming into the world (Rom 5:12), which suggests a transcendent element in it. Apparently Paul found it quite acceptable to speak of the transcendent power of evil under the name Sin.

Therefore, we conclude that Paul did not see Satan as a necessary character in the story. Instead he was a useful character, at times representing the whole of evil. However, that supernatural evil could just as well be expressed (and its immanence even better expressed) in the triple threat of Sin, Death and Law, which are the great forces of evil in Paul's account in Romans.

## (b) Paul's Eschatological Visions Do Not Need Satan

Our second argument for taking Paul as understanding the character Satan symbolically, not as a literal, individual spirit, is that Paul does not depict Satan's end in his detailed eschatological visions. If Paul can describe the End without his character Satan explicitly pictured as coming to an end, then whatever Satan represents was probably represented by other symbols.

In 1 Thessalonians 4–5, Paul depicts the end coming on the world as destruction (*olethros*, 5:3), but he never mentions Satan, or the powers, as objects of that destruction. Presumably, Paul thought the overcoming of all evil is adequately represented in the resurrection of believers. In 2 Thessalonians 2, Satan is in the background. Paul mentions Satan as the one whose powers are at work in the Man of Lawlessness (9), but the destruction of that Man is the center of the story, and no mention is made of Satan's end. Thirdly, in 1 Corinthians 15 Paul speaks of the subduing of the rulers and authorities (presumably meaning both human and angelic), and the final defeat of death, but never mentions Satan. We know that Paul did (at least once) picture Satan as coming to an end, for he (apparently) makes that assertion in Rom 16:20. Therefore we can be confident that in his full myth he included the end of Satan too. But why did he not mention Satan's end in the three main visions, especially 1 Corinthians 15?

Probably because he saw "Satan" as so essentially an aspect of the evil hierarchy that when he spoke of the destruction of part of it he meant the destruction of all of it. Thus when Paul described Christ's final subduing of "every ruler and every authority and power" (1 Cor 15:24), he probably was thinking of the whole evil hierarchy as conquered, including Satan. Perhaps also it is possible that when Paul said that at the very end "the last enemy to be defeated is death" (26), that he was thinking of Satan as the agent of death (as Heb 2:14 describes him). Thus also when he described the resurrection of believers in 1 Thessalonians 4–5 Paul probably assumed that readers would know that the end of all evil was implied. Likewise, when Paul described the destruction of the Man of Lawlessness, he probably believed that his readers would take this to suggest the end of Satan too. Thus Paul probably took mention of any of the evil powers, including Satan, as a reference to the whole mass of evil, the mystery of iniquity which permeated the whole of human social and individual life.

If we are right in saying that mention of any of the powers includes reference to Satan implicitly, and vice versa, we can see a great advantage in this imagery. "Satan" the character is just a single spirit, and while spirits are swift, presumably they are not omnipresent like God.[20] Paul, however, probably imagined Satan as the fountainhead of evil, picturing his tentacles spread throughout every human collective. Thus, if Paul combined the powers with him, seeing them as those tentacles, that suggests how this chief power of evil is at work in all corners of the earth. Thus Paul's Satan is another name for the mass of evil, the Kingdom of Darkness which has enslaved all humankind outside of Christ.

Since Paul did not need to mention Satan's demise explicitly, but implied it in the end of the powers, we conclude that Paul did not see Satan as

---

[20] Russell, though an advocate of a literal Satan, recognizes the substantial problem of conceiving of a transcendent devil: "Such a transcendent Devil is difficult to defend philosophically. It would have to be a person who was not only absolutely evil but also had such enormous knowledge and power that he could extend his operations over the entire universe...But could any created mind, however angelically powerful, have anything like the knowledge required?" (*Mephistopheles*, 299).

the individual, distinct, center and source of evil so completely that his demise had to be explicitly mentioned in the eschatological pictures. Rather, the end of the other forces of evil stands for the end of all evil, including Satan. By contrast, when we think of Churchill during World War II, we can imagine that the real, individual, Hitler was so much at the center of his thoughts that it would have been impossible to consider the war won unless that commander of the evil forces had been captured, condemned and destroyed. For Paul, apparently, no such picture was necessary. Thus it is plausible to conclude that Satan was for Paul a traditional way of depicting the transcendent and (somewhat) unified nature of the evil spread throughout the world.

**Conclusion**

Our conclusion in this debate with literalism is thus that the biblical story itself provides considerable evidence that Paul probably understood the hierarchies of angels, both good and evil, symbolically rather than literally. They probably were for him personifications, or visualizations, of the hidden, mysterious, forces of good and evil, not separate, distinct, individual spirits.

As with other symbolic pictures (e.g. God as the old man on a throne), we recognize the symbolic nature of the good angelic hierarchy because it conflicts with something more basic in the story: God is everywhere and omnipotent throughout the story, not in need of any intermediaries to do the divine work; therefore the picture of such intermediaries, modelled as it is upon spatially limited human kings who need intermediaries, is not to be taken literally. Instead the good angelic hierarchy is to be taken symbolically, as a visual expression of something invisible and mysterious. The positive value of the symbolism is that the good angelic hierarchy helps readers to imagine God as the Emperor of the Universe, as more exalted, powerful, awesome and mysterious than all the human emperors combined. Thus we cannot safely eliminate the symbols, for they have very positive effects on the lives of readers.

Similarly we have shown that Paul probably did not take his character "Satan" literally, for he did not mention him in his major theological argument, and largely ignored him in his three major eschatological visions of the destruction of evil. Thus we conclude that for Paul **Satan and the Powers were probably vivid personifications of the evil that permeates the universe through the corruption of divine justice**. The value of the personification is that it helps human readers to imagine the forces arrayed against them, and thus to take them more seriously as outside enemies to be fought. Just how far outside these enemies are, that is whether they are wholly immanent in the natural world or somehow transcend it, is the issue to which we must now turn in our consideration of the allegorical approach.

## B. ALLEGORISM AND ITS DEFECTS

So far we have concluded that Paul probably did not mean his picture of the angelic hierarchies to be taken literally in the Fundamentalist way, i.e. as referring to millions of individual spirits. Now we need to discuss what this myth of the "evil heavenly army" symbolizes. We will focus on what Paul thought the subject was that lay behind the symbols of Satan and the angelic rulers of this present age.

The major option we need to consider is Wink's theory that the angelic rulers symbolize solely the interiority of the nations, i.e. they do not represent anything that transcends earthly, human realities. This we call the allegorical approach because it interprets the symbol as standing for a subject that can be wholly described without using the symbol.

### (1) Wink's Theory (Allegorism): The Angelic Powers as Wholly Immanent Structures of Human Existence

This second significant approach to the interpretation of the evil hierarchy in Paul's thought is to take his abstractions—principalities, powers, thrones, etc.—to symbolize the structures of society which have become evil because of human sinfulness. A variety of writers have developed this interpretation, but one of the foremost is Walter Wink in his works *Naming the Powers* and *Unmasking the Powers: The Invisible Forces that Determine Human Existence*. In this section we will first summarize Wink's view, then present his argument that evil is wholly immanent, then evaluate the theory.

### (a) Summary of Wink's Theory

His central ideas on the powers of evil, summarized in *Unmasking the Powers*, are these:

> The New Testament's "principalities and powers" is a generic
> category referring to the determining forces of physical,

> psychic and social existence. These powers usually consist of an outer manifestation and an inner spirituality or interiority...every economic system, state apparatus, and power elite *does* have an intrinsic spirituality, an inner essence, a collective culture or ethos, which cannot be directly deciphered from its outer manifestations,

because the outward signs may be deliberately deceptive (4). Thus the mythical spirits, Satan and the principalities and the rest, are apt symbols for something mysterious that lies hidden within these institutions.

In Wink's view, these "powers (are) even more real today than two thousand years ago...(and) largely determine personal and social existence." Examples are "corporate spirits," and "national spirits" and "congregational spirits" (4-5) in our world. Thus Wink argues that the principalities symbolize realities, but not transcendent ones: "What the ancients called 'spirits' or 'angels' or 'demons' were actual entities, only they were not hovering in the air. They were incarnate in cellulose, or cement, or skin and bones, or an empire, or its mercenary armies" (4-5). As spirits of earthly institutions, these powers are wholly immanent: "(They are) powers operative *among and between people*: not transcendent like God, but higher than humans. 'Intermediate beings' they seemed, and the names for them mattered little, *so long as one knew they were there*" (3).

Thus Wink takes Satan as the chief symbol of the experienced earthly reality of evil: "the image of Satan is the archetypal representation of the collective weight of human fallenness." Further he says that Satan is "the symbol of the spirit of an entire society alienated from God, the great system of mutual support in evil" (24). Thus Wink suggests that the symbol "Satan" represents the whole system of evil in the world, a combination of the many other corrupt spirits of institutions which are called rulers, principalities, powers etc.

Wink's major points, for our purposes of understanding Paul's demonology, are these:

(i) The NT's angels, demons and other spirits were apt imaginative expressions, symbols, of real experiences.

(ii) The realities these images pointed to (the subjects behind the symbols) are the inner spirits of collective realities, the "spirit of a nation" for example.

(iii) These spirits are not transcendent like God (i.e. not supernatural, part of another spiritual world) but wholly immanent, the interiority of some earthly institution or structure.[21]

(iv) The spirits are mysterious. Though always immanent in visible institutions, these spirits are not always clearly discernible as to their character. Just as individuals can hide their motives and character behind a persona, so also the spirits of collectives can hide behind whitewashed exteriors.

(v) The spirits can be controlled. As our individual unconscious motives can be constrained when they are brought to consciousness, so also these hidden spirits of institutions can be controlled somewhat when we uncover their presence, power and evil and so overcome some of their mysterious hold.

(vi) In particular, individuals can then choose which spirits, i.e. which institutions, they will be influenced by, for no one can live outside the influence of all the spirits.

Of all these points the main one that may conflict with Paul's view is (iii), the theory that the spirits are all immanent, that without the human institutions they would not exist. We need now to consider Wink's arguments for this purely immanent "Satan and the powers."

**(b) The Argument for Immanence Alone**

Wink's argument for these powers as wholly immanent, with no transcendent component, is essentially this: modern readers (including himself) reject the ancient supernaturalism, and therefore if he is to make sense of the biblical demonology for modern readers he must start with this metaphysical restriction:

---

[21] At times Wink uses language that almost implies the transcendence of the powers. For example he says that Satan represents "a profound experience of numinous, uncanny power" (25). Wink also calls Satan "an archetypal image of the universal human experience of evil," which "is unfathomable; the primordial power of evil" (25). Finally, Wink speculates that "Perhaps in the final analysis Satan is…a function in the divine process…an autonomous spirit that rises out of the depths of the mystery of God" (33–34). When we interpret these passages in the context of Wink's direct assertions that Satan is not transcendent, we have to take them as essentially expressive of the mystery of the powers, not an assertion of their transcendence of the human realm.

> We moderns cannot bring ourselves by any feat of will or imagination to believe in the real existence of these mythological entities that traditionally have been lumped under the general category "principalities and powers"...It is as impossible for most of us to believe in the real existence of demonic or angelic powers as it is to believe in dragons, or elves, or a flat world.[22]

This is essentially a reiteration of Bultmann's approach which used as its standard what "modern man" can and cannot believe. Apparently Wink sees demons and angels as part of the pre-scientific worldview, of the mythology that included dragons and elves. Here, in rejecting literalism he also rejects the possibility that the angels and demons symbolize transcendent but otherwise indescribable powers.

At its heart Wink's argument apparently offers a limited choice of views and then says his is the best one. He offers only three major alternatives, traditional literalism, his demythologizing, and modern blindness to forces of evil. First he rejects modern blindness to evil, since the reality of evil (described at length in the book) is precisely the problem which impelled Wink to write his books. Then he rejects literalism because he believes that modern knowledge has passed that ancient superstition by: modern people cannot believe in angels and demons any more than in elves and dragons. Therefore the only viable alternative left is his demythologizing in which he takes the principalities as symbolizing real, invisible, wholly immanent, inner spirits of human collectives.

## (2) Evaluation of Wink's Theory

Much of what Wink has to say is admirable, especially his tying the principalities and powers to the real, hidden, forces of evil within institutions and other collectives. He seems to express the spirit of Paul's cosmology when he stresses the mystery of these forces, their enormous power over humans, the responsibility humans have to reject their advances, and the hope that in Christ they will all be defeated.

The point at which we wonder whether this view adequately expresses Paul is Wink's assertion that the powers are wholly immanent, solely the

---

[22] *Naming the Powers*, 4.

interiority of collectives. Our counter suggestion is that Paul probably believed that the forces were also transcendent in some respect. Though we agree with Wink's theory to the extent of suggesting that Paul probably did not take the angels and demons literally, he probably did take them as representing something beyond the earthly and human: that something beyond is the divine justice, which we imagine as a standard, impulse and commission coming from God to human collectives, which is then the source and power of the law and order (and often oppression) in earthly institutions. This interpretation is based on the detailed account given above in chapters III and IV, in which we showed that the biblical Satan and the powers are agents of divine justice, not simply forces of evil.

Thus our chief argument is that Wink's three-stop spectrum is too limited, that he is guilty of presenting a false trichotomy. We reject Wink's division of the spectrum into only three groups, supernaturalist literalism on the right, blind materialism on the left, and his immanentist realism in the center. Our view is that between Wink and literalism is a fourth alternative, the True Myth theory. Our presentation of this view in the next section, showing that it differs from literalism and takes modern insight seriously, is thus our chief argument against Wink.

Our second argument against Wink's demythologizing is that his adoption of the modern anti-supernaturalist viewpoint is an inappropriate standard for finding Paul's meaning, which is our goal. Wink is right that many modern readers are skeptics with regard to the supernatural world. Therefore, Wink's adopting their standpoint is an apt *ad hominem* approach, for it may help the skeptics consider the mystery and pervasiveness of evil (which is Wink's goal in writing). However, our goal is different. Our goal in this book is understanding Paul, and he gave no indication that he held the modern skepticism about the supernatural world. His freedom in speaking often about supernatural forces, especially the risen Christ and the Spirit of God, suggests that he did indeed imagine humans as surrounded by mysterious supernatural forces beyond their control. Though we cannot be sure just exactly what he did think, still it is likely that he did believe that Satan and the powers transcended humans and their institutions, because that is the way almost all Jews and Christians of his time wrote.

One further argument for Paul as an advocate of Satan and the powers as symbolizing realities beyond the merely human is this: in Paul's story only the transcendent power of God (through the returned Christ) could finally destroy those powers, which suggests that the powers were also transcendent for Paul. Our argument is this:

(i) Paul's picture of the end of the evil powers is that it happens when Christ returns to earth at the end (1 Cor 15:24-26; 2 Thess 1:7-8), when God crushes Satan (Rom 16:20).

(ii) Paul certainly understood Christ and God as transcendent realities, supernatural beings: they can appropriately be pictured (though not taken literally) as ruling the earth from the heavenly places (Col 3:1), so that the final battle comes when Christ "returns," descending to earth from heaven (1 Thess 4:16).

(iii) If such transcendent, supernatural, powers are necessary for defeating Satan's army, then probably Paul imagined that evil army as also in some respects transcendent, supernatural.

In this section we have given our reasons for believing that Wink's demythologizing (allegorical) approach to Paul's demonology is inappropriately reductionist. Still, Wink's allegorical approach provides substantial insight into the earthly components of the powers of evil. Paul probably did believe that the forces of evil are hiddenly at work within the collectives that dominate society, especially governments and religions. Our task now is to elaborate this true myth approach which we suggest Paul held.

## C. TRUE MYTH

Our purpose in this section is to summarize and support the case for this theory: Paul probably held what we call the "true myth" view of the evil angelic hierarchy, i.e. Satan and the rulers of this present age, etc. We suggest Paul understood his account as symbolic, in fact as mythical in the literary sense of the term. We will elaborate on what we mean by that using the insights of Ricoeur and C. S. Lewis.

Secondly, we suggest that the subject that Paul understood Satan and the principalities to symbolize was this: the transcendent power and guiding light of divine justice which continually becomes corrupted in human collectives. Thus the transcendent reality is the standard, power and impulse of divine justice imagined as a "spirit" sent by God. That spirit, God's justice, Paul saw as incarnate in principalities, powers, thrones, dominions, authorities, and rulers of this present age. The evil aspect of the angelic hierarchy symbolizes the way that the human rulers, the powers in human collectives, use this divinely given mandate for their own selfish ends. In arguing this we will be following closely in the footsteps of Caird and J. B. Russell.

## (1) Authorities on Myth

Calling our theory true myth suggests that it is a third alternative, one that differs both from literalism and from all modern reductionisms. Beker points to such a third alternative in discussing the limitations of Bultmann's approach:

> Bultmann...opposes a literal understanding of myth to its anthropological intent. However, he ignores the historic-cosmic intent of the apocalyptic world-view...The language of apocalyptic myth is more than an existentialist projection of man's plight because it concerns the reality of the cosmic victory of the creator over his created world...the question remains whether the alternative to the "literal" is the "existential."[23]

Beker's implied answer here is that his approach is a third way between the literal and the existential, a way that takes seriously Paul's historic-cosmic intent. Though Beker does not give many details of how his approach works, we believe that he implies an approach like our true myth.

Our approach goes beyond what Beker specifically says because we suggest that a literary approach, through imaginative entertaining of the myth, is appropriate. This approach is in some ways like Ricoeur's "second naivete." Literalism is the first naivete, one which does not take seriously the contradictions among the various mythical pictures. Criticism takes those contradictions seriously, thus recognizing that the stories are probably intended to be symbolic. But then the second naivete goes on to entertain the stories imaginatively, the way we do great literature, because the power of the myth

---

[23] *Triumph*, 141–142.

comes in its whole effect on the imagination.

With Ricoeur we take the view that the biblical myths are symbolic:

> A great discovery: the discovery of the *symbolic* function of the myth..."The story of the fall has the greatness of myth"—that is to say, has more meaning than a true history...the meaning resides in the power of the myth to evoke *speculation* on the power of defection that freedom has.[24]

Earlier he had defined the symbolic function in this way: "symbolic signs are opaque, because the first, literal, obvious meaning itself points analogically to a second meaning which is not given otherwise than in it" (15). Here Ricoeur suggests that biblical (as well as other) myths have symbolic power to evoke insight into transcendent realities, but that we cannot go behind the symbols and describe those realities directly. Thus the defeat of the principalities and powers is a symbolic expression of the triumph of God over evil, but we cannot specify just what form that triumph takes because all we directly have is the myth. That essentially is the theory we call True Myth.

When we entertain the stories imaginatively, the way we do great literature, the power of the myth comes in its whole effect on the imagination. Ricoeur stresses this power when he says: "the myth has a way of *revealing* things that is not reducible to any translation from a language in cipher to a clear language...the myth is autonomous and immediate; it means what it says."[25] While we do not take literally the assertion "it means what it says," because meaning is never identical with expression, nevertheless we agree with what Ricoeur seems to be driving at: the myth is not replaceable by more abstract and literal speech because the myth is the best way to communicate its subject.[26]

Another advocate of this type of understanding is the literary scholar and fantasy writer C. S. Lewis whose appreciation for the mythical power of

---

[24] Ricoeur, *The Symbolism of Evil*, 236.

[25] *Evil*, 163–164.

[26] Other writers who present a similar view of the continuing value of biblical myths when viewed as symbolic are Helmut Thielicke, F. K. Schumann and Austin Farrer writing in Bartsch (ed.), *Kerygma and Myth* (138–174, 175–190, 212–223).

*Paradise Lost* and *The Fairy Queen* enabled him to see biblical myths as equally symbolic and valuable. For example, concerning the biblical visions of the supernatural world he wrote:

> Our sacred books give us some account of the object [Paradise]. It is, of course, a symbolical account. Heaven is, by definition, outside our experience, but all intelligible descriptions must be of things within our experience....heaven is not really full of jewelry any more than it is really the beauty of Nature, or a fine piece of music.[27]

Thus Lewis sees the imagery of the supernatural world as symbolic, not a literal description; then he suggests that this symbolism is the best we can get in understanding the reality, since we cannot know the reality directly. The story is myth, not literal statement; but it is true myth (for the one who accepts the authority of the myth-messengers, as we believe Paul did) for it aptly leads us to imagine (and perhaps in some sense experience) the reality.

Seeing the subject through the window of this myth provides imaginative and emotive power. When we entertain the complete myth in our imaginations, then it is vivid, moving and memorable. The reason for this power is suggested by Lewis's theory of the way myths work:

> In the enjoyment of a great myth we come nearest to experiencing as a concrete what can otherwise be understood only as an abstraction...What flows into you from the myth is not truth but reality (truth is always *about* something, but reality is that *about which* truth is).[28]

By this Lewis seems to suggest that great myths provide experience of the mysterious reality (in the way a dream sometimes does) rather than simply detached assertions (truth) about it.

Lewis looked upon the Christian gospel as an example of the way reality flows into hearers via myth, for he called it "myth become fact." By that he meant that the ancient myths of a dying and rising god had been exemplified

---

[27] Lewis, *The Weight of Glory*, 6.
[28] Lewis, "Myth Become Fact" in *God in the Dock*, 66-67.

(incarnated?) once for all in history in the events of Christ's life, death and resurrection. The central point for our purposes is that according to Lewis the gospel remains myth: "By becoming fact it does not cease to be myth...To be truly Christian we must both assent to the historical fact and also receive the myth (fact though it has become) with the same imaginative embrace which we accord to all myths."[29] In addition Lewis used the phrase "true myth" as one way to express this view of the story of Christ. He wrote:

> I was prepared to feel the [pagan] myth as profound and suggestive of meanings beyond my grasp, even tho' I could not say in cold prose "what it meant." Now the story of Christ is simply a true myth: a myth working on us in the same way as [the Pagan myths], but with this tremendous difference that *it really happened.*[30]

This same imaginative embrace of the myth is the way we propose that Paul took his military gospel, and the way he implicitly invites hearers to take it.

Our true myth theory, following Ricoeur and Lewis, is that the appropriate approach to Paul's battle myth (as to all great myths) is first of all to embrace it with our imaginations, seeing ourselves inside the story as people who are caught up in the battle. In order to facilitate that enjoying we developed Paul's battle myth in detail in the previous chapters. However, all that the reader needs in order to begin this journey is the brief account of the whole given at the beginning of this chapter. Then we can allow this myth to provide a window through which we can imaginatively travel deeper into the experience of God's gracious presence and power through Christ in our world. If Ricoeur and Lewis are right, through this myth we receive a taste of reality, which is more important than truth. However, in order to direct our attention aptly through the window, we must have some idea of what we are looking at. In this chapter we seek to point out what Paul was probably looking at: we suggest that for him the angels (principalities) were symbols for the divine power of justice mysteriously

---

[29] Lewis, "Myth Become Fact," 67. For an exposition and analysis of this theory see Macky, "Myth as the Way We Can Taste Reality: An Analysis of C. S. Lewis's Theory."

[30] "Letter to Arthur Greeves, 11 October 1931," quoted in Roger L. Green and Walter Hooper, *C. S. Lewis: A Biography*, 117–118.

at work in the world, a view suggested by Caird and others.

## (2) Paul's Mysterious Supernatural Subject

As we argued in refuting literalism, Paul probably understood the image of angels to symbolize the divine power and presence in the world. The symbol is a (sometimes fiery, winged, humanlike) spirit that travels between God in heaven and humankind on earth, bringing God's messages and otherwise acting for God. The subject for which this symbol stands is God's own presence and action, including God's Word personally reaching human beings. Thus we suggested that for Paul good angels are the "hands" of God, aspects of the divine reality, not separate spirits which stand between God and humankind. "Angels" in Paul thus are symbols used to enable readers to visualize God as present and active. Further, based on the theory of the principalities that we developed in chapter IV, we conclude that Paul probably saw the original divine ordination of angelic rulers of the nations as symbolizing God's commission, impulse and standard of justice.

Evil angels (including Satan) then should be interpreted in this light, for Paul probably saw them as good angels which had turned bad. Caird made this connection by saying "evil can exist as a force in the world only because it is able to take the powers and authorities of God and to transform them into worldrulers of this present darkness."[31] Further Caird connected God's justice with the symbol of bad angels by saying, "The demonic forces of legalism, both Jewish and Gentile, can be called 'principalities and powers' or 'elemental spirits of the world.'"[32] Thus in the apocalyptic myth the good angels, which symbolized God's gift of justice to the nations, became evil angels, the worldrulers of this present darkness, when humans corrupted the divine justice, using it for their own power-hungry ends.

Once Satan and the powers became pictured as the chiefs of the Kingdom of Evil (in apocalyptic circles), they then represented the great mass of evil. Paul, so we are arguing, knew that the representation was symbolic. He appropriately continued to use this traditional imagery of Satan and the angelic princes of the nations because it was familiar and had imaginative impact. Thus

---

[31] *Principalities*, 53.
[32] *Principalities*, 51.

our theory is that for Paul the evil angels are not distinct, individual, spirits which wilfully cause the evil in the world. Instead they are concrete symbols standing for that evil, especially the evil perpetrated by those collectives (especially religion and government, but perhaps also the marketplace, mass media, and the educational establishment) which wield great (divinely-given) power and so shape the whole of society.

This divinely-given power is the transcendent element in the myth of Satan and the powers for which we argued in opposing Wink's immanentism. As we showed in chapter III, Paul probably imagined Satan as the divinely ordained destroyer run amuck in the pursuit of justice alone, and then in the pursuit of his own enhancement. This image or character Satan is the symbol; God's justice corrupted by humans is the subject symbolized. The transcendent element in the Kingdom of Darkness, then, is God's mandate and impulse for justice, imagined as supernatural spirits corrupted by human powers.

As an element in this divine justice we need to consider divine wrath, which is sometimes the reality behind the symbol of Satan. As we showed in chapter III, in Paul's myth God's wrath in action is very much like Satan's punitive activity. Thus Satan expressed for Paul, as for the Hebrew tradition, the dark side of God. J. B. Russell emphasized this using his Jungian imagery, according to which the Hebraic Satan is "the personification of the shadow of the Lord, of the dark side of the divine nature."[33] That probably was true for Paul also: Paul's Satan was the imaginable agent of the strange (evil-producing) work of God's justice that on the surface conflicts with God's proper work of making people better.[34] Of course Paul's character Satan does not express God's wrath exactly, but God's wrath gone astray, taken too far, used for sinful purposes by sinful human powers. Thus Satan as Paul's symbol partly stands for this mysterious subject: the divine power of punishment when it corrupts instead of redeeming because it is misused (or misunderstood) by sinful human beings.

In using this symbol of Satan and the powers, Paul pictured as concrete and imaginable a mystery that is neither. Perhaps Paul thought of evil as a

---

[33] *The Devil*, 203.

[34] Rom 1:18–32 is Paul's most striking passage describing this divine wrath as making people worse, in contrast to the proper divine work of making people better which is Paul's concern in most of his letters.

"force" that permeates all of the universe, the way gravity does. Perhaps it is a kind of chaos at the root of everything—in the physical realm, in our social groups, in our spirits. Then the overcoming of the chaos would require the annulling of whatever it is that allows such a force to exist, parallel to what would be needed to end all gravity in the universe. Paul could not describe the supernatural force literally anymore than we can, but he followed his tradition in depicting it as Satan and his army, a monstrous enemy hierarchy, the Kingdom of Darkness.

## Conclusion

Paul's evil hierarchy is a serious, apt, emotively powerful, symbolic representation of the evil that people find in their own hearts, in their own groups, and in the whole human race. Indeed, this evil is as powerful as it is because it uses the good, supernatural impulse for justice (including God's wrath on sinners), but corrupts it for self-serving human ends. Thus Paul's characters "Satan" and "the rulers of this present age" symbolize the real, impersonal, mysterious, pervasive and deceptive force of evil—corrupted justice— which is immanent in the groups and structures and processes of culture. This myth continues to be valuable for those who recognize that it is myth, pay attention to its limitations, and then take it seriously. That is the view we will develop in the final chapter.

# IX. THE TREASURE IN PAUL'S EARTHEN VESSEL

## Introduction

St. Paul's cosmic war myth is one of his four major symbolic expressions of the gospel, what we called in chapter I his military window onto the mystery of God's work in Christ. The symbol of multiple windows is intended to emphasize that each perspective provides useful insight but needs to be corrected by the insight gained through the other windows. Thus the cosmic war myth has a central contribution to make, but its limitations also must be recognized. Using Paul's own metaphor we can say that there is treasure contained in the earthen vessel of the myth. So in this chapter we will begin to discern the difference, beginning with **A. The Treasure** and then moving on to **B. The Earthen Vessel**.

## A. THE TREASURE

### Introduction

Paul's battle myth is a highly symbolic version of his gospel, an account using many military images which he did not mean literally but as pointers to a mysterious spiritual process. The subject symbolized by the age-long war between the Kingdoms of Light and Darkness can be described (fairly literally though very abstractly) as "God's agelong conflict with, and final elimination of, the evil that intruded into his good creation." Our task now is to suggest how well this myth communicates this subject, one about which we know a good deal from Paul's other presentations of the gospel.

In order to evaluate this cosmic war myth appropriately we must recognize that myths play a unique role in human life, one quite different from histories, doctrines and sermons. Like parables and poetry, myths use concrete, visual and experiential types of speech which appeal more to the imagination than to the discursive, logical, intellect. They evoke pictures, resurrect memories, and stimulate feelings. Like dreams they can touch the depths of human life.[1] Part of this imaginative power is due to the way a myth makes mysterious realities imaginable, so they seem real. By contrast, abstractions referred to in abstract language often seem ephemeral, mere products of human thought. Thus an effective myth is one that appeals to the imaginations of readers, touching and moving them, as well as one that adequately reflects the way things really are.

Thus, in order to evaluate Paul's myth we need to consider both its imaginative and its intellectual strengths. First of all we will show that the myth itself, the symbolic story we have reconstructed, is **(1) Imaginatively Powerful**, when judged by aesthetic standards, because it is a concrete, dynamic, memorable story that finds a ready home in our modern imaginations since we too know the terrible battles against evil that literally take place in war. Secondly, however, we will show that Paul's myth is **(2) Intellectually Valuable**, since it provides a viewpoint that is complementary to those of the other symbol systems. In particular, it provides distinctive insight in its emphasis on the pervasiveness and power of evil, both the transcendent forces of evil and also the demonic power Sin that insidiously enslaves all the unrepentant. In addition, this myth provides great help in explaining innocent suffering: if believers come to see themselves as actively fighting a war against the darkness, they will understand that the darkness fights back and causes suffering to all its foes. Thus for the soldiers of Christ suffering will not be a sign of God's weakness, but a sign of God's grace, allowing them to take part in the battle, and to suffer as their Lord suffered.

---

[1] For further information on imagination and the powers of concrete speech, see Macky, *Metaphors*, 10–17, 287–294.

## (1) Imaginatively Powerful

When we seek to evaluate a myth, we first consider it as a work of narrative art, and so consider the standards by which other narratives are evaluated. First of all a good narrative needs to be **(a) Both Concrete and Meaningful**, filled with concrete events, yet pointing beyond them to meaningful depths. Next a good narrative should be **(b) Coherent yet Mysterious**. A further common standard for narratives is that they should be **(c) Dramatic and Personally Appealing**. The next important standard for a myth that is going to be the foundation for a religion is that it be **(d) Universal**, not provincial. Further, if the myth is going to be effective then it must be **(e) Distinctive yet Traditional**. The result of high quality in all these standards is that the myth, the symbolic story, will be **Memorable**. It will stick in the memory of hearers because it provides a striking story, but also raw material for the gristmill of contemplation, and a map for living.

### (a) Both Concrete and Meaningful

Concrete elements in a story are those modelled on our immediate experience of the world. The general aesthetic rule is that the more concrete the narrative the more hearers can conjure up the events in their imaginations, and thus the more they can be touched and moved by the story. However, a concrete story by itself does not provide for an adequate myth, for a myth is intended to suggest something about the depths of reality. Paul's most common way of pointing to those depths is by referring directly to his and others' daily experiences when using his battle symbolism. As we shall see, Paul's war myth is highly concrete but at the same time deeply meaningful.

War imagery is highly concrete, for it is filled with action of many different kinds, action which readers can conjure up in their imaginations. For example, Paul's military symbolism for the life of believers pictures them bearing arms and armor, marching out into enemy territory, discovering a fortress, attacking it successfully, then capturing the inhabitants and so gaining more territory for their kingdom.

Behind the concrete war imagery Paul intended hearers to see the meaningful depths—to recognize that his battle story symbolizes the conflict between cosmic good and evil. Evil is the main difficulty that humans face, the reality that causes most human problems. "Evil," however, is an abstraction, not something easy to imagine. Indeed both good and evil are abstractions, and so the bare concepts have little imaginative power by themselves. So Paul (following a long tradition that goes back at least as far as the Babylonian Marduk and Tiamat myth) concretizes these abstractions by picturing them symbolically as two armies in conflict with each other. Thus the war story is both quite concrete and highly meaningful.

Further, the symbol darkness is highly concrete and also deeply meaningful. Darkness conjures up in hearers' imaginations the terrors of the night, when darkness hides dangers, when we cannot see our way, when we are eager to be inside a lighted house and so safe. Further, darkness triggers memories of places where hearers were lost in the dark, in a forest on a moonless night, or inside an unlit cave or building. By using this concrete symbol of darkness Paul (in fact his tradition) makes evil seem far more palpable, far more threatening, far more fear-invoking than the abstraction "evil, i.e. the absence of good" ever can. Thus in Paul's writing it is very clear that this highly concrete imagery is quite meaningful, for the darkness is very obviously symbolic, pointing beyond itself to the mysterious power of evil that permeates so much of the universe.

In addition, the light symbol is highly concrete and very meaningful. Light will remind hearers of the coming of the dawn, when the sun drives away the darkness of the night and brings renewed life, new opportunities, a return to the good that God offers daily. In our description of the Kingdom of Light above we emphasized the image of a fortress, one that advances like a beach-head, for that seemed to express the kind of experience Paul imagined. Such an advancing fortress, taking in more and more territory as the darkness is driven back, provides a quite concrete way to imagine the advance of Christ's army throughout the world of darkness over which the god of this world rules. This aptly symbolizes the Pauline belief that in Christ God's good is reaching out into the evil of the world, overcoming it. Thus Paul's light symbol is both highly concrete and deeply meaningful.

Our conclusion is that Paul's cosmic war myth is a highly concrete story that is at the same time deeply meaningful. He uses the traditional imagery of cosmic warfare but makes it clear that the subject he is concerned with is one humans know intimately—the age-long conflict between good and evil, the process by which the good God has continually opposed the power of evil by rescuing his people from its clutches.

## (b) Coherent yet Mysterious

A coherent plot is one that fits together, its events flowing causally from one to the next, with character, motivations and setting playing appropriate roles. In general, plots are better when they are coherent than when they contain innate contradictions, for the latter inhibit understanding. Still a completely coherent plot may be mundane, uninteresting, so the best plots contain elements of mystery to intrigue readers. Not all questions raised in the narrative need to be answered, for unknowns can aptly point beyond the story to the unknowns in the real world. Thus a good myth should be both coherent and mysterious.

Paul's cosmic war myth, as we have developed it in the previous chapters is quite coherent. That this is not simply an imposed coherence is suggested by the fact that in Paul's inherited Judaism a coherent cosmic war myth was alive in the tradition, e.g. in the War Scroll.

The mysteriousness in Paul's myth is also fairly obvious, for a variety of finally unanswerable questions have appeared as we reconstructed it. For example, the relationship between Satan and the rulers of the nations is not at all certain in the myth—though we tried to decide which among the various possibilities seemed to fit best. Another mysterious detail in Paul's myth is his picture of the Kingdom of Light over which Christ rules. We cannot say for sure just how this earthly kingdom, the protective walls within which believers find themselves, is related to the heavenly kingdom of Christ's reign at God's right hand. This duality is essentially an expression of the older Hebraic way of speaking of God as both transcendent and actively present: God in the tradition is both the King on the throne of the universe and the spirit or angel or hand or name that touched their lives intimately. Thus this ancient mystery of God is reprised in Paul's mystery of the heavenly Christ who is also present within the earthly fortress of light. A third mystery is what exactly happens to the soldiers of light when they die. Paul is confident that in the End they will be raised, but in the meantime he leaves a mystery.

## (c) Dramatic and Personally Appealing

A concrete, coherent narrative may still be deathly dull, one that no one could stay awake to listen to. Therefore a good narrative is one that is dramatic, exciting, dynamic, suspenseful, thereby holding the hearers' attention during the telling. Yet if this dramatic story does not tie in directly to the hearers' personal lives it may arouse excitement without touching them personally. Therefore, a good story combines excitement with personal appeal.

Paul's cosmic war myth is highly dramatic for it postulates two cosmos-wide angelic armies with their visible extensions in people on earth. It describes a conflict between these two armies that has gone on since near the beginning of time and exploded into a cosmos-wide battle in the death and resurrection of Christ. Even more dramatically it foretells a day when Christ the light will single-handedly defeat the army of darkness forever. Thus Paul's dramatic version of the conflict between good and evil has the effect of making the savior, God in Christ, far more exalted than the readers otherwise could imagine.

While the myth is mainly about the cosmos-wide battle that is still going on today, Paul had no difficulty in making the story personal because he saw himself and all believers as soldiers on the front lines. By putting himself in the story, e.g. by picturing his own ministry as one of attacking fortresses and capturing their inhabitants, Paul enabled his readers to find themselves in the myth. Paul's readers, both ancient and modern, can identify with him and so find this war myth a personally involving account. Today the forces of evil that believers must battle if they are to remain free and rescue others are more insidious than the religious inertia and intolerance Paul fought: hedonism, materialism, and self-centeredness (greed) are all vigorously promoted by the advanced economic systems today. Believers find these forces of evil subtly at work within themselves (not just within non-believers) so the battle is a highly personal one.

**(d) Universal**

A universal myth is one that uses as its symbols realities that are known to people from almost all times and places. It stands in contrast to a provincial myth, one that is tied so closely to the time and place of its origin that it dies when attempts are made to transfer it elsewhere. For example, the biblical myth of Christ's death as a Day of Atonement sacrifice in Hebrews, is quite provincial, tied to ancient Jewish practice that no one in the world has experienced since the destruction of the Jerusalem temple. Similarly most Greek myths, e.g. the vegetation myth of Demeter and Persephone, are long since dead.

In contrast to most Greek myths the ancient Hebrew-Christian imagery of a cosmic war is still alive and powerful. One reason for that long life is the pervasiveness of human wars which makes military imagery universal and powerful. No generation passes by without knowing something of war, and the generations of this century have had much more than their share. The symbol of war is thus universal, known by virtually all people of all times, so it can be readily understood and received in all cultures.

Secondly, human wars are often vital turning points in nations' histories. In telling their national myths people select stories of great victories as ways to celebrate the greatness of their nation. Thus a story of fighting and conquering forces of evil, thereby creating a new and better world (e.g. in the American Revolutionary War, or in World War II), is a common and memorable story in most cultures. Thus Paul's story of God's initial victory in Christ, ongoing victories through the Army of Light, and final conquest of evil at the End, is rooted in a very powerful, and largely universal, human experience of war-produced change for the better.

Thirdly, the symbol of warfare is also alive in the imaginative works of this century, both in literature and film. In literature the biblical battle myth came to extraordinary life in Tolkien's *The Lord of the Rings*, one of the most influential books of the middle of the century. It made fantasy mainstream again, and opened the floodgates to the series of highly popular fantastic films that have been created since then. For example, "Jaws" modernized the old Babylonian myth of Marduk conquering the sea monster, and so appealed to viewers that it was the most popular film in history for years. Then "The Star Wars Trilogy" took up a similar fantastic drama, this time setting it in the future, and in the heavens. This myth effectively used the imagery of a heavenly battle between armies of light and darkness which has been central in Western religions at least since the time of Zoroaster. Millions of people poured into theaters to see this drama in three acts, presumably because it was dramatically powerful, and probably because it expressed something meaningful about reality.

Paul's battle myth belongs to some extent in the same literary and imaginative category as do these works of modern, popular art: it too appeals to the imagination using fantastic imagery and the human experience of devastating warfare. One difference between Paul's myth and these others is that it is a myth that is overtly, intentionally, *rooted in history*. In Paul's myth the conquering hero is an historical character, a carpenter from Nazareth in Galilee who was born under Herod and Augustus. The central event in the story is the crucifixion of that historical person under Pilate and Tiberius. Thus Paul's cosmic war myth is tied directly to an event in the history of West that has been taken as pivotal for 2000 years. Evidently the historicness of the event contributes to the age-long life of the myth. In this respect it is quite unlike fictional myths, e.g. of Orpheus' descent into Hell to save Eurydice, which died when its culture faded.

### (e) Distinctive yet Traditional

New stories catch hearers' attentions only when they are novel in some significant respects. The novelty suggests that the story may make a contribution, and thus may be worth listening to. At the same time, however, if a story is to function as a myth, it must be rooted in the deep past, carrying on (and so updating) the tradition in which the hearers find themselves. Paul's cosmic war myth is both distinctive and traditional.

With regard to the Jewish tradition out of which Paul came, the central element of novelty in his myth is that God has in Christ already won the victory that inaugurated the age to come. The Jewish apocalyptic myth prophesied such a victory, but saw it happening only at the End. Thus Paul continued the Jewish cosmic war tradition of a great victory of God over the angelic forces of evil, yet he transformed it by saying it had already happened secretly. Paul's story asserted that into the present evil age of darkness the new age had already dawned, for Christ's death had already defeated (in a preliminary way) the principalities and powers. As a result, in Paul's story, a new Kingdom of Light has appeared (though remaining invisible to the eyes of flesh), a fortress into which believers can enter and be safe from the spiritual forces of evil. He continued the apocalyptic story that in the present the forces of evil persecute and martyr believers, but he also changed the story: now believers cannot be victimized spiritually or eternally, for nothing can separate them from the love of God which they have found in Christ's new Kingdom of Light.

As we argued earlier, the creation of this new Kingdom of Light bears an important resemblance to traditional stories of God's victories over the forces of evil. The Exodus, which was the initial victory in the Moses epic, provided very important background to Paul's myth. The chief traditional element is the translation from slavery to a new kingdom (free Israel), which was at the heart of the Exodus narrative. In addition, the imagery of God conquering Rahab, a monster which symbolized the Egyptian oppression, provided apt traditional background for Paul's story of the conquest of the Satanic Kingdom of Darkness. Secondly, the Maccabean saga provided significant traditional background to Paul's myth: in both God had intervened to rescue his people from tremendous oppression (Seleucids in one case, Satan, Rulers, Sin and Death in the other); in both war was central, with the conquest of fortresses required in order to spread the beachhead of free Jerusalem out to the outermost corners of God's land. Thus Paul's novel myth of the cosmic victory of God in Christ is rooted firmly in the tradition of God's previous victories over the forces of evil.

**Conclusion: A Memorable Story**

For a myth to function effectively as a myth it must be memorable. Since it works by providing a symbolic window onto the mysteries, it must become vividly at home in hearers' memories so they can use it to contemplate their experience using the window of the myth. The way a myth becomes memorable is by exhibiting high quality in the standards just elaborated. It need not be excellent in all of them, but it must be good in them all. As we have argued, Paul's myth is good in them all, indeed of high quality in most respects.

These literary standards are important because Paul's cosmic war myth is myth, not doctrine or history. Myth is literary, i.e. it appeals to something in us that transcends our intellect. It appeals not mainly to the rational intellect (the historian and philosopher in us), but more to the imagination, i.e. to the child, the dreamer, the poet in us. Thus we propose that the appropriate way to receive Paul's battle myth is by entertaining the story in the imagination while remembering that it is symbolic. In this book we have attempted to re-create in detail how Paul may have imagined the complete myth, hoping thereby to enable readers to use it as a symbolic window onto (what Paul believed was) the central event of human history, God's coming to bring salvation through Jesus Christ. Now we will consider the central ideas that the myth symbolizes.

**(2) Appeal to the Intellect: the Theological Value of the Myth**

Though the battle myth appeals first of all to the imagination, still it also can contribute to the theological system constructed by the rational intellect. The ultimate means for discovering this contribution is by interpreting all four of the symbolic versions of the gospel together (along with the minor symbols), using them as complementary windows onto the mystery. Since we cannot attempt that here we will simply show how the battle myth emphasizes some important things that the judicial, familial and organic windows on the gospel do not.

### (a) Life as Conflict

The central image Paul presents in his cosmic war myth is the age-long conflict between the forces of good and evil, with human beings caught up in this conflict on both sides. Paul's own experience taught him how central the conflict with the forces of evil was, for he constantly suffered from the persecution of those who opposed his ministry. Indeed, in the end he was probably one of the soldiers who died in the war.

None of the other symbol systems gives a central place to social conflict, persecution, the struggle between opposing forces that leads to injury and death for some of the participants. Therefore, the cosmic war myth is very valuable since it provides the major expression of Paul's own experience of the ongoing conflict between the people of Christ and the forces of evil.

In Paul's day the chief force of evil he faced was religious, the idolatry and intolerance of the nations, but that is no longer as central as it was then. Today the evil force believers face is more insidious, for it tempts rather than persecuting and coercing. All the propaganda power of the economy is aimed at making voracious, unsatisfied, consumers out of every person. The message that subtly beams out all day and night is that the purpose of life is pleasure, and the way to gain that pleasure is to acquire more possessions and more exciting experiences. Further, this consumerist system tells all that their own self-centeredness is really good, that it promotes the system, so greed is no longer a vice but is now the chief virtue. One consequence of this promotion of greed is that those with power (as in Paul's day) are able to hold down those without it: the lack of adequate jobs, good schools and affordable housing makes the life of the poor in most industrialized countries a never-ending battle against despair.

Most churches today do not recognize themselves as battalions in the war against evil. Rather they have been coopted by their societies, seeing themselves as the religious adjuncts to their nations, the arrangers of Sunday activities, but not soldiers attacking fortresses and risking being killed. Thus Paul's cosmic war myth, with its emphasis on the conflict with the forces of evil, is as important today as it was in Paul's own day, perhaps even more important since the evil is now more insidious.

## (b) Evil as Transcendent: Justice Corrupted

The cosmic war myth presents as its basic conceit a picture of an evil hierarchy headed by Satan, the god of this world. While, as we argued above, Paul probably did not take this image literally, he clearly took it seriously. At its heart it expresses his belief that evil is in some respects transcendent, something supernatural and invisible. None of the other symbol systems adequately expresses this insight. In the organic imagery evil is essentially incarnate in the body of Adam, a disease that has infected all humankind. The legal imagery suggests that human choices bring evil into the world, and that evil is thus a human product. Finally, the royal family imagery echoes the legal one, seeing evil as human rebellion, alienation from the family. The battle myth, by contrast, suggests that evil is far more powerful than individuals, that they are in some respects pawns caught in the middle of a war between supernatural powers.

Paul's cosmic war myth (as we reconstructed it above) pictures the rise of evil in this good creation as due to humans worshipping their angelic rulers. As we argued in the previous chapter, those angelic rulers are symbolic of the divine justice which is God's mandate, impulse and standard spread throughout the whole human world. Justice is good, but when humans get hold of it, become authorities imposing it, they often use it for their own selfish ends and so turn it into an instrument for evil. Therefore this myth, when interpreted, offers a powerful theory of why and how evil is ubiquitous in our world: everywhere that people gain power over others (i.e. in all large groups), the power corrupts, for the powerful use their power for their own benefit while masking (at times) the evil they do to those under them. Today while millions live in poverty, the economically powerful make themselves billionaires and call it justice.

This social myth of the origin and ubiquity of evil provides a very helpful corrective to the individual myth that is presented by Paul's judicial and familial symbol systems: they emphasize Adam's rebellion (the forces of the past) and individuals breaking the law that they know, both of which are very real problems. On the other hand, throughout the biblical story the depredations of tyrannical nations (those which had the power and so authority to impose justice)—Egyptian, Assyrian, Babylonian, Greek and Roman—were central founts of the evil the people of God suffered. Therefore a theory of evil that makes that tyranny and destruction a central problem provides insight into significant elements of the experience of God's people. Thus Paul's cosmic war myth makes the strong suggestion that one major source of the world's evil is the established order (the intertwined system of government, business and religion) especially the more the power in it is concentrated at the top.

### (c) Sin as Enslaving

A third unique and valuable element of Paul's cosmic war myth is its picture of Sin as a demonic agent insidiously at work within human beings. As we argued above, in Paul's cosmic war myth Sin seems to be an agent of Satan, a power of evil that infiltrates the hearts of all members of the human race. The result is that all humans apart from Christ are enslaved to Sin, unable to rescue themselves from its hold. By this imagery Paul ties his myth into the traditional stories of the Exodus and the Return from Exile, for in both of them the people of God were slaves under overwhelming powers, thus unable to rescue themselves.

As we argued above we should hold this enslaved-by-Sin imagery in tension with the individual responsibility picture suggested by the judicial and familial symbol systems. Thus we should not take literally Paul's picture of Sin as a demonic agent of Satan. However, we should take it seriously as an expression of one central aspect of the human condition. The contribution it makes is that it stresses the universal human inability to change oneself from sinner to saint. Old habits become ingrained. The standard practices of our society become second nature. Our past bad choices become written almost in stone in our memories and wills. Bad experiences in childhood can create destructive patterns of behavior that are enslaving. Thus Paul pictures Sin as a demonic agent of the cosmic force of evil, which has invaded the citadel of the human person and taken control. Here is a very valuable image for expressing the weakness of the human condition.

### (d) Salvation by Conquest

Since humans are weak, unable to free themselves from evil, they need a rescuer just as the Israelites in Egypt did. Such a rescuer is pictured in Paul's battle myth in which the conquest of evil takes divine power. By contrast, reconciliation (familial) and justification (judicial) suggest that the major obstacle to salvation is human unwillingness to come home, to repent. That, of course, was a central element in Paul's picture, but it is not enough, for in Paul's mind evil has a hold on the human race that transcends the human will. Thus God in Christ must conquer that evil.

At the heart of Paul's cosmic war myth is the story of how Christ's death and resurrection is the means by which God drove back the darkness: in Christ God created the new Kingdom of Light, the beachhead of freedom into which all believers are translated. Of course Paul did not take literally the imagery of the kingdom as a contiguous piece of physical territory (which was the ancient Israelite image of God's kingdom), but meant the kingdom spiritually. By that spiritual kingdom he meant a realm of safety, a community into which believers could enter and by the power of Christ's presence be protected from all the spiritual forces of evil.

The Kingdom of Light symbol expresses this reality of the conquest of evil (which Paul experienced) better than any of the other symbol systems do. The organic symbol of the body of Christ expresses the community, but not the safety. The royal family symbol expresses the community life within the family, but not the rescue and preservation from attacking forces of evil. The judicial symbol system lays no emphasis on either the community or the forces of evil, for its central concern is with human guilt and repentance, and divine justification producing a new status for the sinner before God. Thus the Kingdom of Light holds together the rescue, community and safety aspects of the experience of believers better than the other symbol systems do.

Another significant contribution the Kingdom of Light imagery makes is that it emphasizes that the post-Easter world itself is now different from the pre-Easter world. A new power has invaded, quite like the way that Alexander put the Greek Empire at the top of the Near Eastern world in a period of less than ten years. With the resurrection of Christ the divine light (the power of truth, goodness and mercy) is now at work defeating the old power of satanic darkness (with its emphasis on lies, evil and the power of justice used to oppress the weak). Thus the world will never be the same again.

Most powerfully of all, the Kingdom of Light, with Christ as its ruler, strongly emphasizes Paul's conviction that nothing external can separate believers from the power and love of God in Christ. When believers see themselves as inside the Fortress of Light, with Christ clothed in heavenly light as their commander, then life is very different from the old way, outside in the world. Instead of seeing the political and economic rulers of this present age as the forces that must be obeyed (because of the harm they can do to the disobedient), the believer sees Christ as the one who must be followed implicitly (because no ultimate harm can come to those who follow him).

### (e) Children of Light: Soldiers of Light

Another valuable element in the light symbol is Paul's image of believers as children of light, clothed in light so that they shine as lights, soldiers of light conquering the darkness of the world. This image suggests how Christ's own qualities of divine goodness, mercy, and sacrifice for others, have come into the lives of his followers, so they represent him, are his presence in the world overcoming evil.

In these various ways the children of light symbol goes considerably beyond the pictures given in the judicial and familial symbol systems. The organic symbol of the body of Christ conveys some of the same ideas because believers are there members of Christ and so his representatives. However, the organic symbol does not stress the truth and goodness which the children of light bring to overcome the darkness. Thus the imagery of God's people as the children of light makes a useful contribution to the Pauline understanding of the Christian community, especially when we add in the image of believers as footsoldiers in the Army of Light.

This picture of believers as members of Christ's Army of Light is very important, elaborating the imagery of them as children of light. The cosmic war myth suggests that the fortress-like Kingdom of Light is an advancing beachhead, a moving wall from behind which believers sally forth to give battle to the forces of darkness. Each believer is clothed with the armor of light which then shines in the darkness, thereby defeating the forces of evil.

This imagery strongly suggests that believers are called to follow in Christ's footsteps, to take up the task of spreading the light that came in Christ, by attacking the forces of darkness. The imagery expresses Paul's practice of carrying the battle to enemy strongholds (attacking fortresses he called it), by means of his evangelistic forays into the cities of the Roman empire. Further, the image makes clear that the task is not easy, for the darkness will resist, so believers must fight (the spiritual forces of evil) and bear the inevitable pain (brought by the physical forces of evil) in order to help achieve the victory.

By these various points the Army of Light symbol goes beyond the contributions made by the other symbol systems. None of the others suggest that attacking enemies, i.e. initiating conflict (by evangelism), bearing armor and weapons (the powers of the Spirit), accepting the inevitable pain (of persecution), and defeating the darkness (by converting unbelievers), are central aspects of the life of the Church. In these respects the Army of Light symbol makes a substantial contribution.

### (f) Hope for Victory Produces Endurance

One final contribution that Paul's myth makes is that its proclamation of final total victory over evil evokes hope and thus enables the soldiers of light to endure the suffering that the war entails.

Nothing is more psychologically important for an army than high morale, the widespread belief that they can win, for that will keep them fighting even when the enemy forces have the advantage. Paul's cosmic war myth provides a substantial boost to the morale of those soldiers of Christ who hold the story firmly in their imaginations. Those who take the battle myth seriously, as a symbolic window onto the depths of reality, may find their spirits energized and their wills strengthened for their ongoing conflict with the evil in their own world.[2]

That strength and energy comes through the imagination taking in and believing the whole of the myth: if believers imagine themselves as soldiers in the Army of Light, with Christ the conqueror at their head successfully driving back the cosmic Army of Darkness, that will help them battle on. By vividly picturing God's initial, ongoing and final triumphs through Christ, the cosmic war myth evokes hope and confidence in Christians for the eventual end of all evil. That hope and confidence then can motivate them to join the battle vigorously. This effect can take place because the myth, through its concrete, dramatic, memorable imagery, enables believers to imagine, and so believe in, God's ultimate victory. Believers hold in their imaginations the myth of Christ on the cross disarming the powers, and at the end destroying the whole mass of

---

[2] Of course, those who find the fighting imagery objectionable, perhaps due to their attitudes towards warfare, will probably not enjoy these benefits. For such readers the other three of Paul's symbolic versions of the gospel will probably be far more fruitful spiritually. Further, in cultures in which men are praised for fighting and women are praised for peace-making there may even be a marked gender difference in the effectiveness of this myth.

evil by a single breath. Those mythical pictures then help to generate confidence in Christ's present power to drive back all the forces of darkness that believers now battle. With that confidence, believers will then stand up and fight, advancing boldly into battle, willing to suffer, indeed to give all they have, for Christ who leads them on.

Such suffering is a necessary part of the soldier's life, so the myth provides the explanation for it and the power to endure it. Once the believer thinks of herself as a soldier, then she will expect to suffer at times, to make sacrifices, for the forces of evil will not give up easily. Thus, when the enemy threatens the believer with harm of some kind, that threat can often be effectively countered by picturing Christ on the cross. That suffering was the necessary way the Commander-in-Chief won the first great battle of the war. Therefore, his fellow-soldiers may even rejoice in their suffering, as Paul did, for it unites them even more fully with Christ than they had been before.

**Conclusion**

Clearly the cosmic war imagery, though not meant literally by Paul, expresses important Pauline themes and so makes a very valuable intellectual contribution. Without this myth Paul's theology would have been considerably less complex and comprehensive. Most of all the cosmic war myth expresses, in a way that none of the other symbol systems do, the conflict between forces of good and evil and especially the experience of Paul and other believers in attacking evil and suffering the consequences. Once believers picture themselves as the Army of Light, then their suffering makes sense, indeed can be embraced enthusiastically as evidence that they have indeed joined Christ's war, for they are suffering as he did in his great battle on the cross.

## B. THE EARTHEN VESSEL

When Paul presents the Christian story as a cosmic warstory, his major purpose is to emphasize central points of positive analogy that we have just discussed. However, in order to recognize them accurately we must put aside the inapplicable details in the symbol by **(1) Discerning Negative Analogies**. Those are not the only limitations of a symbol system, however, for there is further the question of how the readers respond to it. When readers other than the original audience consider the work, then we must work at **(2) Discovering Elements of Provincialism** in the symbol system, those details which the original hearers could immediately grasp but which readers today may not. Those elements must then be translated into terms that present readers know.

## (1) Discerning Negative Analogies

By knowing something about the subject symbolized (God's age-long struggle against evil) readers can discern some of the ways that the symbolism of the cosmic war myth must be discounted, put aside as examples of negative analogies. Experienced readers know about that struggle from Paul's other versions of the gospel, and from the background of the rest of the Bible.

### (a) War's Destruction: Doing Harm v. Doing Good?

War stories carry the central detail that soldiers on one side are fighting enemy soldiers, seeking to kill before being killed. Thus doing harm (sometimes with the theory that good may come from it in the end) is central to war symbolism. By contrast the Royal Family myth suggests that believers are called to reach out in love to help the alienated come home again, leaving no room at all for intentionally doing harm. Further, Paul's organic symbolism suggests that the Church is a tree that bears fruit to provide for the well-being of those outside. No harm is done to other human beings according to those versions of the gospel, which directly correspond with Paul's direct teaching to help enemies (Rom 12:17–20). Together these all provide a central corrective to the war myth.

Indeed this is the greatest weakness of the cosmic war myth as a window on the gospel today, which is a change from Paul's day. He did not expect any of his readers ever to be tempted to harm another human being as part of their Christian calling. Probably he did not expect to be misunderstood on this topic, because all his Christian readers knew that the church was called to be pacific, not warlike. Therefore we find only rarely a specific denial of this element of the symbolism, e.g. when Paul (or perhaps a Paulinist) writes, "Our struggle is not against human enemies (flesh and blood) but against spiritual ones (the angelic rulers of the nations)" (Eph 6:12). Perhaps that denial was called forth by misunderstanding on the part of the readers, but it is unlikely that they had taken up physical weapons to fight evil.

As long as the church was pacific (due to a large extent to its weakness of course), the fighting and doing harm element in the myth was not a big problem, for Christian readers simply discounted it as negative analogy without any further thought. Unfortunately, after Constantine the church's position in society, and its ethical viewpoint, changed to one in which war was an acceptable option for Christians. Therefore Christians could begin to misunderstand Paul, to believe that the war symbolism called them to fight holy wars against other human beings (following thereby the practice of Ancient Israel as described especially in Joshua).

Thus we need to remember when using this cosmic war myth that making war, in its common sense of doing harm to other human beings (usually justified as a means to higher ends), was not meant literally by Paul in his depiction of the Church's role in the world. Instead, Paul meant the war symbolism spiritually, symbolizing the task of confronting and defeating spiritual forces of evil, those which produced the enmity believers sometimes face and the consequent suffering they have to endure. Further, the war between the angelic forces was not meant physically either, for the angelic forces were probably not taken literally by Paul.

**(b) Angels and God's Justice**

We have already decided on one central element of negative analogy in the previous chapter: the picture of angels (in the two angelic armies) as distinct individual centers of mind and will was probably not meant literally by Paul. Instead, as we argued, Paul probably thought of angels as the ancient Hebrews thought of the *malak Yahweh*. That "angel of the Lord" was a periphrasis for God, a way to suggest that God was present and active without implying that God was simply located in that place. Instead of taking the flying, humanlike, individual spirits literally Paul probably took them symbolically: we concluded that for Paul they were traditional, pictorial representations of a divine reality —God's own mandate, impulse and standard of justice at work in the world. Evil angels, including Satan, were probably for Paul that divine justice distorted, corrupted, misused by humans for their own benefit.

Thus a second significant limitation of the cosmic war myth, with its angels intervening between God and humankind, is that it does not adequately express the divine immanence in the world, God's intimate involvement with humankind. God's presence as the Spirit (or Christ) at work within believers (and perhaps throughout the whole creation) was a central Pauline belief, making it clear that Paul believed in God's immanence. Therefore it is essential to provide a corrective to the angel imagery here, for God's immanence very strongly suggests that the divine operation is as intimate as our very own spirits, so there is no room for literal angels between God and humankind. Still the angels play a valuable role, for they enable hearers to imagine something of the great power of God at work in combatting evil.

### (c) God: The Warrior on High v. the Father in our Midst

As we have suggested often above, the chief picture of God in the cosmic war myth is as the one at the head of the Hierarchy of Light, the warrior God who sends his army to destroy the forces of darkness and rescue their prisoners of war. In this picture God is far above the prisoners and soldiers, not knowing them personally at all for they are at the bottom of the hierarchy and important in their numbers, not in their personalities. By contrast, the Royal Family symbol system provides a picture of God as father, one who seeks out his alienated children and personally welcomes them home into his presence. Thus the personal father of the latter myth provides a significant corrective to the distant ruler of the cosmic war myth. God is not literally a distant commander who does not know his soldiers personally, as the mythical picture presents him.

Of course this transcendent-warrior symbol provides a needed corrective to the intimate-father symbol also: God is not literally involved in human lives the same way a human father is either, for human fathers find their own well-being, their own future, their own happiness, tied up with the spiritual and personal success of their children. God is not dependent on humans in those ways. Thus both symbols are valuable when held together: God is and is not a distant commander; God is and is not a member of our household. Something in each symbol provides significant insight into the Divine Reality and a necessary corrective to the other.

### (d) The Demon Sin and Human Responsibility

A second element that we suggested above must not be taken literally in Paul's cosmic war myth is his picture of people as the helpless victims of Satan's powerful demon Sin. Undoubtedly this is a central and powerful element in the myth, one that must be taken seriously, but Paul makes it clear that it should not be taken literally. By using the same word *hamartia* both for this demonic power and for human acts of transgression Paul gives a hint that we are not to take literally the excuse "Sin made me do it!" even though that is what Paul says (Rom 7:17–20). The context of his other symbol systems makes it apparent that Paul is not a determinist in this subject: in the beginning of Romans he makes it plain that he sees humans as responsible (to some extent) for their sinfulness, for knowing God's law they wilfully disobey it (Rom 1:32) so all are guilty before God (Rom 3:19).

This specific corrective thus comes from Paul's legal/judicial gospel which we outlined in chapter I above. Both symbols are important for Paul's complete view: in some respects the human problem is that we are overwhelmed by hidden forces beyond our control; but from another perspective we are people who commit ourselves to concerns that are less than really ultimate and they drag us down into the mire. Paul offers no clear theory connecting these two opposite poles of thought, though of course theologians down through the ages have invented numerous theories.

### (e) Sinfree Believers?

Paul's cosmic war myth clearly pictures Sin as driven out of its rule over believers, though it remains a threat to return if it is allowed back in. In his myth he says that believers are free from Sin, for the Spirit of God has taken over the place that the demon Sin previously occupied as the driver of the human chariot.

However, Paul's own experience of believers (himself included) suggested that they all continued sinning in one respect or another. When he said that he had not yet attained the perfection required for the resurrection, so he pressed on seeking to reach that height (Phil 3:10–16), he showed that he did not think of himself as wholly sin-free.

Possibly we could reconcile the Sin-free symbol with the actual experience by saying that Sin only stands for the coercive forces that force us astray, while all sinning by believers is their own willed sinning. That is unlikely to be the whole picture, however, for Paul presumably knew that old habits die hard, which is why he continually urged his Christian readers to give up their sinful ways.

Therefore we conclude that we should not take literally Paul's picture of believers as wholly free from the power Sin. Instead Paul probably saw believers as free from Sin at the core of their lives. In their capitol city freedom had come. In their conscious wills, by which they had repented and committed themselves to Christ, Sin no longer ruled. But in the provinces, where the will does not have complete control, where old habits, phobias and repressions still lurk in Sin's darkness, complete freedom awaits the End.

**(f) Christ: Victor and Victim**

In the cosmic war myth Christ is the victor over the forces of evil, most of all in the Last Battle but also initially in the victory at Calvary. By contrast, Paul's major emphasis in his other symbol systems is on Christ as the victim, the one who dies by the hand of his enemies to save others. In our normal picturing of life we see victors and victims as contrary images, not ones that can be easily combined.

Thus the picture of Christ conquering the powers must not be taken literally, especially because there are no literal angelic spirits for him to conquer. The great power at work here (or so we argued in the previous chapter) is the divine justice spread throughout all human societies. In Jesus' death that inexorable force for punishment is turned aside, or absorbed, by the divine mercy, as we find Paul expressing it in his judicial version of the gospel.

Both pictures—Christ as conquering hero and Christ as suffering sacrifice—are essential to Paul's gospel, but neither should be taken literally. The victor symbol expresses well the new world that God has created through Christ. The victim symbol emphasizes the cost, the identification of Christ with sinners, his death as a sacrifice for them, that is a striking element in the appeal of the gospel. Thus whenever the cosmic war myth is told, the sacrifice of Christ (a victim of evil forces) is the means to the victory that must be emphasized.

**(2) Possible Elements of Provincialism**

Every ancient symbol system has some elements that are tied so closely to the world of their own day that they are not readily available to the imaginative experience of readers of a later age. Those are the provincial elements in the symbol system, the parts for which interpreters must find more modern equivalents if the symbol system is to have its powerful effect on the imagination. Let us consider some of the possible provincial elements in the cosmic war myth.

**(a) Fortresses**

We suggested that in Paul's imagery God created through Christ a new kingdom that was like an advancing fortress (a beachhead), so its inhabitants could move forward conquering enemy fortresses. In Paul's day that was a common practice in war. Today fortresses are rare. Cities no longer have high walls around them. As a result, most modern readers do not have personal experience to call on which will enable them to understand this fortress imagery. However, we suggested above that the advancing fortress is like a beachhead (e.g. the one formed on D-Day on the Normandy coast), so many people can understand this symbol from the stories and films that have been made to relay that decisive 20th century event. Further, the most deadly battle of the Pacific War was the allied attack on Okinawa, which was in all significant respects a fortress island, one which required a terrible price in human lives before it was conquered.

In addition, even in this day of nuclear bombs, we still have fortresses (by other names): the US government has tunnelled out its war headquarters down in the depths of a mountain near Washington, and the Air Force has a similar underground fortress in Colorado. Like ancient fortresses these modern ones were constructed to provide safety for their inhabitants from the worst that enemies can do. Thus we can still understand fairly well Paul's imagery of fortresses, even though it does not have the same power of suggesting security that it did for Paul's readers.

**(b) Swords, armor and shields**

Not much fighting is done anymore with these exact weapons, but we have not outgrown them completely. Swords have been replaced by bayonets; our armor now is helmets and flak jackets; even shields (now of plexiglas) continue to be used by riot police in cities all over the world. Thus the specific details of ancient armaments do not prevent modern readers from grasping immediately the essentials of this symbolism, especially since films make the ancient forms readily available to our sight.

**(c) Heavenly battles**

In Paul's day the imagery of angelic armies fighting each other was fantasy, not something that people had ever seen. Today it is no longer quite as fantastic, for airplanes have been fighting in the skies for eighty years and space warfare is quite imaginable for those who have seen "Star Wars." Thus the fantastic element still plays a role in modern imaginations through space fantasy films. Probably most readers do not have in their imaginations readily formed images of angels flying into battle, so that specific imagery is quite provincial. Nevertheless, we do have images of heavenly spaceships which provide a very similar symbolic picture. Heavenly battles fought in conjunction with earthly ones are thus readily available to modern imaginations, just as they were to the ancients'.

**(d) War's destructiveness**

In Paul's day a soldier could only kill people one at a time whereas today a single bomb can kill millions. Nevertheless, most modern warfare is still conducted as the ancients did it, one soldier killing another soldier who is trying to kill him first. We still have cities under siege trying to defend themselves but often finding their cause to be hopeless. Thus the changes are not decisive enough to make the Pauline imagery provincial. Indeed one could argue that the new possibility of human warfare destroying the whole earth for the first time provides an adequate symbol for the Last Battle and the end of the earth.

Our conclusion is thus that while the specific details of warfare have changed in many ways since Paul's day, the overall symbol of warfare has not changed much. War today, like war back then, still has soldiers fighting and killing, still has armor and arms, still has fortresses and devastating attacks, still has decisive changes in the political realm coming as a result of wars won and lost. Therefore, Paul's cosmic war symbolism is not very provincial at all.

**Conclusion**

In this chapter we have considered both the limitations and the considerable value of Paul's cosmic war myth. Like all symbolic speech this myth has elements of negative analogy that the reader must discount when seeking to grasp its deeper meaning. In addition, stories out of ancient cultures inevitably are to some extent provincial, though in the case of war the essentials have unfortunately remained much the same. Thus the war myth still has power to touch modern hearers, for it is a vivid, dramatic myth that is tied directly to human experience of the conflict between good and evil forces. Not only does Paul's myth still touch readers, but it also provides substantial theological raw material, for this myth emphasizes a variety of points that the other symbol systems do not.

When the judicial and familial symbol systems are emphasized (as they usually are by the European-founded churches) then the church tends to become a religious adjunct to society, a place where those who wish to can come for therapy. The cosmic war myth by contrast calls the church to recognize that the forces of evil in the world must be fought, that the easy path of making herself at home in the culture is the chief temptation that the forces of evil offer today. If the church today could understand the battle as clearly as Paul did in his own day, perhaps the world-conquering power of Paul's evangelism might not be lost for good.

# BIBLIOGRAPHY

Arnold, C. E. *Powers of Darkness: Principalities and Powers in Paul's Letters*. Downer's Grove, IL: InterVarsity, 1992.

_____. "The 'Exorcism' of Ephesians 6:12 in Recent Research: A Critique of Wesley Carr's View of the Role of Evil Powers in First-Century AD Belief." *JSNT* 30 (1987) 71-87.

Arrington, French L. *Paul's Aeon Theology in I Corinthians*. Washington, DC: University Press of America, 1978.

Aulen, Gustaf. *Christus Victor: An Historical Study of the Three Main Types of the Idea of the Atonement* (translated by A. G. Hebert). London: SPCK, 1961.

Barclay, William. *The Letters to the Corinthians* rev. ed. (*The Daily Study Bible Series*). Philadelphia: Westminster, 1975.

Barrett, C. K. *A Commentary on the First Epistle to the Corinthians* (*Harper's New Testament Commentaries*, Henry Chadwick, ed.). New York: Harper, 1968.

_____. *A Commentary on the Second Epistle to the Corinthians* (*Harper's New Testament Commentaries*, Henry Chadwick, ed.). New York: Harper, 1973.

_____. *A Commentary on the Epistle to the Romans* (*Harper's New Testament Commentaries*, Henry Chadwick, ed.). New York: Harper, 1957.

Barth, M. *Ephesians chs 1-3* (*The Anchor Bible*, v.34). Garden City, NY: Doubleday, 1967.

Beker, J. Christiaan. *Paul the Apostle: The Triumph of God in Life and Thought*. Philadelphia: Fortress, 1980.

Berkhof, H. *Christ and the Powers* (translated by J. H. Yoder). Scottdale, PA: Herald, 1977.

Best, Ernest. *A Commentary on the First and Second Epistles to the Thessalonians*. New York: Harper, 1973.

Bousset, W. *The Antichrist Legend: A Chapter in Christian and Jewish Folklore* (translated by A. H. Keane). London: Hutchinson, 1896.

Bruce, F. F. *1 and 2 Thessalonians* (*Word Biblical Commentary*, v.45). Waco, TX: Word, 1982.

Burton, E. deWitt. *A Critical and Exegetical Commentary on the Epistle to the Galatians* (*The International Critical Commentary*). Edinburgh: Clark, 1921.

Caird, George B. *Principalities and Powers: A Study in Pauline Theology.* Oxford: Clarendon, 1956.

Calvin, John. *The Institutes of the Christian Religion* (translated by Henry Beveridge). Grand Rapids: Eerdmans, 1957.

Carr, Wesley. *Angels and Principalities.* Cambridge: Cambridge University Press, 1981.

Charles, R. H. *Eschatology: The Doctrine of a Future Life in Israel, Judaism, and Christianity. A Critical History.* New York: Schocken, 1963.

Collins, J. J. "The Mythology of Holy War in Daniel and the Qumran War Scroll: A Point of Transition in Jewish Apocalyptic." *Vetus Testamentum* XXV (1975) 596–612.

Cullmann, O. *Christ and Time: The Primitive Christian Conception of Time and History* (Revised edition). London: SCM, 1962.

Daube, David. "On Acts 23: Sadducees and Angels," *JBL* 109 (1990) 493-497.

Davies, W. D. *Paul and Rabbinic Judaism: Some Rabbinic Elements in Pauline Theology.* London: SPCK, 1958.

Day, John. *God's Conflict with the Dragon and the Sea: Echoes of a Canaanite Myth in the Old Testament.* Cambridge: Cambridge University Press, 1985.

De Boer, M. C. *The Defeat of Death: Apocalyptic Eschatology in 1 Corinthians 15 and Romans 5* (*JSOT Supplement Series* 22). Sheffield: JSOT, 1988.

Dibelius, M. *Die Geisterwelt im Glauben des Paulus.* Gottingen: Vanderhoeck and Ruprecht, 1909.

Dillistone, F. W. *The Christian Understanding of Atonement.* Philadelphia: Westminster, 1968.

Dixon, Paul S. "The Evil Restraint in 2 Thess 2:6," *JETS* 33 (1990) 445-449.

Driver, John. *Understanding the Atonement for the Mission of the Church.* Scottdale, PA: Herald, 1986.

Duncan, G. S. *The Epistle of Paul to the Galatians (The Moffat New Testament Commentary).* London: Hodder and Stoughton, 1934.

Dunn, J. D. G. "Echoes of Intra-Jewish Polemic in Paul's Letter to the Galatians." *JBL* 112 (1993) 459-477.

Edwards, James R. *Romans (New International Biblical Commentary).* Peabody, MA: Hendrickson, 1992

Ellis, E. E. *Paul and His Recent Interpreters.* Grand Rapids: Eerdmans, 1961.

_____. *"Soma* in First Corinthians." *Interpretation* 44 (1990)

Forsyth, Neil. *The Old Enemy: Satan and the Combat Myth.* Princeton: Princeton University Press, 1987.

Freedman, D. N. "Strophe and Meter in Exodus 15." In H. N. Bream et al (eds), *A Light Unto My Path: Old Testament Studies in Honor of Jacob M. Hyers.* Philadelphia: Temple University Press, 1974.

Furneaux, R. *The Roman Siege of Jerusalem.* New York: McKay, 1972.

Furnish, V. P. *II Corinthians.* Garden City, NY: Doubleday, 1984.

Gnilka, J. "2 Cor 6:14-7:1 in the Light of the Qumran Texts and the Testaments of the Twelve Patriarchs." In J. Murphy-O'Conner (ed.), *Paul and Qumran: Studies in New Testament Exegesis* (Chicago: Priory, 1968) 48-68.

Grayston, K. *The Letters of Paul to the Philippians and to the Thessalonians (The Cambridge Bible Commentary on the New English Bible,* R. Ackroyd et al gen eds.). Camabridge: Cambridge University Press, 1967.

Green, Michael. *I Believe in Satan's Downfall.* Grand Rapids: Eerdmans, 1980.

Green Roger L. and Hooper, Walter. *C. S. Lewis: A Biography.* New York and London: Harcourt, 1974.

Hall, Barbara. *Battle Imagery in Paul's Letters: An Exegetical Study*. New York: Union Theological Seminary Dissertation, 1973.

Hill, C. E. "Paul's Understanding of Christ's Kingdom in I Corinthians 15:20-28." *Novum Testamentum* XXX (1988) 297-320.

Hughes, P. E. *Paul's Second Epistle to the Corinthians* (*The NIV commentary on the New Testament*). Grand Rapids: Eerdmans, 1962.

Josephus, Flavius. *The Jewish War* (translated by G. A. Williamson). Harmondsworth: Penguin, 1970.

Kabisch, E. *Die Eschatologie des Paulus*. Gottingen: 1893.

Kaiser, Otto. *Isaiah 13-39: A Commentary*. (Translated by R. A. Wilson). Philadelphia: Westminster, 1974.

Kluger, R. S. *Satan in the Old Testament*. Evanston: Northwestern University Press, 1967.

Kuhn, K. G. "New Light on Temptation, Sin and Flesh in the New Testament." In K. Stendahl (ed.), *The Scrolls and the New Testament* (New York: Harper, 1957) 94-113.

Kvanvig, H. *Roots of Apocalyptic*. Neukirchen-Vluyn: WMANT, 1988.

Lakoff, George and Johnson, Mark. *Metaphors We Live By*. Chicago: University of Chicago Press, 1980.

Lee, J. Y. "Interpreting the Demonic Powers in Pauline Thought." *Novum Testamentum* 12 (1970) 54-69.

Leenhardt, Franz J. *The Epistle to the Romans* (translated by Harold Knight). London: Lutterworth, 1961.

Leipoldt, Johannes. "Das Bild vom Kriege in der griechischen Welt," in G. Delling (ed.), *Goett und die Goetter: Festgabe fuer Erich Fascher zum 60. Geburtstag*. (Berlin: Evangelische Verlagsanstalt, 1958) 16-30.

Leivestad, Ragnar. *Christ the Conqueror: Ideas of Conflict and Victory in the New Testament*. London: SPCK, 1954.

Lewis, C. S. *God in the Dock: Essays on Theology and Ethics* (Walter Hooper ed.) Grand Rapids: Eerdmans, 1970.

_____. *Mere Christianity*. New York: Macmillan, 1960.

_____. *Out of the Silent Planet*. New York: Macmillan, 1965.

_____. *The Screwtape Letters*. New York: Macmillan, 1961.

_____. *The Weight of Glory and Other Addresses*. Grand Rapids: Eerdmans, 1965.

Lincoln, Andrew T. *Paradise Now and Not yet: Studies in the Role of the Heavenly Dimension in Paul's Thought with Special Reference to His Eschatology. SNTSS* 43, Cambridge: Cambridge University Press, 1981.

Lind, M. C. *Yahweh is a Warrior: The Theology of Warfare in Ancient Israel.* Scottdale, PA: Herald, 1980.

Longman, Tremper III and Reid, Daniel G. *God is a Warrior (Studies in Old Testament Biblical Theology)*. Grand Rapids: Zondervan, 1995.

MacDonald, George. *Phantastes and Lilith* (with an Introduction by C. S. Lewis). Grand Rapids: Eerdmans, 1964.

MacGregor, Geddes. *Angels: Ministers of God's Grace*. New York: Paragon, 1988.

_____. "Principalities and Powers: The Cosmic Background of Paul's Thought." *New Testament Studies* 1 (1954) 17-28.

Macky, Peter W. *The Centrality of Metaphors to Biblical Thought: A Theory of Interpretation*. Lewiston, NY: Mellen, 1990.

_____. "Myth as the Way We Can Taste Reality: An Analysis of C. S. Lewis's Theory," *The Lamp-Post* (Southern California C. S. Lewis Society) 6 (1982) 1-7.

_____. "St. Paul's Collage of Metaphors in II Cor 5:1-10: Ornamental or Exploratory?" *Proceedings of the Eastern Great Lakes and Midwest Biblical Societies* xi (1991) 162-173.

_____. *The Problem of Sin in Romans: The Relationship in the Thought of St. Paul between Man's Freely Willed Sins and the Demonic Power Sin.* Oxford: Oxford University D. Phil Dissertation, 1967.

Malherbe, A. J. "Antisthenes and Odysseus, and Paul at War." *Harvard Theological Review* 76 (1983) 143-173.

Marshall, I. H. *1 and 2 Thessalonians.* Grand Rapids: Eerdmans, 1983.

McCormick, Patrick. *Sin as Addiction.* New York: Paulist, 1989.

McGinn, Bernard. *Antichrist: Two Thousand Years of the Human Fascination with Evil.* San Francisco: Harper, 1994.

Milton, John. *Paradise Lost.* Franklin Center, PA: Franklin Library, 1979.

Morris, Leon. *The First and Second Epistles to the Thessalonians.* Grand Rapids: Eerdmans, 1959.

Murray, John. *The Epistle to the Romans, vol 1, chapters I-VIII (The New International Commentary on the New Testament).* Grand Rapids: Eerdmans, 1959.

Neville, Robert C. *The Truth of Broken Symbols (Suny Series in Religious Studies,* Harold Coward ed.). Albany: SUNY Press, 1996.

Noack, B. *Satanas und Soteria.* Copenhagen: 1948.

Nygren, Anders. *Commentary on Romans* (translated by C. C. Rasmussen). Philadelphia: Muhlenberg, 1949.

Pagels, Elaine. *The Origin of Satan.* New York: Random House, 1995.

Pfitzner, V. C. *Paul and the Agon Motif: Traditional Athletic Imagery in the Pauline Literature.* Leiden: Brill, 1967.

Ricoeur, Paul. *The Symbolism of Evil* (translated by Emerson Buchanan). Boston: Beacon, 1969.

Ridderbos, Herman. *Paul: An Outline of His Theology* (translated by J. R. de Witt). Grand Rapids: Eerdmans, 1975.

Ringgren, Helmer. *The Faith of Qumran: Theology of the Dead Sea Scrolls*. Philadelphia: Fortress, 1963.

Robertson, A. and Plummer, A. *A Critical and Exegetical Commentary on the First Epistle of St. Paul to the Corinthians (The International Critical Commentary)*. Edinburgh: Clark, 1914.

Roehser, Gunter. *Metaphorik und Personification der Sund: Antike Sundenvorstellungen und paulinische Hamartia*. Tubingen: Mohr, 1987.

Russell, D. S. *The Method and Message of Jewish Apocalyptic: 200 BC—AD 100*. Philadelphia: Westminster, 1964.

Russell, J. B. *Mephistopheles: The Devil in the Modern World*. Ithaca: Cornell University Press, 1986.

_____. *The Devil: Perceptions of Evil from Antiquity to Primitive Christianity*. Ithaca: Cornell University Press, 1977.

_____. *The Prince of Drkness: Radical Evil and the Power of Good in History*. Ithaca: Cornell University Press, 1988.

_____. *Satan: The Early Christian Tradition*. Ithaca: Cornell University Press, 1981.

Sanday, W. and Headlam, A. C. *A Critical and Exegetical Commentary on the Epistle to the Romans (The International Critical Commentary)* 5th ed. Edinburgh: Clark, 1902.

Schlier, H. *Principalities and Powers in the New Testament*. New York: Herder, 1961.

Schniewind, J. "Reply to Bultmann." In H. W. Bartsch (ed.), *Kerygma and Myth: A Theological Debate*. New York: Harper, 1961.

Schweitzer, Albert. *The Mysticism of Paul the Apostle*. (Translated by William Montgomery.) 2nd Edition. London: Black, 1953.

Segal, Alan F. *Paul the Convert: The Apostolate and Apostasy of Saul the Pharisee*. New Haven: Yale University Press, 1990.

Shires, H. M. *The Eschatology of Paul in the Light of Modern Scholarship*. Philadelphia: Westminster, 1965.

Theissen, Gerd. "Soteriologische Symbolic in den paulinishen Schriften." *Kerygma und Dogma* 20 (1974) 282-304.

van der Hart, Rob. *The Theology of Angels and Devils (Theology Today Series, no. 36)*. Notre Dame: Fides, 1972.

Vermes, Geza. *The Dead Sea Scrolls in English*. Harmondsworth: Penguin, 1962.

Vos, G. *The Pauline Eschatology*. Grand Rapids: Eerdmans, 1961.

Wakeman, Mary K. *God's Battle with the Monster: A Study in Biblical Imagery*. Leiden: Brill, 1973.

Webster, Graham. *The Roman Imperial Army of the First and Second Centuries A.D.* London: Black, 1969.

Westermann, Claus. *God's Angels Need No Wings* (translated by David L. Scheidt). Philadelphia: Fortress, 1979.

Whiteley, Denis E. H. *The Theology of St. Paul*. Philadelphia: Fortress, 1964.

Williams, D. J. *1 and 2 Thessalonians (New International Bible Commentary)*. Peabody, MA: Hendrickson, 1992.

Wink, Walter. *Naming the Powers (The Powers, v.1)*. Philadephia: Fortress, 1983.

_____. *Unmasking the Powers: The Invisible Forces That Determine Human Existence (The Powers, v.2)*. Philadelphia: Fortress, 1986.

Witherington, Ben III. *Jesus, Paul and the End of the World: A Comparative Study in New Testament Eschatology*. Downers Grove, IL: InterVarsity, 1992.

Wright, Nigel. *The Satan Syndrome: Putting the Power of Darkness in its Place*. Grand Rapids: Zondervan, 1990.

Yates, Roy. "Colossians 2:15: Christ Triumphant." *NTS* 37 (1991), 575-591.

# AUTHOR INDEX

# SUBJECT INDEX

## NEW TESTAMENT

**Matthew**
7:13 160
9:32 58
13:25 56
17:15 58
18 58
24:8-24 194
25:41 207

**Mark**
3:22 56,58,61
3:23 56
3:27 59,213
5:1-5 99
8:33 59
13:25 59

**Luke**
1:19 235
9:39 214
10 213
10:18-19 59
13:16 58,68
16:19-31 113
18 213
19 213

**John**
12:31 56,60,75
19:36 214

**Acts**
7:10 125
7:34 125
12:11 125
14:15 70
23:27 125
24:15 209

**Romans**
1:11 70
1:16 168
1:18-32 7,257
1:19-23 77
1:21 93
1:24 67
1:24-25 115
1:32 7,278
2:5 8,113,148,150,
195
2:5-6 7
2:6-8 210,211
2:7 10,111,210
2:11 7
2:12 179
2:15 7,114
2:16 7,195
2:19 86,93,121
3:9 86,115,145
3:12 7
3:19 278
3:24 7,12
3:25 7
3:26 13
4:13 9
5 107
5-7 77,100,101,102
5-8 97,135
5:3 159
5:5 9
5:8 97,101
5:8-10 12
5:10 9
5:12 5,86,96,97,104,
107,114,141,145,228,
243
5:12-8:39 106

**Romans (cont.)**
5:12-21 77,100,189
5:13 107
5:14 108,114,145,
208
5:17 9,145,208
5:21 69,97,107,108,
114,145
6 102
6-7 136
6-10 135
6:2 135,139,144
6:2-3 140
6:3-4 146
6:4 139
6:5-6 5
6:6 70,86,96,105,
108,135,139,140,141,
146
6:6-7 134,138,141
6:7 140
6:8 242
6:9 108,111,112,144,
146,148
6:10 138,139,144
6:12 4,97,105,137
6:12-13 182
6:13 97,100,105,169
6:16 70,102,105
6:17 143
6:17-18 109,115
6:19 102,182
6:23 86,98,147,228
7 92,99,102,105,136
7:5 67,143,182,184
7:5,8 103
7:7 103
7:8 86,99,101,102,

## OTHER HEBREW TEXTS

# The Westminster College
# Library of Biblical Symbolism

This series encourages works of scholarship that explore the artistic and theological depths of biblical symbols. "Symbol" here means any well-known reality that is used to illuminate a more mysterious reality by means of the analogy between the two. The symbols can be objects, qualities, actions, roles, events, stories, or systems. "Exploring" symbols entails: painting a full picture of the well-known reality as the original writers and readers would have known it; establishing what the subject of the symbol was in particular instances; and seeing through the symbol to the depths of the subject. The books in this series may focus on a particular symbol (e.g. light, or shepherd, or the Exodus), on a particular type of symbolism (e.g. Paul's legal symbolism, or Hosea's personal symbolism), or on particular themes (e.g. the variety of symbols used to illuminate the mystery of human sinfulness and how those symbols are used to interpret each other). Still others may focus on particular books, such as Ezekiel or Revelation, exploring their main symbols.

For additional information about this series or for the submission of manuscripts, please contact:

Peter Lang Publishing, Inc.
Acquisitions Department
275 Seventh Avenue, 28th floor
New York, New York 10001

## DATE DUE

| | | | |
|---|---|---|---|
| | | | |
| | | | |
| | | | |
| | | | |
| | | | |
| | | | |
| | | | |
| | | | |
| | | | |
| | | | |
| | | | |
| | | | |
| | | | |
| | | | |
| | | | |
| | | | |
| | | | |
| | | | |
| | | | |
| | | | |
| | | | |

GAYLORD | | | PRINTED IN U.S.A.